Being, Time, Bios

SUNY series, Insinuations: Philosophy, Psychoanalysis, Literature

Charles Shepherdson, editor

Being, Time, Bios

Capitalism and Ontology

A. KIARINA KORDELA

Cover image: August Sander, "Bricklayer" / © 2012 Die Photographische Sammlung / SK Stiftung Kultur—August Sander Archiv, Cologne / Artists Rights Society (ARS), New York

Published by State University of New York Press, Albany

For information, contact State University of New York Press, Albany, NY
www.sunypress.edu

Production by Diane Ganeles
Marketing by Kate McDonnell

Library of Congress Cataloging-in-Publication Data

Kordela, Aglaia Kiarina, 1963–
    Being, time, bios : capitalism and ontology / A. Kiarina Kordela.
        p. cm. — (SUNY series, Insinuations: philosophy, psychoanalysis, literature)
    Includes bibliographical references (p.   ) and index.
    ISBN 978-1-4384-4589-2 (hc : alk. paper)—978-1-4384-4590-8 (pb : alk. paper)
    1. Biopolitics—Philosophy.   I. Title.

    JA80.K67 2013
    320.01'57—dc23   2012015235

                        10 9 8 7 6 5 4 3 2 1

Is the task ahead of us to advance towards a mode of thought, unknown hitherto in our culture, that will make it possible to reflect at the same time, without discontinuity or contradiction, upon man's being and the being of language?

—Michel Foucault, *The Order of Things: An Archaeology of the Human Sciences*

Until a new and coherent ontology of potentiality (beyond the steps that have been made in this direction by Spinoza, Schelling, Nietzsche, and Heidegger) has replaced the ontology founded on the primacy of actuality and its relation to potentiality, a political theory freed from the aporias of sovereignty remains unthinkable.

—Giorgio Agamben, *Homo Sacer: Sovereign Power and Bare Life*

One thinks of the perverse arguments of the so-called Capital-logicians: that what Hegel, in the process of making his exhaustive inventory of it, called Absolute Spirit, is now from our perspective rather to be identified as Capital itself, whose study is now our true ontology. It is indeed the new world system, the third stage of capitalism, which is for us the absent totality, Spinoza's God or Nature, the ultimate (indeed, perhaps the only) referent, the true ground of Being of our own time. Only by way of its fitful contemplation can its future, and our own, be somehow disclosed.

—Fredric Jameson, *The Geopolitical Aesthetic: Cinema and Space in the World System*

Contents

Acknowledgments

I would like to thank the State University of New York Press, and especially the editor of the series Insinuations: Philosophy, Psychoanalysis, Literature, Charles Shepherdson, for their unwavering trust in and enthusiastic support of my work. I am equally thankful to the two reviewers of the present work for engaging with it and offering me thoughtful and much appreciated feedback.

My gratitude also goes to all of my colleagues and friends at the Department of German Studies and Russian, as well as several colleagues and friends in various departments at Macalester College, the University of Minnesota, and other universities and colleges both in this country and abroad, of which I would like to name in particular the Writing and Society Research Center at the School of Humanities and Languages, University of Western Sydney, Australia. I am all the more thankful for the fact that, beyond generously supporting the promotion of my work and career, whether as a scholar or teacher or both, many of you have been an inspiration, as well as a source of comfort and pleasure in my life. Regarding new or continued support specifically during the years of the composition of the present work, I would like to express my gratitude particularly to Lin Aanonsen, Frank Adler, Karyn Ball, Aristidis Baltas, Siarhei Biareishyk, Andrew Benjamin, David Blaney, Ernesto Capello, Cesare Casarino, Daniel Cho, Jason Christenson, Justin Clemens, Paula Cooey, Joan Copjec, Stanley Corngold, Erik Davis, Sean Dempsey, Mladen Dolar, Toni Dorca, Ellis Dye, Geoff Gorham, Heiko Feldner, Peter Fenves, Moira Gatens, Jim von Geldern, Ruthann Godollei, Christian Haines, Gitta Hammarberg, Dan Hornbach, Rembert Hueser, Joanna Inglot, Jan Jagodzinski, Eleanor Kaufman, Anna Kornbluh, Sheila Kunkle, Joy and Jim Laine, David Martyn, Tracie Matysik, Mathew S. May, Mark Mazullo, Todd McGowan, Diane Michelfelder, J. D. Mininger, David Chioni Moore, John Mowitt, Kathlyn Murray, Lara Nielsen, Molly Olsen, Kostas Pagondiotis, Jason M. Peck, Robert Pfaller, Brad Prager, Angelo Restivo, Gerhard Richter, Raymond Robertson, Brian Rosenberg, Anthony Uhlmann, Arun Saldanha, Khaldoun Samman, Ahmed Samatar, Jochen Schulte-Sasse, Linda Schulte-Sasse, Simona Sawhney, Ross Shields, Hoon Song, Yannis Stavrakakis, Suzanne Stewart-Steinberg, Henry Sussman, Brynnar and Kristin Swenson, Temenuga Trifonova, Craig Upright, Dimitris Vardoulakis, Joëlle Vitiello, Peter Weisensel, Caroline Williams, and Jack Zipes.

I am also deeply thankful to my students, past and present, for their enthusiastic support and, above all, for their inspiring zeal for learning and questioning. In the context of this work, my gratitude goes particularly to the students who participated in my seminars German-French Dialogues: Phenomenology and Psychoanalysis, and Biopolitics.

Finally, I am thankful to Greece for having instilled a certain mentality in me that, as I come to realize, is likely destined to become extinct if the world of secular capitalist modernity continues in the current direction. Do "sub-races" in general share this or similar mentality? Be this as it may, my thought is with them. Of all my Greek friends I want to acknowledge this time Elias Konstantopoulos for not having had an impact, pleasant or unpleasant, on my life and for having uniquely succeeded—already in a very young and impressionable age—in being truly nothing other than that: a friend.

Preface

In a Nutshell

The present work is concerned with being in our era of secular capitalist modernity. At first sight, framing being within a concrete historical context might seem to contradict the fundamental postulate of ontology that being is transhistorical. But, as we shall see in the course of the present work, being is both transhistorical and historical, insofar as the historical is always a concrete manifestation of transhistorical relations, just as the transhistorical itself is always a retroactive formation effected by historically given epochs. The epoch of secular capitalist modernity is governed by two premises regarding its historically concrete manifestation of being. The first follows from the fact that the mode of capitalist production commodifies everything, that is, it bestows on any concrete being a double ontological quality, as both a material object of utility and an abstract exchange-value that represents it to all other beings as the measure determining its exchangeability with them. This means, as Étienne Balibar succinctly puts it, that a "commodity . . . is preeminently both a representation and, at the same time, an object; it is an object always already given in the form of representation" (2007, 67). In short, the first ontological premise of our epoch is that being does not constitute the dualistic opposite of appearance. Moreover, insofar as being is life—*bios*—being is intrinsic to the politics of our historical era in ways that are again determined by the mode of capitalist production. The latter is based on the commodification of labor and, hence, of the living beings capable of labor. It follows that the second ontological premise of our epoch is that being does not constitute the dualistic opposite of politics and, hence, that ontology includes in itself as its indispensable branch biopolitics.

xi

Predicated on the foregoing premises, the theory developed in the present work adheres to the phenomenological thesis that appearance is not what conceals but what reveals being. Other differences notwithstanding, this thesis defines any phenomenological theory, from Edmund Husserl to Jean-Paul Sartre—even when appearance, as is the case of Martin Heidegger, is reconceptualized as not the aggregation of pure or formal sensations given to perception regarding the matter and form of an entity but as something that is determined by its "equipmental character [*das Zeughafte des Zeuges*]," its "usefulness [*Dienlichkeit*]," which is "the basic feature from which this entity regards us, that is, flashes at us and thereby is present and thus is this entity [*jener Grundzug, aus dem her dieses Seiende uns anblickt, d.h. anblitzt und damit anwest und so dieses Seiende ist*]" (2008a, 348 and 347; 1960, 25 and 21). The reason for Heidegger why "usefulness" must take precedence over sensation in grasping being is that "we never really first perceive a throng of sensations, e.g., tones and noises, in the appearance of things . . . rather we hear the three-motored plane" or "the door shut in the house," and we "never hear acoustical sensations or even mere sounds" (2008a, 346). Because humans are preoccupied with the usefulness of things, usefulness must be the ground of being, just as in Sartre, as we shall later see, consciousness is the ground of being because it is the ground of humans. In extant accounts of phenomenological ontology, being, however annihilated its "thingness" may be, remains trapped within both the presupposition of actuality and anthropomorphic conceptions. The present work turns to Sartre in order to tease out these limitations of phenomenology and to revise it through the line of thought of Baruch Spinoza, Karl Marx, and Jacques Lacan. If of all phenomenologists it is Sartre who is featured prominently in my line of argument, this owes partly to his direct, and pathbreaking, identification of the body as the gaze—an insight which, in the second part of the present work, becomes instrumental in formulating a meta-phenomenological/psychoanalytic theory of biopolitics.[1]

Accordingly, the present ontology can be characterized as "meta-phenomenological." Of course, since Lacan's intervention, psychoanalysis is largely a critical response to phenomenology, and, as such, arguably already meta-phenomenological. At the same time, however, my reading of Lacan and my use of psychoanalytic terms can be seen as either orthodox Lacanian or as a "return" to Lacan, not unlike Lacan's own "unorthodox" return to Freud. The present theory could, therefore, be described as "meta-phenomenological/psychoanalytic," with all the ambivalence of this syntagma, as it can mean either or, possibly, both: "meta-phenomenological, i.e., psychoanalytic" or/and "meta-phenomenological and meta-psychoanalytic."

The first part of this work argues that ontology necessarily involves and is inseparable from three other branches of thought that traditionally are assumed to constitute separate fields of knowledge: a theory of time, a theory of the sign, and a theory of value. The necessity for interlacing these fields results from the purely relational (and, hence, not actual but virtual) character of being, which, albeit being's transhistorical constitution, is particularly pronounced in the era of secular capitalist modernity. The second part focuses on the ontological field of biopolitics, that is, the political function of bios—an Aristotelian term that, since Michel Foucault's introduction of the concept of biopolitics, has been increasingly resuscitated in much contemporary theory. My discussion of bios reveals that an analysis of biopolitics entails as its intrinsic corollary, and as a further indispensable part of the field of ontology, a theory of ethics. The third part presents an analysis of a brief film sequence, as an example of the possible workings of biopolitics in cinema, and draws some logical consequences of the present theory for racism in the international and multicultural world of global capitalism.

Although it is very likely that at this point it will sound unclear or even mystifying, one point of the entire work is that, if beyond appearance there is nothing, there is surplus—and it is because of this and this alone that we can be ethical, but also hoodwinked by the illusion of immortality. It is only by succumbing to the latter that we allow Being (Spinoza's God or Nature) to coincide with Capital.

In Context

This project began out of a sense that, generally, the contemporary *Zeitgeist* or discourse or symbolic order or whatever one may want to call it remains enthralled by the dominant presupposition that being equals mute matter. And this in spite of the by now more than three-centuries-old Spinozian conceptualization of being (or substance) as a sheer *power* (of self-actualization); and in spite of Marx's persistence in his analysis of the political economy of capitalism, one-and-a-half centuries ago, that (abstract) *value* is an aspect of being; and in spite of Sartre's attempts, during World War II, to *dematerialize* being through nothingness or lack;

and, finally, in spite of Lacan's (avowedly indebted to both Heidegger and Sartre) equation of being with the real as a void—to mention just a few of the most eminent interventions that should long ago have incited a different direction in our ontological assumptions. Concomitantly, this project is also motivated by a sense that extant accounts of biopolitics are predicated on the same, so far triumphant, naturalist premise regarding being, as they treat bios in an essentialist-materialist way which, sooner or later, as if in a twist of a Moebius band, yields to its underside, where bios becomes a purely discursive construction. In response to this theoretical paradigm, the itinerary indicated in the title and pursued in the present work, from ontology through a theory of time and history, to biopolitics, constitutes an attempt to formulate a systematic *monistic ontology* and, as its corollary, a *Marxian-psychoanalytic theory of biopolitics*, for which body and thought are neither opposites nor supplementary alternatives, but two expressions of being that, to recall Georg Simmel's words, "are as alien to each other as are thought and extension for Spinoza," "precisely because they have the same formal relation to," and "express[,] the same absolute substance" (Simmel, 62).

At this point I should pause to stress that, in spite of several affinities, by being monist, this Marxian-psychoanalytic theory is fundamentally distinct from Slavoj Žižek's theorization of Lacanian Marxism, which is informed by Hegelianism. Nevertheless, beyond my extensive reference to Sartre, whose thought is in many ways Hegelian, in this work I also often draw on Žižek's work, insofar as it facilitates the development or formulation of certain lines of my argumentation. Yet, in proposing a monist ontology and theory of biopolitics, I take distance from Hegelian dialectical thought and, when appropriate, I delineate its relevance to my work, or its limitations.

Moreover, this project endeavors to fill a conspicuous gap in contemporary discussions of bios and its relation to power. This breach is exemplified in the bilateral disregard or strife between, on the one hand, the biopolitical approach based on discourse analysis, as introduced by Foucault, and further elaborations of biopolitics by thinkers usually associated with Spinoza (e.g., Gilles Deleuze, Antonio Negri, Michael Hardt, Giorgio Agamben), and, on the other hand, Lacanian psychoanalysis. Although both sides examine the ways in which life and the body are inscribed by power, there has been no attempt to bring these two bodies of knowledge into a productive dialogue that would reveal their intrinsic relation and would allow them to enhance mutually their insights.

I maintain that a productive dialogue among these major theoretical camps is indispensable to any analysis of biopolitics, and propose to this effect a psychoanalytic theory of biopolitics, which moreover, as I will argue, alone can justify the necessity of a biopolitical theory and analysis in the first place, beyond extant theories and analyses of ideology and institutional, social, and individual practices and behaviors.

I will conclude this section with a few introductory remarks regarding the deficiency of Foucault's account of biopolitics. In the 1970s, Foucault linked bios to political power to indicate a transformation in power's mechanisms since the seventeenth century, whereby political control over "juridical" matters extended to include and focus primarily on "the administration of bodies and the calculated management of life," that is, the "biological" body and "existence of a population" (Foucault 1990, 137 and 140). In an interesting twist, however, Foucault's innovative turn within his discussion of power's shift from the legislative level to the physical or biological body brings about the opposite effect, as the permeation of the body by power leads to the total de-organization of the body (in the sense of biological organs), and its concomitant complete organization (in the sense of its discursive constitution and regulation). Eventually, Foucault's conception of power as biopower entails a slippage from the traditional, naturalist or essentialist, treatment of the body as a physical fact that precedes culture to the historicist conceptualization of the body as yet another historical construction that, like clothing and other cultural norms, can change according to fashion and circumstances. But if nothing escapes history and culture under Foucault's historicist and constructivist view, then, as Charles Shepherdson puts it, we are led back to the old "humanistic (narcissistic) notion that 'man is the maker of all things'" (163).

Psychoanalysis objects to this historicist reduction of the body to discourse not on the basis of the claim that the body is a natural fact, but by arguing that, although the body is indeed nothing but an effect of history and culture, it is a surplus effect, an effect that is not realized in, and hence cannot be reduced to, them. Psychoanalysis concurs with historicism that the body, far from being given, must be constructed and "cannot take form without undergoing this subjection to representation" which is thoroughly historical, but, going beyond historicism, psychoanalysis rejects the total subjection of the subject and the body to the control of representation (Shepherdson, 170). Or, to put it in the Heideggerian idiom, the body constitutes itself around a lack or void—for either term, lack or excess, simply signifies that the body and representation never coincide. The starting point for grasping the true workings of biopolitics is the body as a surplus or excess by-product of history. A psychoanalytic theory of biopolitics, therefore, requires that Foucault's account of biopolitics be revised through a reconceptualization of the body and bios as the excess to, or lack in, discursive construction.

And a brief postscript to "surplus." As is indicated in the previous paragraph, this term can designate either more or less than the elements required for a system to sustain its equilibrium. That the body and representation never coincide means that there is a *disequilibrium* in representation itself—whether because it is more or less that is said about the body—so that the body is either lacking in or supernumerary to representation. The term "surplus," therefore, is employed in this work to designate this disequilibrium, regardless of whether the latter manifests itself as lack or excess, so that these two concepts themselves, lack and excess, become interchangeable in this context and, hence, synonyms of surplus. Of course, this indistinctness between lack and excess is true only of the ontological level, whereas on the ontic (empirical) level, as we shall see in the context of enjoyment (*jouissance*), the distribution of enjoyment between subject and the Other, and the fact that the subject must lack enjoyment in order for the Other to harvest it as surplus, are crucial functions in the relation of subjectivity to power in secular capitalist modernity.

In Parts

Part 1 of the present work shows that the key to bridging the rift between being and thought that continues to dominate secular thought is a historical ontology that accounts for the changed character of being under the conditions of secular capitalism, while, nevertheless, remaining faithful to the primary ontological principle that being is transhistorical. For a historical ontology does not compromise the transhistorical and immutable character of being, which is indeed the object of any ontology worth its name. Rather, a historical ontology is capable of discerning being as a transhistorical entity in and through its various specific historical manifestations, which alone can provide ontology with its starting point.

Such a historical ontology entails as an indispensable part of itself a theory of time. For, contrary both to the Kantian paradigm, for which time is a pure a priori category of perception (appearance), not of being-in-itself, and to the later historicist inversion of Kantianism, for which time is an a posteriori category of pure perception (appearance)—a non-dualistic conception of being and appearance (thought) recognizes time as intrinsic to both being and appearance, and postulates accordingly that ontology be inseparable from a theory of temporality. If we understand properly the consequences of Sartre's statement that "the essence of the appearance is an 'appearing' which is no longer opposed to any *being*," then the categories through which we perceive appearances must be intrinsic to being itself (Sartre, 7). By the same token, if being and appearance/representation are not severed, an ontology is always also a theory of representation (and vice versa). And since representation consists always of values, whether linguistic (signs) or economic (exchange-values), then our ontology is also inseparable from a theory of value. This explains why the present work positions centrally and intertwines four major modern schools of thought for which being and appearance are not conceived dualistically: Spinozian monism, Marx's theory of value, phenomenology, and psychoanalysis.

It is important to note here that the aforementioned monistic conceptualization of being and representation entails a radical revision of the concept of *representation* itself. The term can no longer designate either phenomenon (appearance) or language, as has traditionally been the case, but rather it now comes to stand for *value*, both exchange-value on the economic level, and semantic value (sign) on the linguistic level—both of which are *systems of arbitrary differential relations*—as opposed to use-value and the (phenomenological) in-itself—that is, this aspect of being that is not determined through arbitrary differential relations—whereby *both value or representation and the in-itself are the two equivalent aspects of being.*[2]

By inserting among my four primary interlocutors—Spinoza, Marx, Sartre, Lacan—Paolo Virno, part 2 shows the historically specific mode in which being emerges as a biopolitical object in secular capitalist modernity. My meta-phenomenological/psychoanalytic reconceptualization of bios leads to the thesis that, contrary to what current biopolitical theories maintain, the object of biopolitics is not the regulation of body and life as biological conglomerations but rather the human being's relationship to a specifically modern (i.e., secular) illusion of immortality. This relation, in turn, is liable to biopolitical administration through discursive constructions and deconstruction of gazes. Moreover, while phenomenology operates on the axis finitude-infinity, the present meta-phenomenological/psychoanalytic biopolitical theory argues that a third category of time—what Spinoza refers to as the "species of eternity"—is required in order to account for being. It is under this species of eternity (*sub specie aeternitatis*) that Spinoza's "third kind of knowledge" occurs, as the sole knowledge that gives us access to truth and Joy, and which constitutes the culmination of his theory of ethics. By differentiating between the species of eternity and infinity, and by linking the former to the ethical dimension and the latter to the illusion of immortality—understood not as the belief in afterlife but as a fetishistic disavowal of one's mortality, which we could call properly "secular immortality"—I advance the following thesis regarding the biopolitical administration of the subject's relation to mortality and immortality. The structural similarity and slippery conflation between infinity (the dimension of immortality) and the species of eternity (the ethical dimension) enables the biopolitical mechanism through which human subjects give up their ethical mode for the sake of (the illusion of) immortality—or, to put it in the Lacanian idiom, the mechanism by which subjects give up their enjoyment (Spinoza's Joy) for the sake of the enjoyment of the Other.

Part 3 demonstrates that this monist meta-phenomenological/psychoanalytic theory of ontology and biopolitics has portentous significance for the analysis of culture and politics. The first chapter of this part turns to film, and specifically to Paul Verhoeven's *Total Recall* (1990), to examine the function of cinema as a major biopolitical apparatus due to its direct dependence on the gaze (camera). The chapter advances a theory of "biocinema" that addresses the cinematic capacity of (de)constructing gazes as a means of administering the illusion of immortality. My discussion of biopolitics and its mechanisms concludes, in the last chapter, by examining the ramifications of the insight that biopolitics administers (the illusion of) immortality for Foucault's thesis that all biopolitical states are necessarily racist. A brief comparison of the media representations of violent death occurring in the West and its "other" after 9/11 reveals the necessity to reconceptualize radically our notion of "race" in postmodern capitalism in terms of what I call "biorace." The bioracial theory developed here remains predicated on the racist division between, in Foucault's words, "what must live and what must die" (Foucault 2003, 254); yet, going beyond to either ethnically or (Foucault's) biologically based modes of discrimination, this distinction is now shown to reflect the struggle between the super-race of the (self-perceived) immortals and what it perceives as its other, the sub-race of the mortals. Since they "*must* die," the sub-race consists not of those who bear mortality as the inevitable conclusion of life, but of those whose mission, destiny, and *raison d'être is* to die. Thus, their violent death does not constitute, often even in the most humanitarian eyes of the Western super-biorace, a crime.

PART I

MONIST META-PHENOMENOLOGICAL ONTOLOGY

Being and Time

Phenomenology is the most eminent modernist school of thought that attempted to produce a systematic ontology in which being is not opposed to its appearances. Mainly responding to two of the most influential figures of phenomenological thought, Edmund Husserl and Martin Heidegger, Jean-Paul Sartre adopted as his starting point their shared principle that there is no "dualism of appearance and essence," that is, that the "appearance does not hide the essence." Rather, the "essence of an existent . . . is the manifest law which presides over the succession of its appearances." The "being of the phenomenon" (as opposed to the "phenomenon of being") is nothing other than this "principle of the series" of its appearances. And though Sartre's phenomenological devotion initially tempted him to assert that "essence, as the principle of the series, is definitely only the concatenation of appearances," and hence "itself an appearance," he soon had to recognize that essence spills out from the contained "well connected series of its manifestations" due to nothing less than *infinity*—something which cannot ever appear. For "the existent . . . cannot be reduced to a *finite* series of manifestations since each one of them is a relation to a subject constantly changing." Although "an *object* may disclose itself only through a single *Abschattung*"—in a single adumbration, shading, aspect, or profile—"the sole fact of there being a subject implies the possibility of multiplying the points of view *on* that *Abschattung*," and "[t]his suffices to multiply to infinity the *Abschattung* under consideration." Thus, Sartre concludes, what the phenomenological enterprise has succeeded in doing is not "overcoming *all* dualisms" that oppose "interior to exterior" or "being" to "appearance," but rather "converting them all into a new dualism: that of finite and infinite" (Sartre, 3, 5, and 7). In short, one first thing

3

that phenomenology shows is, in Jacques Lacan's summarizing phrase, that "where there is being, infinity is required" (1998, 10).

If it were creeping into our phenomenological immanence from some out-worldly heaven it would be fairly easy for secular thought to get rid of infinity; but this is not the case. Infinity is stubbornly wedded to phenomenological experience as such, insofar as the appearance presupposes a perceiving subject, and hence a theoretically infinite multiplicity of "points of view" from one of which any given subject may perceive the appearing object. Of course, as the fact that this infinite multiplicity of gazes is posited only "theoretically" indicates, *infinity* remains also within phenomenology a *transcendent* category, that is, a category that is never given empirically—there can never be empirically an infinite number of people perceiving an object—yet, this transcendence is enfolded in immanence, insofar as it does not emanate from some extra-empirical beyond but is rather the effect of empirical experience itself. This *enfolding of transcendence within the plane of immanence* is constitutive of what can properly be called *secular* thought.

Eventually, Sartre concludes this section of *Being and Nothingness* by acknowledging that, even though "there is nothing behind the appearance," nevertheless, the being or "the essence of the appearance is an 'appearing' which is no longer opposed to any *being*." Well, then, as he subsequently wonders, "there arises a legitimate problem concerning *the being of this appearing*" (Sartre, 6–7). The answer to this question is arguably summarized in Lacan's statement: "if beyond appearance there is nothing in itself, there is the gaze" (1981, 103)—by which I emphatically invite us to understand the gaze "of the Other, the capital Other, [which] is already there in every opening . . . of the unconscious" (130). This "capital Other" is not simply the symbolic order, understood as a given society with its ideological systems, laws, and so forth, as in many of Slavoj Žižek's or Ernesto Laclau and Chantal Mouffe's, and others' writings. True, no society is ever given in its totality as an object to be perceived by an empirical subject, and, by that token, we can say that empirically " 'society' is impossible" as a whole—and is, hence, transcendent to experience (including several other inferences that Laclau and Mouffe draw from this, such as that society consists of "purely relational identities," something that, as will eventually become clear through the line of argument presented here, results from the fact that being itself is relational) (Laclau and Mouffe, 114). But what is often missed in this all-too-easy reduction of Lacan's "capital Other" to society—a phenomenon in which we are immersed in our everyday experience—is the fact that here we are speaking of the *totality* of society. And the moment we speak of (the) *totality* (of whatever)—just as when we speak of infinity—we enter a realm that operates according to entirely non-empirical modes of temporality and laws. That the "*the unconscious is outside*" certainly means that it is society, the external world itself—but *qua totality*, that is, as something that is altogether outside experience itself (insofar as experience is given to consciousness) (Lacan 1981, 123). In turn, that neither totality nor infinity can be given empirically (consciously) means that in order to talk about them presupposes above all figuring out their spatio-temporal coordinates and specific structures—which pertain not to actuality (consciousness) but to a virtual (unconscious) transcendence that is inseparable from the empirical (conscious) plane of immanence. "Secular" does not mean the elimination of transcendence; rather, *the "unconscious" is the Freudian/psychoanalytic term for indicating precisely this enfolding of transcendence within immanence* required by thought in order for it to become truly secular. To introduce a reference to which we shall have plenty of opportunities to return, "the true formula of atheism is not *God is dead*" but "*God is unconscious*" (Lacan 1981, 59). And it is this unconscious or total or infinite multiplicity of gazes—an all-seeing omniscient gaze—that, no matter how secular thought is, renders being conjunctive with infinity and, hence, with immanent transcendence.

We can find a concept that offers us a good idea of what immanent transcendence is in Walter Benjamin's "Absolute." As Fred Rush writes, "for Benjamin, the profane world of finitude is of an entirely other order from the Absolute," so that "an 'infinite approach' of the profane to the Absolute is an impossibility" (70). Paraphrasing Rush's statement, I would say that the "empirical" world of "human looks" or gazes is of an entirely other order from transcendent Infinity, so that an infinite approach of the empirical to Infinity is impossible. In other words, the gaze *qua* real is not an infinity of human looks, but, as Sartre will point out further on, the place from which the subject cannot see itself.

Returning to Sartre, immanent transcendence is a way of going beyond simply "replac[ing] the dualism of being and appearance" with "a new opposition, the 'finite' and the infinite," since the relation in question is actually that of "the infinite in the finite." For "the appearance, which is *finite*, indicates itself in its finitude, but at the same time in order to be grasped as an appearance-of-that-which-appears, it requires that it be surpassed toward infinity" (Sartre, 6). In other words, and specifically in terms of set theory, being is not-all, that is, a non-totalizable set insofar as what is supposed to be enclosed within the set is also outside it. As Sartre proceeds to write:

> What appears in fact is only an *aspect* of the object, and the object is altogether *in* that aspect and altogether outside of it. It is altogether *within*, in that it manifests itself *in* that aspect; it shows itself as the structure of the appearance, which is at the same time the principle of the series. It is altogether outside, for the series itself will never appear nor can it appear. Thus the outside is opposed in a new way to the inside, and the being-which-does-not-appear, to the appearance. (6)

There is nothing behind appearance, but the appearance offers itself in two ways: on the one hand, as appearance in its finitude, and, on the other hand, as being-which-does-not-appear, the series itself of infinite appearances and their points of view, which "will never appear" and which allows for any concrete appearance that, by simply appearing, functions as the principle of the series. On the one hand, we have finitude, appearance, and the concrete point of view from which it appears; on the other hand, we have infinity, the all-seeing gaze under which the entire series of appearances would appear, but never does. Hence Lacan's two other succinct formulations: "there is no Other of the Other" and "the gaze I encounter . . . is not a seen gaze, but a gaze imagined by me in the field of the Other" (1998, 81; 1981, 84). "There is no Other of the Other" is another way for saying "there is no gaze of the Other," for the gaze of the Other (i.e., the gaze of the entire series of appearances) is the infinity of all possible points of view; as far as experience is concerned, therefore, there is no such gaze, since the infinity of all possible points of view could never determine me to perceive the appearance from any finite point of view. On the other hand, I do nevertheless perceive appearances only from a finite perspective, and if I am capable of doing so it is only because I imagine a specific (finite) gaze on the part of the Other. It is by imagining a specific gaze there where there is only an infinity of gazes that the object can appear at all and that the series of appearances is subjugated to a principle and obtains the structure specified by this appearance. The gaze, therefore, is altogether *within*, in that it manifests itself *in* the aspect of the finite gaze I imagine in the field of the Other; but it also is altogether *outside*, for the gaze itself, as the infinite series of possible points of view, cannot appear.

Let us also note a further point about the gaze that will become crucial in the discussion of biopolitics in part 2. If I can imagine a specific gaze in the field of the Other it is precisely because no such gaze is given to experience, for in truth the gaze is the non-appearing infinity of gazes. The finite gaze emerges due to its reference to the infinity of gazes, which is itself entailed through its reference to the finite gaze. In one word, *the gaze is the cause of itself and, as such, it is both self-referential and the power or potentiality of actualizing itself.* In fact, that the gaze is the potential of self-actualization entails the (Spinozian) principle that the essence of the whole world (substance, in Spinoza's terms) is itself the power of self-actualization. For, as Sartre writes, the body as "a point of view supposes a double relation: a relation with the things *on which the body is* a point of view and a relation with the observer *for whom the body is* a point of view" (Sartre, 433). In other words, "my being-in-the-world, by the sole fact that it *realizes* a world, causes itself to be indicated to itself as a being-in-the-midst-of-the-world by the world which it realizes" (419). In realizing the world which, at the same time, is what realizes ("causes") my body as a being-in-the-midst-of-the-world, my body and the world are one and the same "flesh" which is both the cause and the effect of itself.[1]

Turning now to the temporality of being, once we are beyond the dualism of being and appearance, and we conceive of being in monistic terms—according to which being "is altogether *in* that aspect [of appearance] and altogether outside of it"—then we are forced to acknowledge that *being pertains to two distinct spatio-temporalities*: finitude, *qua* appearance, and infinity *qua* gaze of the entire series of appearances or being-which-does-not-appear.

This ontological thesis is far removed from the basic Kantian premise that time and space are transcendental categories of perception (appearance), not of being or the thing-in-itself (the latter standing for Kant in a dualistic opposition to appearance). Kant's premise that "space and time, together with the appearances in them" are "nothing existing in themselves and outside my representations," is the logical conclusion deriving from the dualism that opposes representation (appearance) to being-in-itself (1977, 82, §52c). Since this dualism has now collapsed, we can no longer maintain that the categories of appearance are not also categories of the being-in-itself. Rather, if appearance involves two spatialities and temporalities, it is only because being itself involves two: *finitude, insofar as it appears, and infinity insofar as it does not.* Going farther back than Kant, the old (Platonic) hierarchy in which appearance is inferior to being collapses, as the appearance cannot be considered an adulterated simulacrum of the being-which-does-not-appear or of the series to which it belongs, since the given appearance and the entire series of appearances presuppose one another.

Our preliminary conclusion therefore is that the (Kantian) *a priori categories of thought* through which we perceive appearances are in truth *intrinsic to being itself.* It is being in itself that appears and does not appear. Being is the appearance and the series of appearances that can never appear. Finitude and infinity, therefore, are being's own temporal attributes.

Sartre arrived at the same conclusion: "temporality can be only a relation of being at the heart of this same being. . . . Temporality *is not.* Only a being of a certain structure of being can be temporal in the unity of its being" (194–195). Yet, as we shall have the chance to see throughout part 1, Sartre's conception of temporality is limited by—and his phenomenological ontology after all fails to grasp entirely the relation between time and being partly due to—the fact that he reduces the "being of a certain structure of being" to the being of a for-itself exclusively conceived as human consciousness.

Monist Being and Atheism

Given the historical emergence of phenomenological thought in modernism, many would tend to attribute the possibility of a monistic conception of being to circumstances ranging from the massive industrialization of capitalist production and the concomitant urbanization to the outbreak of two World Wars. Undoubtedly, this association is true regarding many aspects of phenomenological thought, and particularly Sartre's existentialism, but we do also know that the first systematic articulation of a monistic ontology dates back to the seventeenth century, specifically in the philosophy of Baruch (Benedict de) Spinoza.

The primary phenomenological postulate regarding the ontological equality between being and its appearances is expressed in Spinoza's monistic conceptualization of substance (and its attributes) and its modes, that is, the way substance appears in its empirical actualizations. For Spinoza, substance *is* both its attributes *and* its modes, even as there is a conceptual difference in their ontological status. It is for this reason that Spinoza can infer that God *is* the world, and that there is only one substance, which is "*Deus, seu Natura*" [God, *or* Nature]," or that "in Nature there is only one substance," and "*Except God, no substance can be or be conceived*" (1990, 436; 1985, 544; *Ethics*, part IV, pref.; and 420; *Ethics*, part I, prop. 14 and cor. 1). It is particularly in propositions 21–23 of the first part of the *Ethics* that Spinoza stresses that there is an absolute univocity between the attributes of substance and its empirical modes, because of which (unlike both Platonism and Judeo-Christianity) the former cannot be more perfect than the latter. As Gilles Deleuze puts it:

> [T]he attributes are strictly the same to the extent that they constitute the essence of substance and to the extent that they are involved in, and contain, the essences of mode. For

example, it is in the same form that bodies imply extension and that extension is an attribute of divine substance. In this sense, God [i.e., substance] does not possess the perfections implied by the "creatures" [modes] in a form different from that which these perfections have in the creatures themselves: thus Spinoza radically rejects the notions of eminence, equivocity, and even analogy (notions according to which God would possess the perfections in another form, a superior form . . .). The Spinozian immanence is therefore no less opposed to emanation than to creation. And immanence signifies first of all the univocity of the attributes: the same attributes are affirmed of the substance they compose and of the modes they contain. (1988, 52)[1]

Spinoza explicitly opposed creationism by stating that: "God is the immanent, not the transitive, cause of all things" (1985, 428; *Ethics*, part I, prop. 18). That is, rather than being a cause that precedes its effects (creation) in linear or diachronic time, God is a cause that is itself the effect of its own effects. In other words, being both its cause and effect, the transcendent (God or substance) is in a differential relation with the empirical and, thus, pertains to the same plane of immanence as it.

Throughout the present work, the term "transcendence" will be used in this monistic sense, as conceptually distinct from empirical reality and, yet, as pertaining to the same plane of immanence as empirical reality, for it is at once its cause and effect and has positive ontological status nowhere else but in its effects, the modes of empirical reality. Moreover, insofar as the transcendent always necessarily entails (as both its effect and cause) that in relation to which it is transcendent, it can no longer be differentiated from the transcendental. This distinction was crucial to Kant, precisely because he wanted to sustain transcendence as something that escapes the plane of immanence, and hence he needed a further term (the transcendental) in order to designate the logical or metaphysical preconditions of the empirical domain. Given that for monism God is these logical or metaphysical preconditions (attributes) of empirical reality (modes), the transcendent and the transcendental overlap entirely—in fact, in monistic terms, the transcendental is all transcendence can mean.

This non-creationist concept of God as the immanent cause of the world (which is another way of asserting the identity of God and the world) follows necessarily from any monistic conception of being for, as Sartre argued, if God is conceived as a "divine subjectivity" capable of a "creation *ex nihilo*," then "[s]uch subjectivity cannot have even the *representation* of an objectivity, and consequently it cannot even be affected by the *will* to create the objective." Hence, Sartre concludes,

> being, if it is suddenly placed outside the subjective . . . can only affirm itself as distinct from and opposed to its creator; otherwise it dissolves in him. . . . If being exists as over against God, it is its own support; it does not preserve the least trace of divine creation. In a word, even if it had been created, being-in-itself would be *inexplicable* in terms of creation; for it assumes its being beyond the creation. (26–27)

A creationist conception of divinity entails God's subjectivization and thereby renders (objective) being inexplicable. There remain, therefore, two options for any ontology: either, following the Nietzschean attitude of "God is dead," to ignore the concept of God altogether—the so-called death of metaphysics—or, following the Spinozian path, to equate God with nature by conceiving of God not as the (subjective) creator but as the (objective) immanent cause of nature—the enfolding of metaphysics or transcendence within the plane of immanence. This difference does not in the least imply that Spinoza was any less an atheist than Nietzsche; on the contrary, it indicates that he was more properly monist *and* atheist than the latter. For to ignore God means nothing other than to be blinded by appearances to the point of ignoring the series itself of all appearances, the being-that-does-not-appear. Which is why Lacan insisted that "the true formula of atheism is not *God is dead* . . . [but] *God is unconscious*," that is, God is the entire series of appearances (or thoughts) that will never appear (1981, 59). Like the infinite gaze, the unconscious is another term for the entire series of appearances.[2]

Atheism is the inclusion of infinity within the plane of immanence, something which is possible only through a monistic conception of being. This is why such an ontology is particularly apposite to the era of secular (and capitalist) modernity, since the seventeenth century. To say so, however, amounts to the claim that the relation between being and appearance is historically determined—and, yet, as is the postulate of any proper ontology, this historical relation must account for being also transhistorically. We shall return to this point.

Value—Being—Surplus

Now we shall see why, beyond being a theory of time, a monistic ontology is always also a theory of value, and hence of the sign. As this "hence" indicates, there is an intrinsic relation between value and sign, which we must approach first.

As Michel Foucault has extensively argued, "[e]ver since the Stoics, the system of signs in the Western world has been a ternary one, for it was recognized as containing the significant, the signified, and the conjuncture." This state of affairs prevailed also over the entire period of theocracy, up to and including the "Renaissance," insofar as God, as the Creator or transitive cause of the world, was the guarantor of the conjunctures, that is, "the similitudes that link the marks [significants] to the things designated by them [signifieds]," so that the link between the "mark" and the "thing" was "organic." It is this organic, divinely grounded bond that raised the status of the word to that of the Word—as is indicated in the fact that in this paradigm the signified is taken as being directly the *thing* designated by the significant. "From the seventeenth century," however, "the arrangement of the signs was to become binary, since it was to be defined . . . as the connection of a significant and a signified," without any organic link between the two, whereby the relation between significant and signified became, as Ferdinand de Saussure would put it in the context of structural linguistics, "arbitrary" (Foucault 1970, 42; Saussure, 120–121). Henceforth, signifiers and signifieds "are purely differential and negative when considered separately," that is, each is determined within its own synchronic system through its differences from all other elements (signifiers *or* signifieds) of the system, and in itself, without this differentiation, it would be nothing (Saussure, 118–121). By the same token, henceforth, far from enjoying the status of the Word, the word becomes what we know as the signifier,

13

which in "modern thought" was to become the object of "the analysis of meaning and signification," as opposed to the object of ontology (being) (Foucault, 1970, 43). The collapse of the organic divine bond entailed that henceforth representation was to be considered as separated from being by what eventually became an unbridgeable abyss.

This modern object known as the (arbitrary) signifier emerged in the seventeenth century, that is, at the same time at which, with Spinoza, the discourse became capable of conceiving of God as no longer the transitive but the immanent cause of the world. If the world is not created, then there is no divine link between "marks" and "things," and hence the word is an arbitrary signifier. The non-creationist conception of God entails the destruction of the "organic" link between words and things, or, in Foucault's words, that "[t]hings and words were to be separated from one another," so that the "profound kinship of language with the world was . . . dissolved" (Foucault 1970, 43).

However, as I will presently argue, this conclusion is correct only insofar as it accurately describes *the major error of modern epistemology and ontology*, according to which, the signifier (representation) was indeed to become a self-referential system, severed from being—an error raised to the indisputable principle of philosophy since Kant, who, precisely, reduced space and time to the *a priori* categories of representation, and not of being. To be sure, it would be a preposterous epistemological fallacy within modern thought to consider the signifier, as one used to do with regard to the Word, as "a stigma upon things, a mark imprinted across the world," as "part of its most ineffaceable forms," and as such, as "unique and absolute" (Foucault 1970, 42). As Foucault admonishes us, right after having raised the question cited earlier as one of the epigraphs of this work: "If that is so," that is, if the task at hand is to "reflect at the same time, without discontinuity or contradiction, upon man's being and the being of language," then: "we must take the very greatest precautions to avoid anything that might be a naïve return" to past theories of discourse, be they "the Classical theory of discourse" or the theocratic (1970, 338). The crucial point, however, is that the discursive collapse of the organic link between things and words, *pace* Foucault and the vast majority of modern epistemology, amounts to something more than itself. That is, its true effect is not the severance of the thing from the word but, rather, a radical and unforeseen *reconfiguration of the relation between the thing and the word or being and appearance*—one that Karl Marx was the first philosopher to represent systematically.

To enter Marx's line of thought we need first to return briefly to Spinoza and what is known as his "pantheism"—which is the first philosophical model that grasped, even before Marx, this new configuration of the relation between thing and word. In Lacan's succinct formulation, Spinoza's "pantheism" means nothing other than "the reduction of the field of God to the universality of the signifier" (1981, 275). For, to conceive of God as the immanent cause of the world amounts to conceiving of the world as a system of differential relations, in which there is no cause transitively preceding and determining them. This is exactly what the signifier is: a system of differential relations. To say that God is Nature entails that nature *is* a system of signifiers. This is the sole possible meaning of "pantheism" once God is the immanent cause of the world.

However, to equate God or nature with the universality of the signifier does not in the least mean, as in some unexpected idealist sleight of hand, to reduce the world to thought or ideas, thereby denying its materiality. Rather, it means that *nature is thinking matter*, that is, that thought—the existence of a system of signifiers—is not the exclusive prerogative or distinctive characteristic of the human being. If this has always so easily been assumed to be the case it is due to a persistent reduction of thought to consciousness. And, although it is above all Freud who is known for having introduced the idea of "unconscious thought," we find one of its earliest and quite extensive presentations in Marx's pantheism, as presented in *Capital, Volume 1*. In other words, Marx invented not only, as Slavoj Žižek has argued, the symptom, but also the unconscious, and he did so in a way that makes amply clear that no reduction of the world to ideas is involved in the concept of pantheism.[1]

But before we turn indeed to Marx, let us note parenthetically that Spinoza's pantheism also entails that there is no room for any possible teleology in the world, in accord with the absence of a transitive first cause. For if there is no first cause, there can be no final cause either. This is a point to which we shall return in the context of the analysis of historical time.

If Marx, unlike his contemporary economists, grasped the mechanism of capital, it is because he replicated the Spinozian reduction of the world to the universality of the signifier on the level of economy: he subjected all (commodified) nature to (exchange-)value, whereby nature—including humans and their labor as "objectified," "congealed," or "abstract human labor"—is not only the vast flock of "objects of utility" (use-value, i.e., no abstract value but a concrete physical, material thing) but also the aggregation of "sensuous things which are at the same time suprasensible or social," that is, "values . . . as their [men's] language" (Marx 1990, 150, 165, and 167). The transformation of objects into commodities entails that they no longer are only material things but also signifiers, by dint of the fact that they now become abstract exchange-values. Marx is emphatic about the ontological difference between the realm of exchange-value and that of use-value:

> Not an atom of matter enters into the objectivity of commodities as values; in this it is the direct opposite of the coarsely sensuous objectivity of commodities as physical objects. . . . When . . . we said in the customary manner that a commodity is both a use-value and an exchange-value, this was, strictly speaking, wrong. A commodity is a use-value or object of utility, and a "value." (1990, 138 and 152)

Empirical reality, Marx argues, consists of two distinct universes: in the one there is no room for even "an atom of matter"—this is the universe of the circulation of exchange-values, with its own category of synchronic time (circulation-time); the other is the universe of material objects, that is, the universe of the production of physical objects by specific, specialized, labor, and as subject to material decay in the linear temporality of physical life (production-time).[2] Circulation-time reigns in the "noisy sphere" of circulation and self-valorization, "where everything," that is, the production of surplus-value, "takes place on the surface and in full view of everyone," whereas production-time marks "the hidden abode of production," in which "the secret of profit-making" remains hidden from the public view, just like the thing-in-itself is traditionally assumed to remain veiled under its representation (1990, 279–280).

Commodities *qua* exchange-values become "suprasensible" or the "language" of humans since both exchange-values and signifiers are determined purely differentially within their synchronic systems, in which there is not "an atom of matter." By being economic values, commodities become also signs, *linguistic* or *semantic* values, since both obey the same laws.

But Marx's point about economic value (and implicitly semantic value, since values are "men's language") is that these two universes, (exchange-)value and material objects, are the precondition for another kind of value: surplus-value. For surplus-value must "have its origin . . . in circulation and not in circulation," in exchange-value with its synchronic circulation-time, and not in it, that is, in the realm of the production of material objects with concrete and inherent physical properties, which are subject to the linear and finite production-time (1990, 268). *A fortiori*:

> the money [exchange-value] and the commodity [use-value] function only as different modes of existence of value itself [surplus-value], the money as its general mode of existence, the commodity as its particular or, so to speak, disguised mode. (1990, 255)

Exchange-value and use-value are the "modes" in which "value itself" (surplus-value) manifests itself empirically. In other words, there is only *one substance or being-in-itself, "value itself,"* whose attributes cannot manifest themselves empirically as such, but rather appear in two different modes, as exchange-value and as objects of utility.

Here we see that Marx adopted not only Spinoza's pantheism but also his monism regarding being-in-itself or substance, according to which "in Nature there is only one substance" that has two attributes, "thought" and "extension," which appear in the empirical modes of "an extended thing [use-value]" and "a thinking thing [exchange-value]" (1985, 420 and 448–449; *Ethics*, part I, prop. 14, cor. 1, and part II, prop. 1 and 2). Indeed, empirically, both objects of utility and exchange-values or signs are *given*, for even if the latter are abstract symbols, symbols too make their appearance in reality (as money or letters and sounds). By contrast, surplus-value is a purely *metaphysical* category, something that cannot ever be given in empirical reality as such. Marx stresses this point by writing that "[a]t the end of the process" of "buying in order to sell" for more money, "we do not receive on one hand the original £100, and on the other the surplus-value of £10. What emerges is rather a value of £110," where the originally advanced exchange-value (£100) and the surplus-value (£10) it yielded are empirically indistinguishable—both "the end and the beginning [of the process being] the same, money or exchange-value"—so that the final £110 "is in exactly the same form, appropriate for commencing the valorization process [anew], as the original £100," the "value of the

£110 ha[ving] the same need for valorization as the value of the £100," since both are exchange-values (1990, 252–253). In other words, in capitalism surplus-value manages to appropriate the function of the one substance of which everything in the world is a mode of manifestation. We shall return again to this point.

For now let us rephrase Marx's ontology in terms of Sartre's phenomenological ontology, a process which will also reveal the fundamental shortcoming of phenomenology. Use-value corresponds to the *phenomenological* being-in-itself, about which Sartre, following Hegel, writes that it "*is what it is . . .* it is *solid* (*massif*) . . .* the synthesis of itself with itself," without having a "*within*" which is opposed to a "*without*" (28). Use-value is a material object which, unlike signs or exchange-values, does not need differential relations to a "*without*" in order to constitute itself, and thus seems to be given in its plenitude. Exchange-value, on the other hand, corresponds to what Sartre calls the "for-itself," which is "perpetually determining itself *not to be* the in-itself," that is, not to be matter, not to allow even an atom of matter to enter itself (134). The "*for-itself* is defined . . . as being what it is not and not being what it is," just as both the exchange-value and the concept of this apple on my table are defined as being what the apple is not and as not being what the apple is (28). Closer scrutiny, however, undermines the in-itself's plenitude by revealing that in truth the in-itself is posited as such by the for-itself's nihilation, or, as Hegel puts it: "this *in-itself* turns out to be a mode in which the object is only for an other" (Hegel 1977, 104; §166). In Sartre's own words: "the for-itself includes within its being the being of the object which it is not inasmuch as the for-itself puts its own being into question as not being the being of the object" (244). Put even more strongly: "The for-itself . . . is the nothing by which *there are things*" (555). It is the nihilation of the for-itself—consciousness, for both Hegel and Sartre—that brings about the being-in-itself.

Here we begin to see how Marx parts way from the Hegelian tradition. To be sure, Marx asserts that if there are material commodities (the in-itself) it is because they are the "particular or, so to speak, disguised mode" of immaterial value. But, crucially, he asserts the same also about exchange-value (the for-itself), which too is a "mode of existence of value," albeit not the "particular" but the "general." In other words, unlike Hegel and Sartre, in Marx the in-itself (being or use-value) and the for-itself (consciousness or exchange-value) are modes of a third: surplus-value. Through Marx we understand that, while use-value and exchange-value are the phenomenological in-itself and for-itself, respectively, value-in-itself (surplus) is the *meta-phenomenological or metaphysical* being-in-itself-for-itself, the substance whose attributes are expressed empirically in the phenomenological being-in-itself and being-for-itself. And since both use-values or the phenomenological in-itself and exchange-values or the phenomenological for-itself are the two modes in which surplus or the meta-phenomenological in-itself-for-itself manifests itself empirically, it is more accurate to say not that the in-itself is posited through the nihilation of the for-itself but that both, in-itself and for-itself, are posited through a primary nihilation—which is simultaneously an actualization—of the meta-phenomenological in-itself-for-itself. *Phenomenology cannot grasp the proper relation of being and appearance because it ignores precisely this meta-phenomenological being-in-itself-for-itself.*[3]

At this point a subtle, yet crucial distinction must be made explicit. This being-in-itself-for-itself is *not* what Marx calls "value in itself" or surplus-value *per se*; rather, it is its adulterated equivalent insofar as, as mentioned earlier, in capitalism surplus-value succeeds in appropriating the role and function of the meta-phenomenological being-in-itself-for-itself. The latter, like Spinoza's substance, is the cause of itself, and, hence, it is the *power of self-actualization*. By contrast, surplus-value is a function within a specific historical formation that is itself the effect of external causes—unless we want to claim that the cause of the emergence of the capitalist mode of production was capitalism itself, as is tacitly claimed in the ideological narrative of "a primitive accumulation," that is, "the 'previous accumulation' of Adam Smith," to which we shall return in the chapter "Historical Time" (Marx 1990, 873). In other words, surplus-value is the actualization of one historical appearance, whereas the meta-phenomenological being-in-itself-for-itself is the power of the series of all appearances to actualize itself. To distinguish *substance or being*—the being-in-itself-for-itself—from surplus-value, I will employ for the former the term "surplus."

There will be further opportunities to approach the difference between surplus-value and surplus in more detail throughout this work, but as an introductory remark I would like to refer to Lacan's comment in 1970, that: "It's not because one nationalizes the means of production at the level of socialism in one country that one has thereby done away with surplus value, if one doesn't know what it is" (2007, 108). Lacan's contention in this seminar is that Marx discovered something more profound and wider than what he, in a rather reductionist approach, called surplus-value and defined as a purely economic category specific to capitalism. *Surplus-value is only the specific modulation of surplus or the being-in-itself-for-itself under the capitalist economic organization.* In other words, one cannot get rid of surplus, but this does not mean that it must by any ontological necessity take the form of the capitalist surplus-value. Returning to Fredric Jameson's words cited in one of the epigraphs of the present work, in order to fathom the world order of "Capital" we must first understand that the object of "our true ontology" is not capital but surplus, and that capital is only one of its historically possible modulations. What is ontologically necessary (and, hence, transhistorical) is surplus, and this, as we shall see in the chapter "Historical and Transhistorical Aspects of Being," can entail historical realities as diverse as the ancient Greek democracy with its slaves, theocratic feudalism, and capitalism, so that it would be both arrogant and narrow-minded to assume that one could anticipate being's future historical modulations and, hence, socio-politico-economic organizations.

Recapitulating, surplus, therefore, is our third term, next to the gaze and the unconscious, for being, which is the entire series of appearances insofar as it is the cause of itself, or, which is the power of the series of all appearance to actualize itself.

In the specific capitalist modulation of surplus as surplus-value, the unconscious of capital becomes surplus-value. One might object here, isn't capital's most conscious intention the accumulation of surplus-value? No: capitalism's conscious intention is the increase of exchange-value. The two statements may be taken as saying the same thing *practically*, but, as we saw Marx emphatically insist, they do not *ontologically*, since surplus-value is not something I can ever have in my hand, unlike exchange-value (money) which I can. The "cunning" of capital, in precisely the Hegelian sense, is that, while it sees its essence and sole purpose of existence in the perpetual accrual of exchange-value, in truth and generally without knowing it, it serves the perpetual accumulation of something transcendent to its empirical reality, surplus-value. What remains unconscious in capitalism is that its support is metaphysical: the being-in-itself-for-itself or surplus, albeit only a disfiguration thereof. The true formula of materialism, as well as of pragmatism, is not "transcendence is dead, there is only matter" or "profit," but, quite the contrary, *matter and profit are the empirical manifestations of transcendent surplus*, whether the latter is distorted or not.

Finally, this homology among being, sign, and value—the ontologi-cal, semantic, and economic series—owes to the fact that the semantic and economic series are historical modulations of the transhistorical being, surplus, which will always already have emerged as the effect of the two historical series. History is a name for the modulations of surplus in the economic and semantic fields, which is in turn reflected in our historically concrete ontological accounts. The economic modulation of the ontological surplus as surplus-value within capitalism entails that a similar distortion must occur also in the semantic field and, by extension in human subjectivity, insofar as the human "subject is the subject of the signifier" (Lacan 1981, 67). As will become evident in part 2 here, grasping the specific historical modulations of surplus in secular capitalist modernity is instrumental in fathoming two intersecting, yet radically divergent functions of human subjectivity, ethics and biopolitics. For now, let us continue to examine further being and time, and to reflect on this project of expansion and revision of phenomenology through Spinoza, Marx, and Lacan.

Matter

Post-Kantian philosophy has been dominated by the assumption that being in itself is matter in its self-plenitude. Consciousness, accordingly, has been conceived as the agent of a contagious lack that infests matter itself by merely perceiving it. This enduring illusion, nevertheless, points to the truth. It is because being is the power of its self-actualization, *absolute potentiality*, the overlap of lack (of actual materiality) and excess (of power of actualization), or, rather, lack only insofar as it is excess, that the moment it is actualized in its empirical modes it splits itself into the two empirical givens of irrecoverable lack (thought, conceived as consciousness) and unmitigated plenitude (thoughtless materiality). In other words, the truth pointed to by the illusion is that the division between matter and value is modal or empirical—in the substance itself, these two attributes are inseparable—so that any ontological conception of matter as severed from value is doomed to be illusory. Nevertheless, to the extent that we also need to account for the fact that in our empirical reality matter and value constitute two distinct modes, we must find appropriate concepts to express this distinction without compromising our monistic ontology. The development of both science and capitalist economy indicate that chemical consistency can no longer provide a tenable criterion for defining matter ontologically. If, according to the relativity theory, matter is energy, and if, as we see in everyday late capitalism, all possible forms of information are sold and bought like other material commodities, we have to revise our concepts of use-value and exchange-value so that the distinction between materiality and immateriality becomes a derivative of the object's function.

We have to replace the distinction of use-value *qua* material object of utility, which corresponds to the phenomenological in-itself, with a meta-phenomenological in-itself and conception of matter, defined as anything insofar as it functions as a use-value, that is, as it exists in the world of production time—however immaterial (in the canonical sense of the word) this object may be, from pure energy, quanta, MBs, to words and images. Objects of utility may sometimes appear as "immaterial" as the signifier, electricity, and information—leaving aside the fact that, chemically speaking, even these presumably immaterial entities do involve matter. But this does not change by a farthing the eternal law of the commodity to have a double empirical manifestation, as use-value (in-itself) and as exchange-value (for-itself), both of which are the empirical manifestations of surplus-value, the capitalist modulation of surplus, which is undifferentiated immaterial-matter. Kojin Karatani rightly stresses that the assumption that the stage of informatized capitalism renders Marx's analysis obsolete is entirely misled and misleading. Karatani's reason for arguing this is that information, "as the father of cybernetics, Robert Wiener, suggested," is "originally nothing but *difference*," and capital "lives on by the difference," that is, "surplus value," regardless of "whether it gets [it] from solid objects or fluid information." Consequently, "the nature of capital is consistent even before and after its dominant production branch shifted from heavy industry to the information industry" (2003, 267). But we should add to Karatani's argument that just as any product, "solid" or "fluid," is in its essence always "fluid" (difference or surplus-value), taken as an empirical use-value it is essentially always "solid," however "fluid" it may be chemically, insofar as it is precisely a use-value—an in-itself (in our meta-phenomenological sense). Concomitantly, whatever functions as exchange-value will constitute the meta-phenomenological immaterial for-itself. In short, regardless of their physical qualities, all use-values are material, and all exchange-values are immaterial, while surplus is the doublet material-immaterial or in-itself-for-itself, of which they are the two empirical manifestations.

In more tangible economic terms, the distinction between use-value or the in-itself and exchange-value or the for-itself corresponds to the distinction between the inability and ability of procuring surplus-value. Information, for instance, taken as use-value consists of symbols (words, images, etc.) that express semantic values (signifieds or concepts), but it is not in this quality that they can contribute to the accumulation of surplus. The function of the symbol to express a concept is merely its use-value: signifiers are things whose use-value is to evoke concepts. In order for information to procure surplus-value, the additional quality is required that all these semantic values expressed through the informational material can and must be expressed as a further value, the exchange-value proper of these semantic values, whose circulation in the market alone can procure surplus-value. As we shall see later, the same distinction can be made within the semantic field itself, without any recourse to economic surplus-value. In addition to their function to signify concepts, words, too, have the additional quality of being represented by a further value which alone can procure what Lacan, by analogy to Marx's surplus-value, calls surplus-enjoyment—something to which we shall return in later chapters.

Historical Time

In order to specify the historical and transhistorical aspects of the being-in-itself-for-itself or surplus we first need to specify what is historical time and what is subject to it or not. I mentioned in passing that history designates the modulations of surplus in the semantic and economic fields. But if such modulations can occur in the first place, there must be an attribute in surplus (substance) whose empirical manifestation is historical time. The question becomes, therefore: what are the temporal attributes of surplus?

Let me frame the question within extant debates. When speaking of specifically *historical* time, the first question that poses itself is whether this time is supposed to have a directionality, a *telos* toward which historical events are supposed to converge. This is another way of posing the question about the existence or not of a meaning in history, to which, as is amply known, Hegel responds affirmatively by animating history as the time that unfolds under the guidance and for the sake of its notorious Spirit. Drawing on Pierre Macherey's exposition of the difference between Spinoza's and Hegel's conceptions of historical time, Eugene Holland concludes that "finally, and most importantly, a Spinozian-Marxist politics would reject all forms of teleologism" (§27).[1] Such a "Spinozian-Marxist" conception of history presupposes an understanding of temporality other than the Hegelian "*dialectical*" struggle of the positive and the negative "in the teleological sense . . . i.e., as destined for synthesis/resolution at some shining moment in the future" (§28). The reason why the Spinozian theoretical edifice precludes all forms of teleologism lies in the very conception of substance as radically non-teleological. As Spinoza states of substance, which we recall is another word for God or Nature: "Nature has no end set before it, and . . . all final causes are nothing but human fictions." Referring to those who believe in God's will, Spinoza writes, not without sarcasm, that they think that:

> [I]f God acts for the sake of an end, he necessarily wants something which he lacks. . . . For example, if a stone has fallen from a roof onto someone's head and killed him, they ["the Followers of this doctrine"] will show . . . that the stone fell in order to kill the man. For if it did not fall to that end, God willing it, how could so many circumstances have concurred by chance . . . ? . . . And so they will not stop asking for the causes of causes until you take refuge in the will of God, i.e., the sanctuary of ignorance. (1985, 442–443; *Ethics*, part I, prop. 36, appendix)

The first postulate of monism regarding historical time is that it be not teleological.

The next question is then whether historical time must be conceived in linear or other terms. Taking the capitalist modulation of surplus as surplus-value as our lead, we see that it manifests itself empirically in two modes, as exchange-value and as use-value, of which the former is determined differentially within the synchronicity of circulation-time, and the latter is subject to decay within the diachrony of linear production-time. The evident inference would be that the historical time of secular capitalist modernity must also consist of these two modes of temporality.

I have presented elsewhere a more extensive exposition as to why secular historical time must be conceived in synchronic terms, so I will only recapitulate the relevant points here, while also expanding on the diachronic aspect of historical time.[2]

The shift from the presecular to the secular mode of historical time is reflected in, among others, the shift from *mythos* to *logos* as the narrative form capable of representing historical truth. *Myths*, whose diachronic narratives had for centuries, from biblical time through all antiquity and theocracy, remained the unchallenged purveyor of truth, lose their epistemological legitimacy within secular reason and become the realm of fiction. The legitimate source of truth becomes now *logos*, that is, logical deduction, which the secular discourse has traditionally assumed to consist of a sequence of causes and effects in a transitive connection within diachronic time, where A is the cause of B, B the cause of C, and so on, without reversibility. In truth, however, logical thinking is a differential mode of thought that takes place within synchronic time: if A necessarily entails B, then B also necessarily entails A as its presupposition. As Kenneth Burke puts it, "though there is a sense"—the physical or biological sense—"in which a Father precedes a Son, there is also a sense"—the logical sense—"in which the two states are 'simultaneous,'" since "parents can be parents only insofar as they have offspring, and in this sense the offspring 'makes' the parent" (32). The realm of logic is not that of biological diachrony but that of the signifier, which is also to say, the realm of the law, as is evident in the fact that in legal adoption the son and the father are literally made simultaneously. Since *logos*, like the signifier, operates in synchrony, it can grasp and represent history only synchronically, considering historical events in their logical simultaneity. The fact that, as Heidegger writes, "an entity for which . . . its Being is itself an issue, has, ontologically, a circular structure," so that all "interpretation operates in Being towards a totality of involvements which is already understood," means that our conception of history is always circular, and that, therefore, this circularity must be taken into account, rather than denied (2008, 195 and 188, and 190–191; 2006, 153 and 149–150). Yet, historiography has demanded throughout the secular era that historical causation and genealogy be presented in diachronic terms.

But, one might justifiably wonder: okay, if logical deduction indeed operates in the mode of synchronic time, shouldn't then there be another kind of thought, operating in a different temporal mode that would be capable of accounting for the fact that in history certain facts predate others and can therefore be considered as the cause of the facts that postdate them? After all, it is plausible to argue, as many historians have, that, say, WWII was at least partly caused by the failed 1848 revolution, the delayed constitution of the German state, and the German defeat of WWI, but wouldn't it be utterly absurd to argue conversely that WWII was the cause of any of these preceding events? Well, the tragedy or farce of history is that the latter is what we *do* say, even if mostly without knowing it. It is no accident that it was Marx who exposed this procedure through which we cover the logical simultaneity of historical causes and effects under the façade of an ostensible diachronic deduction. In debunking the notorious "historical genealogy" of capitalism, the "so-called primitive accumulation," Marx made obvious that the historical narrative meant to explain the generation of capitalism is, in Slavoj Žižek's words, pure "fantasy": "Long, long ago there [was] . . . [a]

diligent, intelligent, and above all frugal" agent "who 'act[ed] like a capitalist' " prior to the existence of capitalism, and "who did not imme-diately consume his surplus but wisely reinvested it in production and thus gradually became a capitalist" (Žižek 1991, 210–211; citing Marx 1990, 873). This, in Marx's words, "original sin" of capitalism, far from being a historical truth, is, in Žižek's words, an "*ideological* myth," a "fan-tasy," which "has, by definition, the structure of a *story* to be narrated" and is "produced by capitalism retroactively to explain its own genesis and, at the same time, to justify present exploitation: the myth of the 'diligent saving worker' " (Marx 1990, 873; Žižek 1991, 211). So-called historical causality is in truth expressed through the "logic of *fantasy*," which, albeit disguised as a diachronic (and usually progressivist) *story* to be narrated, is "circular," since it "presupposes what it purports to explain" (Žižek 1991, 211). Hence, far from expressing the truth about the linear genealogy of any given historical state, it only reaffirms (or, alternatively, depending on its political agenda, challenges) the ideology sustaining this state.

The fact that the secular era raises *logos* to the sole epistemologically legitimate vehicle of truth renders secular thought incapable of providing diachronic or transitive causes. All secular causality, logical and (presum-ably) genealogical, is "circular," that is, synchronic.[3] This is to say that true answers to genealogical historical questions are fundamentally impossible, or, differently put, the necessity of a historical epoch's genesis emerges purely contingently. Which is why, as Laclau and Mouffe put it, "the relations between 'necessity' and 'contingency' cannot be conceived as relations between two areas that are external to each other . . . because the contingent only exists within the necessary" (114).

The circularity of historiography has two crucial consequences. First, that secular thought always arrives there from where it starts, the conclusion *is* the premise, or, in Lacan's famous words, "the real is that which always returns to the same place" (Lacan 1981, 49). Second, if truth emerges only as a synchronic refinding of itself, then the true empirical fantasy is the illusion that it emerges in a diachronic succes-sion. *History conceived as a diachronic narrative is an empirical fantasy.* To "traverse the fundamental fantasy" of ideology means to get out of diachrony, *to translate diachrony into such synchronic terms that explain the possibility of their own manifestation as the given diachrony* (Žižek 1991, 271). *History proper is real fantasy*—that is, the synchronic fantasy that underlines the fantasy of diachrony.[4]

This conclusion, however, does not mean that whatever presents itself as a diachronic narrative should be dismissed as an epistemologically illegitimate mode of thought. Quite the contrary, it means that it should be reduced to its synchronic logic so that the truth underlying its fantasy is revealed. The lesson of Marx's debunking of capitalism's "original sin" is not just that ostensibly diachronic genealogical explanations are epistemologically illegitimate, but that they are *ideological*. That is to say, their truth-value lies not in what they purport to explain but in the *desire animating their presumed explanations*. To traverse the ideological fantasy means to reveal the (real) desire that motivates the ostensibly diachronic genealogy.

Yet, the fact remains that even as secular thought cannot produce narratives that indeed represent a diachronic explanation of historical facts, historical facts *do* nevertheless occur in a diachronic succession with irreversibility. There should therefore be a secular temporal mode that accounts for the succession of events in linear time, while it should simultaneously be a mode of the attributes of surplus. Evidently, such an irreversible diachrony of events that occur in succession of one another *must exclude any causal (i.e., genealogical) relation* between them, since, first, the latter can be established only through "logical deduction," that is, in synchronic temporality, and, second, if causality is permitted entrance to diachrony it will inevitably transform itself into teleology, something which, as we saw earlier, is inadmissible within any monist conceptualization of history. Indeed, we can find accounts of such noncausal diachrony in secular capitalist modernity, both in the semantic and the economic fields.

But prior to examining these accounts of diachronic temporality, let us turn once again to Sartre, to revisit his phenomenological conception of time. In Sartre, there is no room for diachrony, and all time is synchronic. Sartre begins with the accurate observation that the phenomenological in-itself and the for-itself cannot share the same temporality; in fact, the in-itself, what he also calls "facticity"—the being that is in itself, in its own plenitude, insofar as, as we have seen, it is posited as such through the nihilation of the for-itself, as that which the for-itself cannot be—must pertain to a mode of temporality that the temporality of the for-itself cannot be.[5] As Sartre argues, if the for-itself is that being whose "being is in question in so far as this being implies a being other than itself"—that is, the phenomenological being-in-itself—then "every revelation of a positive characteristic of being is the counterpart of an

ontological determination as pure negativity in the being of for-itself"
(Sartre, 239 and 248). Sartre's next step is Hegelian, that is, he infers
that the temporality of the in-itself, the "other" or the "pure negativity"
of the temporality of the for-itself, is no time whatsoever. According to
monism, this is impossible because if the temporality of the for-itself is
to be limited by something else, this something else must itself be of
the same nature, that is, some form of temporality, and not no time
whatsoever. The "other" of the temporality of the for-itself, the time of
the phenomenological in-itself, cannot be "pure negativity" but rather
the "other" of synchrony and its imaginary causes, diachrony as a non-
causal succession. This, however, is not Sartre's reasoning, whose stunning
itinerary in the chapter "The Ontology of Temporality" deserves pursuing closely. There he concludes that there can be no temporal relation
between (phenomenological) in-itselfs for the following reason:

> If A is to be prior to B, it must be, in its very being, *in* B as
> A's future. Conversely, B, if it is to be posterior to A, must
> linger behind itself in A, which will confer on B its sense of
> posteriority. If then we grant *a priori* being in-itself to A and
> to B, it is impossible to establish between them the slightest
> connection of succession. (190)

For the *a priori* being in-itself is complete in its closeness and cannot
be *in* another in-itself, either as its own priority or posteriority. We see
here that Sartre's conception of priority and posteriority is intrinsically
one of causality and teleology: if A's prior in-itself were already in B's
in-itself then A would necessarily cause the emergence of B, and the
in-itself in general would be teleological. It is because, for Sartre, time
necessarily involves causality that he has to negate all temporality in the
in-itself, lest everything in the world has a purpose.

Sartre then proceeds to dismiss "the possibility that this relation
before-after can exist only for a witness who establishes it," because he
wants to bypass Kant's thesis that time is a category of representation
and not of the thing-in-itself, and to argue instead that "the relation
of the Present to the Past is a relation of being, not of representation"
(190 and 207). Here one might want to object that in truth Sartre
remains within the Kantian paradigm, inadvertently reducing time to a
category of representation, insofar as time "is the intra-structure of the
being which is its own annihilation—that is, the *mode of being* peculiar

to being-for-itself," which for Sartre is nothing other than consciousness (202). In his attempt to preempt this objection, Sartre frames his thesis that "Temporality exists only . . . as the intra-structure of a For-itself" with the admonition that: "Not that the For-itself has an ontological priority over temporality. But Temporality is the being of the For-itself in so far as the For-itself has to be its being ecstatically. Temporality is not, but the For-itself temporalizes itself by existing" (195). Sartre argues here that his model differs from Kant's insofar as there is not first a consciousness that posits temporality; rather, temporality itself *is* the being of consciousness, insofar as consciousness cannot emerge but in the distance from its in-itself, in a "way of projecting itself vainly toward its Self, of being what it is beyond a nothingness . . . , of being this fall of being, this frustration of being which the For-itself has to be" (196). The for-itself can long to be the Self that it has to be only within temporality, which is thus presupposed for, rather than posed by, consciousness (196). In other words, in a somewhat ironic way, it is only via consciousness that Sartre can claim that time is not just a category of consciousness but an intra-structure of being. More specifically, the in-itself emerges through its intra-structure with the for-itself as the latter's past: "The In-itself is what the For-itself was *before*" (198).

This phenomenological explanation of time works only insofar as the for-itself (consciousness) is given absolute priority over both the in-itself and time. For, one may ask: before, when the for-itself was not yet the in-itself, how was it possible for the for-itself to delineate itself as a for-itself unless there was already an in-itself? This could lead to a regression to a "bad infinity," unless, of course, as Sartre does—when he writes that, to repeat, "the For-itself temporalizes itself by existing"—one equates the for-itself (consciousness) not with itself, as opposed to the in-itself, but with the temporalizing process in which both, the in-itself and the for-itself, perpetually (re)emerge. What we have here, then, is one of Žižek's favorite Hegelian points: the appropriation of the genus by one of its species. Of the two species (the in-itself and the for-itself) under the genus of temporality, the one (the for-itself) emerges as the genus of temporality itself. Thus Sartre offers us one of the most brilliant accounts of the ideological fantasy of the temporality of the for-itself (consciousness), comparable perhaps only with Hegel's.

Sartre's fallacy lies not in his conception of "temporalization" as such, but in that he attributes it to *consciousness*, and *not*, as Marx does, to *surplus-value*, which, being the capitalist modulation of the being-in-itself-for-itself, approaches its attributes, even if only asymptotically. The following comparison between Sartre's and Marx's accounts will illuminate their difference. Let us start the comparison again with Sartre, who argues that there is "no consciousness without a past," but: "[t]his does not mean . . . that every consciousness supposes a prior consciousness fixed in the In-itself." Rather, "it is as the nihilation of the In-itself that the For-itself arises in the world, and it is by this absolute event that the Past as such is constituted as the original, nihilating relation between the For-itself and the In-itself" (198). In short, "Present, Past, Future" occur "all at the same time," for "the For-itself dispersing its being in three dimensions is temporal due to the very fact that it nihilates itself" (202). Sartre's line of thought culminates in the statement:

> Thus the time of consciousness is human reality which temporalizes itself as the totality which is to itself its own incompletion; it is nothingness slipping into a totality as a detotalizing ferment. This totality which runs after itself and refuses itself at the same time, which can find in itself no limit to its surpassing because it is its own surpassing and because it surpasses itself toward itself, can under no circumstances exist within the limits of an instant. There is never an instant at which we can assert that the for-itself *is*, precisely because the for-itself never is. Temporality, on the contrary, temporalizes itself entirely as the refusal of the instant. (211)

On the other hand, Marx's writes (note that in this passage "value" stands for surplus-value):

> [T]he circulation of money as capital is an end in itself, for the valorization of value takes place only within this constantly renewed movement [buying in order to sell]. The movement of capital is therefore limitless. . . . [Value] thus becomes transformed into an automatic subject. . . . [V]alue is here the subject of a process in which, while constantly assuming the form in turn of money and commodities, it changes its own magnitude, throws off surplus-value from itself considered as original value, and thus valorizes itself independently. For the movement in the course of which it adds surplus-value is its own movement, its valorization is therefore self-valorization

[*Selbstverwertung*]. By virtue of being value, it has acquired the occult ability to add value to itself. It brings forth living offspring, or at least lays golden eggs. . . . [I]n the circulation M—C—M′, value suddenly presents itself as a self-moving substance which passes through a process of its own, and for which commodities and money are both mere forms. But there is more to come: instead of simply representing the relations of commodities, it now enters into a private relation with itself, as it were. It differentiates itself as original value from itself as surplus-value, just as God the Father differentiates himself from himself as God the Son, although both are of the same age and form, in fact one single person; for only by the surplus-value of £10 does the £100 originally advanced become capital, and as soon as this has happened, as soon as the son has been created, and, through the son, the father, their difference vanishes again, and both become one, £110. . . . [T]he circulation M—C—M′ presents itself in abridged form, in its final result and without any intermediary stage, in a concise style, so to speak, as M—M′, i.e., money which is worth more money, value which is greater than itself. (1990, 253–257)

We can never say that (surplus-)value *is*. Instead, it "temporalizes itself as the totality which is to itself its own incompletion," as the "totality which runs after itself and refuses itself at the same time, which can find in itself no limit to its surpassing," because it always throws off more surplus-value, which is what makes it capital, that is, "because it is its own surpassing and because it surpasses itself toward itself," so that "under no circumstances [can it] exist within the limits of an instant." It "temporalizes itself entirely as the refusal of the instant," for it is always "greater than itself." It is an "autonomous subject" "for which commodities [in-itself] and money [for-itself] are both mere forms"; it is a "self-moving substance" not because it is human consciousness, but because it thinks, and thought itself is *not* human. What Marx grasps, thus going beyond Sartre, is that the *for-itself is not consciousness but thought*—a system of differential signifiers, whether exchange-values or the semantic values of language. It is because thought permeates everything, from God to matter, that Marx is compelled to invoke all four kinds of metaphors—economic (commodities, money), anthropomorphic (self, subject), natural (offspring, eggs), and supernatural (God and Son)—in order to describe the "occult" character of self-valorizing (surplus-)value.

Now we can return to the semantic and economic accounts of non-causal diachrony. Beginning with the economic, Marx introduces the distinction between synchronic and diachronic time by addressing the difference between exchange- and use-values not in general, that is, not with regard to all commodities, but with regard to one exceptional commodity, insofar as it is presupposed for the production of any other commodity: *labor*. From the perspective of production (i.e., within diachronic production-time), labor is an "object of utility," that is, a unique, specialized, non-exchangeable activity, which is bound to specific materials and takes place within a finite span of time, having a beginning and an end (the production of a specific product). If we want to generalize this aspect of labor *qua* use-value to any use-value, any product of labor is, from the perspective of production, an "object of utility," that is, a concrete, non-exchangeable object that requires specific materials and specific kinds of labor in order to be produced, and whose production also takes place within a finite span of time, from the beginning of its production to the moment that it is ready to enter the market. In short, and in our meta-phenomenological terms, labor and any other commodity are here matter. The moment a commodity enters circulation it becomes an exchange-value, that is, something that can be exchanged for anything else, regardless of its specific inherent physical qualities. This is the case also of labor which, too, can enter circulation not as any specific kind of labor (matter) but as "abstract human labor" or "*congealed labour-time*," incorporated in the product, which counts directly as exchange-value (Marx 1990, 150 and 130). At this moment, the commodity, be it labor or any other, dies as a physical object of utility and enters the realm of immaterial or symbolic, and hence immortal, values within circulation-time.

While this double aspect, *qua* exchange- and use-value, applies to any commodity including labor, what differentiates labor from the rest of the commodities is that it *reflects this double aspect on the level of its remuneration*. That is, labor has *two* distinct *prices*: the price at which it is sold (its exchange-value) and the price at which it is bought (its remuneration or cost, or what Marx used to call "wages"). It is sold in circulation time as "congealed" labor or exchange-value, but it is bought in production-time as labor-power, that is, as at once the potential to actualize itself in some concrete form of labor and—an exquisite overlap that will become crucial to our examination of biopolitics in part 2—(meta-phenomenological) matter. The exchange-value against which labor is sold, once its products enter circulation—that is, the exchange-value of the labor "congealed" or objectified within any commodity which happens to be its product—is determined arbitrarily and differentially, as commodities obtain an exchange-value in relation and comparison to other commodities. This process takes place within circulation-time (synchrony). By contrast, labor-power is bought (i.e., the laborer is remunerated) at a price that is *not* arbitrary, that is, a price not determined through purely differential determinations among units of abstract labor-time. The *cost* of labor-power is determined outside circulation, within production-time, in which, as Marx writes, "labour . . . is measured according to definite social laws" that determine "the value of labour-power" according to its specific kind, in a way that "contains a historical and moral element," insofar as it takes into account the "known *datum*" in "a given country at a given period" about "the average amount of the means of subsistence necessary for the worker" to continue to live and labor (Marx 1990, 286 and 275). Thus, for instance, it is possible that an hour of highly specialized labor-power is paid more than an hour of unskilled labor-power, regardless of whether the latter might, within circulation-time (i.e., as a "congealed" exchange-value), actually contribute to the accumulation of more surplus-value than the former. What matters instead, is the "moral" judgment of a given society that considers, for instance, skilled labor-power worth more than unskilled. While the cost of labor-power is determined *outside* of circulation, as a specific object of utility, by given moral and historical laws, *within* circulation, as exchange-value, the value of the same labor, which is now "congealed" labor, becomes autonomous, "free," so to speak, from historico-cultural norms or "social laws," and is instead determined by the arbitrary, differential and synchronic laws of exchange-values. If the surplus-value accrued through unskilled labor-power is more than that accrued through skilled labor-power, the value of the former *within* circulation (as congealed labor) is more than that of the latter, regardless of whether the same unskilled labor-power may be remunerated as an object of utility within production-time at a lower cost than the same skilled labor-power.

Surplus-value does not presuppose that, say, the working hour of a lawyer must necessarily be remunerated higher than that of a construction worker; it does not even presuppose that some people must necessarily be underpaid compared to others. These are purely "moral" matters.

The sole presuppositions (cause), as well as effect, of surplus-value are: *first, that any commodity, including labor, have the peculiar ontological quality of being both a use-value and an exchange-value; second, corollary to the first, that the specific commodity of labor manifest itself as use-value in the form of labor-power, and as exchange-value in the form of congealed labor; third, corollary to the second, that labor have, on the one hand as labor-power, a cost determined by diachronic factors (the "moral" laws of a given society) and, on the other hand as congealed labor, an exchange-value determined differentially in the synchronic time of exchange-value; and, forth, that the total cost of labor-power be lower than the total exchange-value of its equivalent congealed labor.*

We can conclude, therefore, that the specific modulation of the being-in-itself-for-itself as surplus-value on the economic level entails a historical shift with regard to temporality. *On the one hand*, the realm of exchange-value introduces *synchrony into historical time*. This shift, as we have seen, is reflected on the semantic level in the replacement of myths with *logos* as the legitimate incubator of truth. In this regard, history is conceived as change or a linear series of causes and effects that appear as such through fantasy. *On the other hand*, the realm of use-value with its production-time introduces diachrony, a linear and finite time, structured neither as the recurrence of seasons, as in the agricultural conception of time, nor as a directional sequence leading to some *telos*, but, as the remuneration of labor-power indicates, as sheer contingency. While exchange-value is determined arbitrarily through synchronic differential relations, the cost of labor-power depends on historical contingency, the social and moral laws that happen to be operative in a given society. In terms of value, the at once ontological and historical event of the configuration of being-in-itself-for-itself *qua* surplus-value entails the emergence of two *radically different types of value, differential exchange-value* and *contingent cost. Differential arbitrary value and contingent cost and their respective temporalities are the two modes in which the attributes of being-in-itself-for-itself manifest themselves empirically in capitalism.*

To examine how these two structures of historical time emerge also on the semantic level, and to make more clear their radical difference and codependence, let us now turn once again to Saussure, who offers us a closer examination of the distinction in question.

Like Marx, Saussure also takes as his point of departure the synchronicity and differentiality of the semantic values, that is, signifiers and signifieds. Yet, his point is that even though there is nothing positive in

any differential system, and everything is constituted purely synchronically, negatively, and differentially, value itself is something that transcends
the system's differentiality, arbitrariness, and synchronicity, and produces
facts. As Saussure puts it: "the statement that everything in language
is negative is true only if the signified and the signifier are considered
separately." When, by contrast, "we consider the sign in its totality, we
have a "value" that is defined, on the one hand, through the "combination" of two "dissimilar," arbitrarily chosen things (signifier and signified)
that can be mutually exchanged, and, on the other hand, through being
set in an equally arbitrary comparison to "similar" things (the values
of all other signs). Only taken together do this combination and this
comparison determine a sign's value, which itself is "positive in its own
class," "a positive fact"—in fact, "the sole type of facts that language has"
(Saussure, 115 and 120–121). For instance, in French, *mouton* signifies
"sheep," while in English *mutton* signifies only a piece of sheep "ready to
be served on the table," because there is a second sign, "sheep," whose
value stands for the living animal. This different value of *mouton* in the
two languages is a "fact," in the sense that one cannot refer to a living
sheep in English arbitrarily using the word *mouton/mutton* (115–16).

Historical contingency may change the value, and hence the use,
of the word in either language; this is to say, although its signifier and
signified are each purely arbitrarily defined, once a value is established,
it becomes a "fact" that can change not arbitrarily, but only if at a point
in history something contingent happens because of which a new sign
is introduced whose value effects the value of *mouton*. Signifier and signifieds are purely arbitrary effects of synchronic differentiality, but their
"combination" or "value" is the effect of both this differentiality and
historically contingent factors. This is "how . . . value differ[s] from signification," yet, value is always appended to signification (Saussure, 114).[6]

Having established the conceptual distinction between synchronic
signification and the diachronic mutation of value, Saussure proceeds to
specify further the laws governing each. The "linguistic institution" is a
purely synchronic system, whose "function" lies in "maintaining the par-
allelism between the two classes of differences [signifiers and signifieds]"
(Saussure, 121). Nevertheless, the same institution produces as its own
effect something that transcends itself insofar as it is "a positive fact"
which, as such, can be effected only by something transcendent to the
arbitrariness of synchronic differentiality, namely, historical contingency.
For "diachronic facts" are "particular," they are "events which are not

only outside the system [of language] . . . but are isolated and form no system among themselves" (95). Therein lies the difference between the laws that govern the synchronic and the diachronic "facts" of language: "synchronic facts . . . evidence a certain regularity but are in no way imperative; diachronic facts, on the contrary, force themselves upon language but are in no way general" (95). One cannot therefore "speak of laws in linguistics," if by "law" one means "social law," which "has two basic characteristics: it is imperative and it is general" or universal (91). For the *diachronic facts* are only *imperative*, and the *synchronic facts* are only *universal*. Nevertheless, Saussure continues, we can speak of "synchronic laws," not in the sense of "social laws," which are both imperative and universal, but in the sense of being a universal "simple expression of an existing arrangement," of "report[ing] a state of affairs," like, for instance, "a law that states that trees in a certain orchard are arranged in the shape of a quincunx," or, say, Marx's synchronic laws governing the structure of the commodity, the accumulation of surplus-value, and so on, both of which are "not imperative," and, yet, "[n]othing is more regular than [these] synchronic law[s]" (92). But it is absurd to claim that diachronic laws evidence regularity, since diachronic developments do not even constitute a system, and simply force themselves upon language without either regularity or generality. In other words, diachrony is not guided by any causal, let alone teleological, laws or principles. By the same token, there are no "synchronic facts," if by "fact" we mean, with Saussure, an event that could as well have happened otherwise but did not (such as the introduction of *mouton* into English). For events are by definition imperative and not universal. This is why Saussure concludes that the only fact in language is value, whose engendering involves, in addition to its synchronic systematic constitution ("signification"), diachronic contingent factors.

It is, therefore, as wrong to infer, as is traditionally the case, that historical time is diachronic, as it is to reduce history to pure synchrony. As Saussure shows us, facts (values) can undergo change within diachrony, while they are themselves produced out of synchronic differentiality (among signifiers and signifieds); as such, they are governed by the laws of the synchronic system that produces them, while there are absolutely no laws of regularity governing their changes within diachrony. Moreover, as Saussure emphatically stresses, both the immutability and the mutability of language are due to its synchronic, arbitrary character. In Saussure's words, unlike a "symbol," which "is never wholly arbitrary"—

for example, the "symbol of justice, a pair of scales, could not be replaced by just any other symbol, such as a chariot"—"language is a system of arbitrary signs and lacks the necessary basis" which would provide "the solid ground for discussion" about why a sign should change. That is, while there is a rational justification of the combination between signifier and signified in a symbol, "there is no reason for preferring *soeur* to *sister*, *Ochs* to *boeuf*" or any other signifier in whatever language (Saussure, 68 and 73). This lack of a rational basis for change "protects language from any attempt to modify it" and makes it immutable (73). Nevertheless, experience teaches us that diachronically there is a "more or less rapid change of linguistic signs," paradoxically caused by this same absence of any "reason" why a signifier and a signified should be attached, which also gives no reason for its value not to change either, so that "the two facts are interdependent: the sign is exposed to alteration because it perpetuates itself" (74). The "fact," which transcends the arbitrariness of the universal, is something that can change by a diachronic factor, but the cause of this factor is itself the synchronic differential system itself, with its arbitrary character and absence of "necessary basis." In other words, value is subject to diachronic mutations that are governed by no system of regularities precisely because language is a synchronic, differential, and arbitrary system governed by its own universal laws regarding its existing arrangements or relations.

In short, *diachronic change is contingent and presupposes the regularity of a synchronic system.* What is perceived as historical causality or genealogy consists of contingent diachronic changes that, at the same time, presuppose a system of necessary logical causality. Historical facts are *random* events that, to repeat Saussure's words, "are isolated and form no system among themselves"; yet, at the same time they are *not random* insofar as the synchronic system presupposed for this diachronic contingency provides the background that determines the realms of the possible and the impossible regarding change within diachrony. This, I think, is the meaning of Marx's notorious statement that: "Men make their own history, but they do not make it just as they please; they do not make it under circumstances chosen by themselves, but under circumstances directly encountered," which are, of course, "given and transmitted from the past" but crystallized in the synchronic laws of the present they encounter (1998, 15).

This is why, as Spinoza argued against the Aristotelian tradition, the modes (and, hence, the historical facts and changes) of the substance, *are contingent only insofar as they are necessary*, that is, insofar as they must be manifestations of the attributes of substance. This is to say that there is change in time, or as Lacan puts it, "new things do emerge in the symbolic order," not because of any diachronic law, but because several (although not *any*) realities can emerge as the empirical manifestations of the attributes of substance (1991a, 61). Yet, which of these specific potential realities becomes actual fact remains contingent, since there are no diachronic universal laws. This is why *contingency is not sheer randomness*, for although there are no diachronic principles of regularity and, hence, no telos or predictability in history, there are synchronic laws determining the possible realm of contingency. By saying that historical facts are contingent, we mean that they are *transitively random* (i.e., there are *no* diachronic laws determining the occurrence or non-occurrence of a fact) and *synchronically necessary* (i.e., there *are* synchronic laws that define the realm of the possible and the impossible with regard to the occurrence or non-occurrence of certain facts).

Because of the double representation of the value of labor as exchange-value and cost (wages), as well as the double linguistic quality as (purely differential) signification and (also diachronically contingent) fact, Marx's eternal laws of capital (and, we can add, Saussure's eternal laws of the arbitrary sign) are always, as Eugene Holland puts it, "profoundly *contradictory*," and it is only "these contradictions . . . [that] may indeed constitute the *motor of history*." But it is important to understand that they cannot be "construed as *dialectical* contradictions in the teleological sense" (§28). Holland infers from this that, once within capitalism, "the only universal history is the history of capitalism as a mode of production; and its motor, for better and for worse, is the ongoing (and contradictory) self-expansion of capital itself: history *without* a subject, whether a class subject (the proletariat) or a transcendental one (species-being)" that would somehow guarantee the advent of a "decisive (i.e., revolutionary) contradiction leading dialectically to resolution" (§28). While agreeing that history is "*without* a subject," it is also crucial to clarify that, far from being the substance of history, *capital is just a contingent diachronic fact*, one of the possible modulations of surplus or the being-in-itself-for-itself. The "only universal history" is the *history* not of capital, but of *surplus*, which, unlike a subject, has no will or intention. *The sole motor or telos of "universal history" is the empirical realization of the attributes of surplus, their actualization in contingent modes.* This is the fundamental law determining the realm of the possible within "universal history."

Meta-Phenomenological Fact

In this chapter I am returning to a distinction I alluded to in an end-note earlier, between ideological and primary fantasy. The former is the modal empirical, and contingent, actualization of the latter. If ideological fantasy is that which makes circular thought (*logos*) appear as (if it were) transitive deduction, and hence allows for the illusion of epistemologically legitimate genealogies and anticipations, then it is fantasy itself that constitutes the sole meta-phenomenological fact. To clarify this point we need to differentiate between two Lacanian concepts, the gaze and the Master-Signifier.

As we have seen by bringing together Sartre and Lacan, the *gaze in itself* (the gaze of the Other, which does not exist) is the infinity of the points of view from which an appearance can appear, and, as such, it cannot determine from which of these points of view an appearance will actually appear to a given subject within empirical reality. The gaze, therefore, is equivalent to the laws governing the synchronic system of value, which too cannot determine which of all the possible facts will actually occur. An actual historical (phenomenological) fact is diachronically contingent, that is, transitively random (radically inexplicable as to its causation and, hence, also unpredictable) and immanently necessary (it can occur only if it belongs to the realm of possibility delineated by the synchronic laws). The *meta-phenomenological fact* is the *specific* gaze or *Master-Signifier* that *makes the contingent phenomenological fact appear as (if it were) necessary in diachrony*, that is, as necessarily caused by its past or as the necessary future outcome of the past and the present.

In other words, meta-phenomenological facts are not what we traditionally call "facts," that is, empirical facts, either in the sense of the (phenomenological) fact-in-itself, which simply *is*, and as such cannot open itself to interpretation, or in the sense of the (phenomenological) fact-for-itself, which is always other than itself, since it has already been mediated by interpretation and its ideological distortions. Rather it is *the gaze of the specific ideology under which the fact-in-itself becomes the fact-for-itself*, that is, represented and interpreted in a certain way. This *ideological gaze* is the *Master-Signifier*: that because of which contingent events or states appear as being bound with one another through organic or necessary causal links in a transitive deduction, and hence as having a diachronic telos. It is such a Master-Signifier that allows, for instance, "primitive accumulation" to appear as (if it were) the diachronic cause of capitalism.

Here the reader might raise the objection: why raise the illusion of the Master-Signifier to the level of the meta-phenomenological fact when, at the same time, we ascertain that there is no diachronic causality, necessity, or telos? In other words: why raise the ideological gaze to the level of a meta-phenomenological fact when substance has no end in itself? Because it is the (imaginary) stuff that fills the void of the real (infinite gaze), and, as such, its status pertains also to the real, even as it is imaginary. For, albeit imaginary, the meta-phenomenological fact has real effects.

Let us explain this by starting with the real gaze (the infinity of viewpoints), which corresponds to what Kant calls the "I of transcendental apprehension," and whose "status," as Žižek writes, "is that of a *necessary* and simultaneously *impossible* logical construction . . . in short: of the Lacanian *real.*" The real gaze is a logical presupposition "necessary" in order to account for the possibility of all concrete empirical gazes, and simultaneously " 'impossible' in the precise sense that its notion can never be filled out with intuited experiential reality," that is, with any specific empirical gaze, without ceasing to be the real gaze and becoming an ideological Master-Signifier (Žižek 1993, 14). Now, this Master-Signifier, too, pertains to the status of the real, that is, it, too, is both impossible and necessary, albeit for the exact opposite reasons: The ideological gaze is "impossible" from the transcendental perspective of the real gaze, which provides no grounds on the basis of which one could ever opt for any particular among the infinite points of view; and it is also "necessary" for empirical experience, which cannot take place without specific gazes that render the world meaningful in some way or other. The distinction between (real) gaze and Master-Signifier, therefore, "corresponds perfectly to the Lacanian distinction between the Real qua *Ding*," the Thing or gaze, and the Real *qua* "*objet a*," the "object which gives a body to the lack of positive objects," the stuff that fills in the void opened up in experience through the "Real" in its first sense, as the infinity of all possible points of view (Žižek 1993, 18). To put it in terms of Jacques-Alain Miller's by now classical distinction within the realm of the Real between R_1 and R_2: the gaze, which is purely real and, hence, a void or non-existent, pertains to R_1, whereas the Master-Signifier, which is imaginary but has real effects, pertains to R_2.

Like surplus-value—the specific modulation of surplus (the being-in-itself-for-itself) in secular capitalist modernity—the Master-Signifier makes the world and history meaningful from the perspective of secular thought, and capitalist economy is a specific modulation of the gaze *qua* infinity of all possible points of view. We call the secular modulation of the gaze ideological because its Master-Signifier assumes the form of secular ideas posited as Ideals (e.g., State, Nation, Democracy, Communism, and even God, insofar as the latter is posited as one among other Ideals), whereas we call the specific modulation of the gaze in the Middle Ages, for instance, theocratic because its Master-Signifier found its condensation in God's absolute, omniscient gaze. Within any historical modulation of the gaze, further subordinate Master-Signifiers, that allow for sub-beliefs or sub-ideologies within their overarching paradigm, emerge contingently, that is, insofar as they belong to the realm of the possible and as a-systematic diachronic factors allow them.

Our conception of history as a diachronic causal succession of events is fantasmatic, purely ideological, which is why we should revise our conception of history so as to take into account its diachronic contingency and its synchronic determination. Part of this revision, however, is to identify the function of the Master-Signifier that allows for the representation of history as diachronic genealogy, and to raise it to the level of the meta-phenomenological fact. For although the Master-Signifier is impossible from the perspective of a synchronically conceived history, it is also a fantasy necessary for the enterprise of diachronic genealogy and teleology to appear as if it were consistent. Teleology's *objet a* is the ideological desire underpinning it. The Master-Signifier is a meta-phenomenological fact because desire is meta-phenomenological. Invoking once again "primitive accumulation," Marx's gesture consists in revealing that the sole fact in this otherwise imaginary narrative is a specific desire: the desire to ground capitalism tautologically on itself, and thus, to transform it into a Law. For nothing can function as Law—a historical inevitability or necessity—unless its "character," in Žižek's succinct summary of a thesis advanced by an abundance of thinkers since early modernity to Kafka and beyond, is "constitutively senseless," so "that we must obey it not because it is just, good or even beneficial, but simply because *it is the law*—this tautology articulates the vicious circle of its authority," as well as the vicious circle of desire (Žižek 1989, 37).[1]

Only Master-Signifiers and their entailed necessary diachronic causes are meta-phenomenological facts, for only they are ideological (both impossible and necessary, as well as both imaginary and teleological). Any "organic genealogy" in history is ideological, regardless of whether it happens to be Lukács's "organic genealogy of the bourgeois collective project" or the postmodern "vast collection of images," where "the past as 'referent' finds itself . . . effaced altogether" (Jameson 1991, 18). For, as Fredric Jameson himself makes clear elsewhere, the "past" in question is not a Rankean "faithful" reconstruction, but, in properly Benjaminian fashion, an "allegory" of the present, an "intent" and a "desire" "to hypothesize" it (Jameson 1992, 3; Benjamin, 255). Lost in postmodernity, therefore, is not a Lukácsian historical consciousness with its "bourgeois collective project" but the "past" as an object of desire, that is, as something that introduces a lack in the present. The self-representation of postmodernity as the plenitude of a "vast collection of texts" *is* a "collective project"—the project to represent the present as not lacking, as the ultimate fulfillment of all genealogical deduction, which, as such, desires (or, at least, appears to desire) nothing but its own self-perpetuation. The difference between postmodernism and Lukácsian modernism lies not in the absence or presence of a "collective project," but in the Master-Signifier giving meaning to and motivating each project, as well as determining its specific strategies.

One may attempt to explain the difference between the two eras as follows. In modernism, the dominance of capital was not global, as a result of which there was more than one possible place for "objective knowledge" and for claims to the true meaning of history to enunciate themselves, the historically ex-existing "communism" having been eminently one such place. It is the coexistence of competing "objective knowledges" and their corollary Ideals that invited the modernist rhetoric of self-justification by means of genealogical narratives that were meant to prove the historical necessity of their chosen socio-political agenda and to discredit similar claims by other narratives. Global capitalism, by contrast, takes its "organic genealogy" for granted: if the present state *is* the global domination of capital, then the entire march of history will always already have taken place in order to realize this end. Any attempt of global capitalism to justify itself by means of an "organic genealogy" would only be a reminder that the state of affairs could as well be otherwise—that is, it would be a reminder that its basis is not the gaze of the Other (equated here with the gaze of some providential Spirit of History) but just one Master-Signifier among others. Any recourse to "organic genealogy" on the part of global capitalism would only undermine the "objectivity" of a body of knowledge unchallenged by considerable competitors—and the moment competition becomes visible, the postmodern discourse, too, can invoke organic genealogies.[2] Depending on historical context, the rhetoric of "organic genealogy" is one of the strategies that can be used with the aim of either sustaining or challenging the *status quo*.

But the previous account of postmodernism's desire is just epiphenomenal, limiting itself within the realm of appearances and the strategies employed in it, such as postmodernism's self-presentation as desiring only itself. For one cannot know in advance the real of desire underlying any appearance of desire, be it modernism's seeming desire for something other than itself or postmodernism's apparent desire for itself. After all, whatever lack and desires modernist capitalism might presumably have had, even someone who believes in an "organic genealogy," whether of the bourgeois or any other "collective project," would have to admit by looking back into history that, its revolutionary intentions and desires notwithstanding, all that the modernist project caused as its actual effect is the present state of postmodernist global capitalism. Insofar as the real referent of "organic genealogy" is the contingent diachronic succession of events, in which there are in truth no laws but only the limitations posed, on their possibility of being actualized, by the synchronic laws of the given modulation of the surplus, the desire to cause this or the other effect in history is liable to misfiring. And so may be the desire to sustain the *status quo*. What matters are *not desires inscribed within diachrony* but the *desire* (and fantasy) *that makes diachrony appear* as a level *appropriate for the function of desire*. Another way of putting it is: what matters is the fantasy that makes past, present, and future appear as diachronic categories, thus also making desire appear as something that can be fulfilled only in some later point in diachrony, a "last instance," which by definition, as Althusser would put it, "never arrives." But to conceive of past, present, and future in terms other than sheer diachrony, we need to develop a new concept of historicity and historiography.

Historiographical Project

Giorgio Agamben has argued that "Marx did not elaborate a theory of time adequate to his [revolutionary] idea of history," which "clearly cannot be reconciled with the Aristotelian and Hegelian concept of time as a continuous and infinite succession of precise instants" (1993, 99–100). An aspiration of the present work is to show that Marx's ontology entails a theory of temporality that offers a radical alternative to the centuries-old tradition of a historiography that is based on the conception of time as continuity of instants. Agamben's remark instigates us rather to differentiate between Marxist historiography and Marx's own work. As Cesare Casarino writes:

> [Marx] is a thinker who found it indispensable to grapple explicitly and directly with the possibility of another temporality that would be qualitatively different from as well as antagonistic to that homogeneous temporality of quantifiable and measurable units. . . . There is a Marx who understood well what Agamben accurately claims that many—perhaps most—Marxists have never understood, namely, the necessity to change time. (189)

A fortiori, time has already changed since being-in-itself-for-itself obtained its modulation as surplus-value, and it is this change that enabled the emergence of several of the theoretical models referenced here, which however implicitly or explicitly presuppose this new time. At stake in this change is the shift from the feudal theocratic paradigm, which was organized around the divine organic link between signs (semantic and economic) and things, to the pantheism of the secular capitalist paradigm, with its arbitrary binary signs and exchange-values. In terms of temporality, this is a shift from the theocratic division between the linear, finite time of earthly life and heavenly eternity to the secular overlap of infinity and finitude or synchrony and diachrony within the domain of earthly life—which, as we shall see in part 2, also entails an unforeseen reconfiguration of eternity. It is, therefore, against the matrix of this new time that also a temporality adequate to a revolutionary history must be thought of.

The widely spread assumption that the revolutionary moment involves an interruption of the linear continuum of homogeneous instants only perpetuates the Aristotelian and Hegelian concepts of time, since it presupposes it. The amply praised Event—in all its recyclings, from the *kairós* of the Stoics, through Heidegger's *Ereignis* and Benjamin's *Jetztzeit*, back to Agamben's reprised kairological time—"the abrupt and sudden conjunction where decision grasps opportunity and life is fulfilled in the moment"—has no revolutionary potential within secular capitalist modernity, unless not only the "past" but all history be "blasted out of the continuum of history" (Agamben 1993, 101; Benjamin, 261). One might think that, because linear time, invariably cast in terms of progress, nevertheless continues to provide a central ideological veil for capital's internal and external legitimization, the Event's eruption should challenge capitalism insofar as it would blast one of its fundamental ideologies, progressivism. But, as Antonio Negri remarks: "*Jetzt-Zeit*, innovative precision, utopia: capital considers them as its own. Progress is the eternal return lit-up by a flash of a *now-time (Jetzt-Zeit)*. Administration is illuminated by charisma" (108). In Casarino's more emphatic commentary:

> Negri seems to be saying—since when have not epiphanies and illuminations of all sorts been ultimately useful for oppressive and exploitative systems of command? Since when has capital not been able to learn and bounce back from revolutionary impulse thus conceived? (191)

Nothing revolutionary emerges out of the attempt to blast the continuum of history through the eruption of a moment, an innovative momentary Now that is nevertheless just a part of that very continuum of history on whose outbursts and crises capitalist history has been thriving all along. Rather, if one persists on a conception of time as a continuum, then capitalist history itself will have to be understood as a continuum punctuated by flashes of illumination and revolutionary innovation.

However, it is not necessary, arguably not really accurate, to read Benjamin's *Jetztzeit* as an interruption of a historical continuum understood as linear time. This is particularly indicated in the first appendix following the last of the eighteen theses on the philosophy of history, where Benjamin writes: "Historicism contents itself with establishing a causal connection between various moments in history. But no fact that is a cause is for that very reason historical. It became historical posthumously, as it were, through events that may be separated from it by thousands of years." Benjamin reproaches historicism for its lack of consciousness regarding the arbitrary and retroactive constitution of facts as *historical* causes. By contrast, "a historian who takes this" differential constitution of historical facts "as his point of departure stops telling the sequence of events like the beads of a rosary," as if they were concatenated in a linear fashion. "Instead, he grasps the constellation which his own era has formed with a definite earlier one," not because it follows it but because it returns to it through a "leap" that the present takes "in the open air of history" (Benjamin, 263 and 261). It is in this retroactive loop, the "tiger's leap into the past," that the present finds "a past charged with the time of the now [*Jetztzeit*]" (261). Nevertheless, just as Agamben adequately represents the standard Marxist understanding of Marx's concept of historical time, Negri's reading, too, accurately represents the standard understanding of Benjamin's theses.

To undermine irrevocably such an understanding of history as a homogenous continuum, in which historical events and their conglomerations as historical periods succeed one another, with or without flashes of revolutionary epiphany, we have to overturn entirely our concepts of historical event, period, and periodization themselves.

To do so, let us bring together our insights regarding both historical causality or genealogy and historical facts. Regarding historical causality, we have concluded that any explanation as to why a historical event or period is succeeded by another is always fantasmatic, that is, circular, presupposing that which it is supposed to explain. Regarding historical facts, we have seen that they are contingent, which, on the one hand, means that within a specific realm of the possible they are random (which is why historical genealogy is necessarily fantasmatic), and, on the other hand, means that they are necessary insofar as they are always manifestations of the one substance, surplus. This double condition of contingency is presupposed for every historical period to be a concrete

manifestation of the attributes of the one substance, without simultaneously endowing history with a direction.

While it would be vain to attempt to explain why one historical
period yields to another, it is mandatory to be able to explain the formal
differences between any given periods. If, to take two grand periods,
feudalism and capitalism are both different modes of the attributes of the
same substance, we must have a methodological and conceptual apparatus that will enable us to differentiate between them. That is, in addition
to being able to describe any given historical period in terms of its being
an empirical manifestation of the attributes of the one substance, we also
must be able to distinguish formally this concrete empirical manifestation (period) from any other concrete empirical manifestation of the
attributes of substance. Finally, given that there is change also within
any given period, we must be able to differentiate changes internal to a
period from changes that indicate a shift from one period to another.

The present ontology and theory of time indicate that history can
be conceived only as a system whose elements are, not periods succeeding
one another in diachrony, but *synchronic blocks*, all of which are concrete
modulations of one and the same substance. This means that all known
history, from tribal life to antiquity, theocracy, and secular modernity,
occurs *now*, even if not in the same degree of actuality. "Ancient Rome"
may be a virtual past or future to several historical blocks, but "to
Robespierre" it "was a past charged with the time of the now," to the
point that "the French revolution viewed itself as Rome reincarnated,"
that is, as (re)actual(ized) Rome (Benjamin, 261). Moreover, each block
is distinguished from the rest by its own *formal logic* which articulates
both the general structure in which the modes of this block express
the attributes of the one substance and the specificity because of which
this block distinguishes itself from other blocks. Thus, each "*past*" block
is defined by its own formal logic, whose structure, however, can be
described only in terms of the formal logic of the *present block*—that
is, the presently *actual* block—as one of the *virtual* alternatives to itself,
or as a virtual copy of which the "present" block is an *actual* reincarna-
tion. The "past" is that which the "present" or actual block determines
itself not to be, for, to recall Sartre, the relation between "present" and
"past" is the relation between the for-itself and the in-itself: "The In-
itself is what the For-itself was *before*" (198). But that the "present" or
the actual block "is defined . . . as being what it is not and not being
what it is" *can also mean* that it can be "what the For-itself was *before*."

Both, "what it is not" and "what it is" without being it, are the "present's" virtual "past" and "future" blocks, and both are contemporaneous with the "present" block, as its virtual bygone or reincarnated block, or its potential "future" block. For "Present, Past, Future" occur "all at the same time," as the empirical virtual or actual manifestations of the same being-in-itself-for-itself (Sartre, 202).

Which of all blocks happens to be the present or actual block, or of all its virtual and potential blocks the one that will always already have been its former block, or, finally, the one that will at some point in the "future" become actual—all this is a matter of contingency. It is by dint of this contingency that the emergence of any historical block as past, present, or future, constitutes a historical fact, in Saussure's sense, and that (directionless and a-systemic) diachrony intertwines itself with synchrony to form history.

Moreover, there is change also within each block, so that each historical block may consist of any number of *phases* or *stages*, insofar as the latter, too, are not to be understood teleologically. Each stage may exhibit any number of contingent differences from the others, but all of them constitute stages of one and the same block because, whatever their concrete contingent shapes, they are *all manifestations of one and the same formal modulation of surplus*, being governed *by one and the same set of "eternal laws,"* such as those described by Marx regarding all stages of capitalism (Marx 1990, 301). *Historical eternity* coincides with the duration of the block to which it pertains. If one could speak of a *telos* motivating stages, this would be to *actualize in its fullest the potential of the formal structure* of the block to which they belong. And if one could speak of a *telos* guiding blocks, this would be to *embody a modulation, virtually or actually, of the attributes of the one substance*.

If this is so, one might ask what happens then to "revolutionary history"? If the realm of the possible historical blocks is once and for all determined by the synchronic laws that govern the attributes of the substance (surplus), how can a historical block emerge that would constitute a revolutionary overthrow of its past? *Revolutionary movements in history are possible only because they, too, belong in the realm of the possible.* If theocratic feudalism, which was a revolutionary overthrow of the pagan and Roman *status quo*, or secular capitalism, which was in turn a revolutionary overturn of theocratic feudalism, could emerge, it is only because all these historical blocks are part of the realm of the possible. The assumption that the revolutionary transgression is not part of the field of immanence is predicated on the Hegelian dualism, according to which the positive (actual historical block) can be transgressed only by something conceived as the negation of the field of immanence of the positive. Translating the issue into topological terms, this dualism conceives revolution as the leap from a positive space into, not another space, but no space at all. As Robert Pfaller succinctly puts it, the "Hegelian solution . . . presupposes topologically that the only transgression of certain spaces is a negative transgression; that the only beyond of a closed space is an empty beyond" or that "what limits the positive" is "something negative." By contrast, "the Spinozian principle" of monism entails "that something can only be limited by something else that is of the same nature," namely, also "positive." Therefore for Spinoza, Pfaller concludes, "the solution of a problem of transgression can never consist only in the 'empty gesture' of a negation"; "if we want to transgress a space we must arrive at another space . . . (whereas a space that cannot be transgressed at all, cannot be transgressed by negation either)" (234). The plane of immanence cannot ever be transgressed; all possible transgressions, like all possible transcendent spaces, are within the plane of immanence. A transgression, therefore, is not a sheer negation but, what we could call in order to distinguish it from Hegelian negation, a *positive negation*, a negation that negates a space by means, not of the elimination of space whatsoever, but of another positive space. Every transgression conceived as negation, including the Hegelian revolution, is impossible (which is why, if it nevertheless manages to emerge as a possibility within the actual, it is doomed to fail). It is another problem, worthy of its own treatise, that people often mistake the impossible for the prohibited.

In the next chapter we shall see how the aforementioned conceptualization of history is implicitly operative as the methodological premise of Lacan's account of historical "periodization."

Historical and Transhistorical
Aspects of Being

If surplus or being-in-itself-for-itself is the one substance, then it must be something transhistorical of which every historical block is one concrete empirical manifestation. With regard to the specific historical block of capitalism, Marx tells us that its defining formal eternal law, whatever contingencies its various stages may involve, lies in procuring surplus-value. Capitalism is the first economic system in history that entails and relies on this accumulation of surplus-value. This means that capitalism's past blocks, ever since the emergence of society—that is, ever since the emergence of exchange, economic and semantic—from the earliest societies of tribes and clans, and the slave systems of pagan antiquity, to theocratic feudalism with all its stages including Renaissance, Humanist, and other reformational modifications, can be conceived only as the positive negative of this eternal law defining our present historical block: if capitalism involves surplus-value and is thus a *system of disequilibrium*, then its *past* can be conceived only as an economic *system of equilibrium*, with no surplus-value. If capitalism is that specific historical block in which the modulation of surplus becomes surplus-value, the past blocks of capitalism must be such that their modulation of surplus does not involve surplus-value. And, yet, all, past and present blocks, must be manifestations of the same substance, surplus or being-in-itself-for-itself. Concomitantly, due to the structural homology between economic and semantic systems of exchange, the past absence of surplus-value must also be reflected on the semantic level, which must also be conceived in positive-negative terms, as one of equilibrium, with no unconscious surplus required to ground truth. We have already had a glimpse of this difference as it is reflected in the distinction between *mythos* and *logos*, the latter being a "circular" mode of reasoning which, as such, always presupposes the (unconscious) surplus of fantasy. But a detour through Lacan's "periodization" will help us obtain a more precise description of the difference between the secular capitalist block and its past with regard to both economic and semantic systems of exchange.

Evidently, I insert the word "periodization" in quotes to indicate that it designates the description of the formal laws governing historical blocks taken in their synchronic juxtaposition. It is for this reason both that I will henceforth employ exclusively the term "historical block," rather than "period," and that I am now turning to Lacan's discussion of the "four discourses" as a means of clarifying further the present conceptualization of history as a set of synchronic blocks. The "discourses" in question are conceived by Lacan precisely as not successive but synchronic discourses, which are distinct from one another in terms of their formal structure and efficacy or function. As Bruce Fink puts it, "Lacan's 'four discourses' seek to account for the structural differences among discourses" and focus on the differences regarding the "efficacy," "function," or "effect" they can have "on others" (i.e., on the subjects they address), depending on "the effect allowed by" each discourse and "the obstacles and shortcomings endemic to that discourse" (129–130). The relevance of Lacan's discourses to the ontology (and, hence, theory of temporality and history) presented here lies primarily in the fact that all discourses consist of the exact same elements (attributes), as well as in Lacan's selection of these specific (four) elements. On the one hand, the appearance of the same elements in each discourse safeguards the unity of the substance of which all discourses are the empirical manifestations; on the other hand, the specific four constitutive elements represent and shackle together the central constituents of the present ontology: first and second, the two fields of exchange, economic and semantic (or, in Lacan's parlance, power [S_1] and knowledge [S_2)]); and third and fourth, being-in-itself-for-itself or surplus, and the human subject (or, again in Lacan's words, "*objet a*" [a] and the [truth of the] subject [$]).

Given that there are four elements or "mathemes" constituting every discourse and that each discourse distinguishes itself from the others formally only by dint of the different positions the mathemes can assume by rotating within a specific sequence or order, "other discourses than the four" ones on which Lacan focuses "could be generated by changing the *order* of the four mathemes," so that instead of having the order S_1, S_2, a, $—as is the case in the four discourses—we could have, say, the order S_1, a, S_2, $. Even as "a total of twenty-four different discourses are [therefore] possible," Lacan focuses primarily on the four discourses that he finds "particularly important": the discourse of the Master, of the University, of the Hysteric, and of the Analyst (Fink, 198). It is the difference between two of the four discourses—the discourses of the University and the Master—that is directly relevant to the present argument, for they reflect the difference between the present historical block of capitalism, in which surplus takes the specific form of surplus-value, and the past blocks in which surplus's modulations allowed for economic and semantic equilibrium.[1]

Beginning with the past, the formal structure of the discourse of any pre-capitalist block can be represented through the discourse of the Master:

$$\underline{S}_1 \rightarrow \underline{S}_2$$
$$\$ \ a$$

Here, knowledge (*savoir*) and vassals are effectively indistinguishable (S_2), since the unambiguous *raison d'être* of both is to serve the master (S_1). The master's address ($\rightarrow$) to the slave is tantamount to the command that the latter put all the knowledge he might possess and all his labor to the service of the master. And by working, the slave produces ever more products and knowledge (a)—what we could call a surplus of products and knowledge—but, crucially, the latter play no role in the slave's knowledge of what the master wants, his truth ($). For above and beyond any practical knowledge (*savoir*) and the "many things" he "knows," the slave "knows even better still . . . what the master wants," he knows the truth of the master which is that the slave should work for him. In short, "the slave knows [that] that's what his function as slave is." This is so, "even if the master does not know it himself," even if he himself is inconsistent ($—the bar in the matheme for the Subject symbolizing this inconsistency), "which is the usual case, for otherwise," as Hegel has made amply clear, "he would not be a master" (Lacan 2007, 32). What remains hidden or "unconscious" (placed in the lower left position in the formula) is the master's own inconsistency ($), of which the slave knows nothing. In other words, the truth of the master *for* the slave—and hence the ground of the master's legitimacy in occupying the position of authority vis-à-vis the slave—does not depend on some fantasy (surplus) on the part of the slave's knowledge, for it is presupposed *a priori* (as the truth that the slave must work for the master), beyond and above any body of knowledge produced in the discourse of the Master. The concrete manifestation of the fundamental ignorance of the master's own will or desire within the theocratic era of the discourse of the Master takes the form of God's unknowable will; and here too, this impossibility of knowing God's will remains inoperative with regard to the slave's knowledge of the *a priori truth* that he must serve the Master (God). The truth of the theocratic slave could be expressed as: "Whatever God's will may be, one thing is certain, that he wills that I serve Him."

Lacan's model in formulating the discourse of the Master is clearly Aristotle, whose basic premise is that proper slaves are "natural slaves." Lacan's innovation lies in dismissing Aristotle's "difference between the rule of master over slave and the rule of a statesman," and in applying the logic of the "natural slave" to the "naturally free men" (Aristotle, 74; 1255b16). Lacan's conception of knowledge—*savoir*, as opposed to *connaissance*—is also predicated on Aristotle's conception of the slave's knowledge:

> A man is not called master in virtue of what he knows but simply in virtue of the kind of person he is; similarly with slave and free. Still, there *could* be such a thing as a master's knowledge or a slave's knowledge. . . . house-boys . . . cookery and other forms of domestic service. . . . All such fields of knowledge are the business of slaves, whereas a master's knowledge consists in knowing how to put his slave to *use*. . . . But the use of slaves is not a form of knowledge that has any great importance or dignity, since it consists in knowing how to direct slaves to do the tasks which they ought to know how to do. (Aristotle, 74–75; 1255b16–1255b30)

Occasionally, there are "those masters whose means are sufficient to exempt them from the bother" of overseeing the slaves as to whether they indeed know how to do the things they ought to know, and who "employ an overseer to take on this duty" (75; 1255b30). But no one needs to oversee that the slaves do work and are put to use, since, whether or not the slave really knows the "many things" he is supposed to know, one thing is always certain, namely, to repeat Lacan's words, that "the slave knows . . . what his function as slave is." By contrast, the "essence of the master" remains throughout all history the fact "that he does not know what he wants" (Lacan 2007, 32). By the same token, the essence of the slave remains throughout history to obey a master who must, therefore, appear to the slave as wanting to be obeyed, to be the master. But the crucial point lies in *whether the slave knows* a priori *that this is what the master wants*—in which case this knowledge is part of his overall knowledge (*savoir*)—or *whether it is a further kind of knowledge (*connaissance*) that must be produced by the discourse in order to justify that this is what the master wants*. In short, the point is whether the slave takes it for granted that his essence is to obey the master or whether a further knowledge is required in order to justify to the slave why he must obey the master. In the discourse of the Master, the slave knows *a priori* what the master wants, and the latter's inconsistency remains totally hidden to him, so that it could be called unconscious only catachrestically, since it is a *non-functional "unconscious"* that plays no role in sustaining truth and authority. Dylan Evans helps us clarify the distinction between the two kinds of knowledge by pointing out that "the unconscious is simply another name for symbolic knowledge," which is "*savoir*," as opposed to "*connaissance*," which is "imaginary knowledge." *Savoir* is an " 'unknown knowledge,' a knowledge which the subject does not know he knows" (94). In the discourse of the Master, the slave *knows* what the truth of the master is for him, while he *knows nothing, not even unconsciously*, of the master's inconsistency. Rather than being a knowledge that the slave has without knowing it, the master's inconsistency is completely not known. In short, in the discourse of the Master, *savoir* and *connaissance* (symbolic or unconscious and imaginary knowledge) coincide, which is why the unconscious is not an operative function here.

A juxtaposition with the discourse of the University, which represents the historical block of secular capitalism, will help us establish the difference between the two historical blocks. The difference between the "classical master [*maître antique*]" and the "modern master, whom we call capitalist, is a modification in the place of knowledge" (Lacan 1991, 34; 2007, 31). With capitalist modernity, the position of mastery or the "dominant" position, which is always "installed in the place on the left" top in the graph of a discourse, comes to be occupied by knowledge itself and, thus, to form what Lacan calls the University discourse (2007, 34):

$$\underline{S_2} \rightarrow \underline{a}$$
$$S_1 \ \$$$

Now it is the master and knowledge that are effectively indistinguishable (S_2), for now knowledge is "not knowledge of everything . . . but all-knowing [*non pas savoir-de-tout . . . mais tout-savoir*]," that is, "nothing other than knowledge," not mastery or power, but *pure* knowledge, which, as such, is said to be "objective knowledge" or "science" or what "in ordinary language is called the bureaucracy" (1991, 34; 2007, 31). Whereas "in the initial status of the master's discourse knowledge is on the side of the slave," in the next status of the discourse of the capitalist master, all knowledge is the "master's knowledge" (*connaissance*), so that "[c]apitalist exploitation" amounts to the fact that "the proletarian has been dispossessed of something," which beyond "communal property, of course," consists of "his [the slave's/proletarian's] knowledge," which the discourse of the capitalist master "render[s] useless" (2007, 31–32). Thus, whereas in the discourse of the master what was hidden was ($\$$)—the fact that the master himself does not know what he wants—what is hidden in the discourse of the University is that knowledge *is* mastery and power (S_1). How is this possible? Because knowledge is now secular, that is, both "objective"—presenting itself as (if it were) operating on pure transitive deduction (*logos*)—*and* lacking (a ground), so that it requires a surplus fantasy (*a*), in order to sustain itself as (presumably) "objective," since, as we have seen, it is not truly transitive deduction but "circular." Thus the participation of the secular subject-slave in the university discourse entails his split ($\$$), since he speaks through something that presents itself as "objective" knowledge, while in truth it involves fantasy. It is only insofar as the slave's fantasy adjoins the truth of the master, that this truth comes to appear as (if it were) "objective knowledge." And the slave accepts this knowledge as truth because of his conviction that it is, precisely, objective—the product of non-circular reason—and not because it supports and legitimizes the authority of any master. In short, the university discourse produces, and is predicated on, the illusion that the function of knowledge is to reveal objective truths rather than to sustain authority—at the very moment when the function of knowledge for the first time becomes precisely a means for sustaining authority. The specific characteristic of the discourse of the university or of modern mastery is that "all-knowing" (*tout-savoir*), "the idea that knowledge can make a whole"—that is, can exclude power and be instead pure or objective knowledge—is "immanent to the political as such" (2007, 31).

In other words, unlike in the discourse of the Master, what is hidden in the University discourse now fulfills a function necessary for the slave to sustain the truth of the new master, the "truth" that knowledge is "objective," or, what amounts to the same, that there is no master. This is why, in contrast to the discourse of the Master in which the "hidden" (unconscious) remained non-functional, in the secular capitalist block the "hidden" must be taken into account as an epistemological function. The unconscious is an exclusively secular epistemological function, just as, on the level of economy, surplus-value is again an exclusively capitalist function. The modern slave's labor produces not only the objects of utility required for the sustenance of the master but also surplus-value, something which goes far beyond the means of the master's subsistence, constituting that which sustains the master in his position of politico-economic power in the first place.

Thus, we see how surplus—which in the present context can also be formulated as the "hidden" truth that the master (from any "natural master" and God to any secular political power) "does not know what he wants"—is transhistorical, while it can manifest itself historically in forms that entail equilibrium or disequilibrium in both the semantic and the economic fields.

The brief description of the University discourse therefore is: knowledge (S_2) addresses the unconscious fantasy (a) of the subject, which, at the cost of splitting itself ($\$$), provides the required ground so that said knowledge appears as "objective," and not as a body of knowledge serving a certain power (S_1). If, to repeat, "knowledge," as something that "can make a whole [*puisse faire totalité*]," is ever since the advent of secular capitalist modernity "immanent to the political as such," it is because knowledge, the new locus of power, can make a (consistent) totality only if the subject provides it with a surplus (fantasy) (Lacan 1991, 33; 2007, 31). The moment knowledge requires an unconscious surplus in order to obtain the appearance of consistent "objective knowledge," ideological fantasy emerges as an indispensable political factor. Ideology is predicated on a fetishistic split between (unconscious) knowledge and (fantasmatic) belief: "although I know that my acts and thoughts are dictated by the master (power), I believe that they are dictated by objective knowledge."[2] (As Žižek has rightly pointed out, it is knowledge, not belief, that is unconscious and wherein the real of one's desire lies.[3]) The irony is that, although the unconscious knowledge or the real of the subject's desire is to have a master (i.e., to be a slave), it so turns out that, if the subject believes in knowledge as objective and power-neutral, then he or she also believes that there are no masters but just free individuals, masters of themselves. This is the widely praised secular fantasy of the "freedom of the individual."[4]

Capitalism and secular reason, with their whole array of accompanying new, specifically modern, phenomena, ranging from ideology and hegemony to non-coercive coercion and biopolitics, entail that in the past historical blocks, the sustenance of authority did not depend on the subjects' drawing on the available knowledge. Knowledge was rather a derivative by-product of the *a priori* self-posited truth of authority *qua* authority. This picture was radically transformed with the actualization of the historical block of secular capitalist modernity, in which the new fact that the subject is the subject of the unconscious, and hence split, is to be taken literally: the secular subject is the embodiment of an imaginary *coincidentia oppositorum*, both free master and deceived slave. While the classical slave was above all convinced that the truth of his master lies "in knowing how to put his slave to *use*," the modern slave believes, above and beyond all, that everything is ruled by objective knowledge, not by a master for whom she must work (even as she unconsciously knows that this is the case). The notorious Hegelian dialectic of (read: reversibility between) the master and the slave finds its full realization in the historical block of the "modern master," which is also the block of the "modern slave," insofar as it is only in this block that the slave is convinced that the true master is no other than himself. *The Hegelian dialectic of the master and the slave* is an accurate description of the central ideological illusion organizing the *logic of internalized power and non-coercive coercion*, the properly modern democratic forms of power.[5]

Aristotle's Discourses

Οικονομια *versus* Χρηματιστικη

Surplus-enjoyment (*plus-de-jouir*) is the fantasy required for knowledge to appear both consistent (without involving a contradictory split) and objective (without supporting a specific power position). And, as mentioned earlier, Lacan introduced this concept as the semantic equivalent of the economic surplus-value. Just as the latter's condition of possibility lies in the split character of commodities as both use-values and exchange-values, surplus-enjoyment emerges out of the primary fact that "objective knowledge" is split, appearing as a transitive deduction, while requiring, in order to sustain this appearance, a fantasy that presupposes the purported outcome of the deduction. And although surplus is transhistorical, in the past historical blocks it did not manifest itself as either surplus-value or surplus-enjoyment because exchange, economic and semantic alike, was based on and motivated by the perpetual sustenance of an *a priori* or "natural" equilibrium, both with regard to the values of the exchanged products, which remained equilibrate since they did not procure surplus-value, and with regard to power hierarchies, in which power positions were both explicit and stable.

It is this difference between the capitalist and the past blocks that Marx attempts to foreground in his reading of Aristotle. Aristotle had already argued that value existed since the most primitive societies, since "the technique of exchange can be applied to" all "pieces of property," and exchange "has its origin in a state of affairs often to be found in nature, namely, men having too much of this and not enough of that" (Marx 1990, 151; Aristotle, 82; 1257a5). Nor did value have to wait until the invention of currency to emerge in the world. As Marx puts it commenting on Aristotle's analysis of value, when the latter writes

" '5 beds = 1 house (Κλιναι πεντε αντι οικιασ)' is indistinguishable from '5 beds = a certain amount of money (Κλιναι πεντε αντι . . . οσου αι πεντε κλιναι),' " what he thereby presupposes is that " '[t]here can be no exchange' . . . 'without equality, and no equality without commensurability' ('ουτ' ισοτησ μη ουσησ συμμετριασ').' " This means, Marx continues, "that the house should be qualitatively equated with the bed, and that these things, being distinct to the senses could not be compared with each other as commensurable magnitudes if they lacked this essential identity," which is expressed in the "concept of value" (1990, 151). Nevertheless, Aristotle "abandons" here "the further analysis of the form of value," concluding that " 'it is, however, in reality, impossible . . . that such unlike things can be commensurable,' " so that "this form of equation can only be something foreign to the true nature of the things"; it can only be " 'makeshift for practical purposes' " (151; citing throughout Aristotle's *Nicomachean Ethics*, bk. V, ch. 5). Aristotle falls short in understanding "what is this homogeneous element, i.e., the *common substance*, which the house represents from the point of view of the bed, in the value expression of the bed," for the fact remains that: "Towards the bed, the house represents something equal, in so far as it represents what is *really* equal, *both in the bed and in the house*" (Marx 1990, 151; emphasis mine). This "common substance" which is value, and which is the real substance of both the bed and the house, Marx identifies as "human labour," insofar as "in the form of the commodity-values, all labour is expressed as equal human labour and therefore as labour of equal quality"—the quality of value. "Aristotle himself was unable to extract this fact" and to complete his analysis of the form of value, Marx continues, "because Greek society was founded on the labour of slaves, hence had as its natural basis the inequality of men and their labour-powers" (151–152). The emergence of a value that produces surplus-value is possible only in a society in which "men" appear equal. Lacan makes the same point in the context of energy, a concept of similar structure and history as value:

> Not that energy hasn't always been there. Except that people who had slaves didn't realise that one could establish equations for the price of their food and what they did in their *latifundia*. There are no examples of energy calculations in the use of slaves. There is not the hint of an equation as to their output. Cato never did it. It took machines for us to realize

they had to be fed. And more—they had to be looked after. But why? Because they tend to wear out. Slaves do as well, but one doesn't think about it, one thinks that it is natural for them to get old and croak. (1991a, 75)

Like value, energy has "always been there," but the concept of energy as a quantifiable abstract entity that would allow for the emergence of modern science could not be incepted prior to the replacement of slave-labor with remunerated labor, since only for the latter does one need to establish equations "as to their output," the "price of their food," and so on, in order to calculate their required means for the laborer's physical and "moral" subsistence. And these equations presuppose the equality of all human labor, which, in turn, presupposes the idea of equality among humans. In Marx's words:

> The secret of the expression of value, namely the equality and equivalence of all kind of labour because and in so far as they are human labour in general, could not be deciphered until the concept of human equality had already acquired the permanence of a fixed popular opinion. (1990, 152)

The establishment of this "fixed popular opinion" "becomes possible only in a society where the commodity-form is the universal form of the product of labour, hence the dominant social relation is the relation between men as possessors of commodities" (Marx 1990, 152). It is the "commodity-form" and possession that make the human "free." Here we evidence once again Marx's anti-genealogical thought and methodology: the concept of value as objectified, and hence exchangeable, human labor presupposes the commodity-form, that is, the product specific to objectified labor. In other words, what Marx offers us is not the cause that led to the emergence of either of the two (commodity-form and objectified labor), but: (1) the formal laws that structure the commodity-form and objectified labor in the historical block that is not based on the labor of slaves; and (2) the formal reasons why value, even though already existent, could not be structured, let alone grasped and described, in the same way in the blocks in which slavery was the dominant mode of labor. The genealogical shift itself from slave labor to capitalist "free" labor can methodologically constitute only an *a priori* and unexplainable fact, whose possibility (though not necessity) lies in that both slave labor and commodified labor enable economic organizations whose modes are manifestations of the attributes of surplus. Surplus (value and the unconscious) existed always, but in the former case as non-operational or virtual, while in the latter as operational and actual. As Lacan puts it in his seventeenth seminar:

> Something changed in the master's discourse at a certain point in history. We are not going to break our backs finding out if it was because of Luther, or Calvin, or some unknown traffic of ships around Genoa, or in the Mediterranean sea, or anywhere else, for the important point is that on a certain day surplus *jouissance* [*plus-de-jouir*] became calculable, could be counted, totalized. This is where what is called accumulation of capital begins. (1991, 207; 2007, 177)

Intertwining more closely the economic and semantic fields of exchange, Lacan describes this shift further by saying:

> the impotence of conjoining surplus-enjoyment [*plus-de-jouir*] with the master's truth . . . the impotence of this conjunction is all of a sudden emptied. Surplus-value adjoins itself to [*s'adjoint au*] capital—not a problem, they are homogenous, we are in the field of values. (1991, 207; 2007, 177–178; translation modified)

Both realms, semantic and economic, are, and have always been, domains of value, but it is only in capitalism that the impotence of conjoining their surplus to value itself is canceled, so that value is actually increased.

In a sort of premonition of the capitalist block, Aristotle expressed the difference between his own and the capitalist blocks by using as his criterion (which was meant to become pivotal in Marx's thought) the existence or not of a *limit* in the act of *exchange*. Aristotle juxtaposed limited and limitless modes of exchange as contemporaneous phenomena, as the threat posed already at his time to the dominant practice of limited οικονομια ("household-management") by that of limitless χρη-ματιστικη or chrematistics (the "acquisition of goods/wealth" or, more accurately, the trade for the purpose of acquiring profit or interest—*tokos*, which Marx translates literally as "offspring" [1990, 255]). In the first case, the end or purpose of the exchange is defined "by the proper use of the article in question," which is always limited, such as the use of a "shoe" which is to "put [it] on your foot" (81; 1256b40). But the same shoe can also be used "to offer in exchange," and "both," Aristotle admits, "are uses of the shoe, for even he that gives a shoe . . . and receives in exchange" something else "is making use of the shoe as a shoe." But, Aristotle adds here, this latter is "not the use proper to it, for a shoe is not expressly made for purposes of exchange" (81–82; 1256b40). Nevertheless, this act of exchange can remain within the limits of what belongs to "nature" (οικονομια) as long as it is "carried on far enough to satisfy the needs of the parties" involved in the exchange, unlike the "form of money-making," χρηματιστικη, which is not part of nature because it is concerned with "how the greatest profits might be made out of the exchanges" (82–83; 1256b40). In the first case, even as the shoe is not used for its proper or original purpose, the "technique of exchange" is natural because "it keeps to its original purpose: to reestablish nature's own equilibrium of self-sufficiency" (82; 1257a28). In this way, οικονομια is a practice that remains faithful to the discourse of the Master, whereas by focusing on what "a great deal of money may be procured," χρηματιστικη introduces disequilibrium, and thereby transforms exchange into a limitless process, since money can always procure a greater amount of money. In short, χρηματιστικη deals not with money but with capital, thus intimating its adjacent virtual discourse of the University, an anathema to "natural slavery," which Aristotle feels compelled to condemn and, thus, misses his chance of completing his analysis of value in its potentiality beyond οικονομια.

Aristotle often seems to deem the introduction of currency as the root of all the evils accompanying (interest-bearing) trade: "Once a currency was provided, development was rapid and what started as a necessary exchange became *trade*," in which "wealth" is "regarded as being a large quantity of coin because coin is what the techniques of . . . trading are concerned with" (83; 1257a41). But it is clear that he deems currency not to be the true cause of the disequilibrium, for "coinage [*nomisma*]" becomes "convention [*nomos*] and artificial trumpery having no root in nature" only "if those who employ a currency system chose to alter it," and instead of using it for its proper or original purpose, they use it so that "coins cease to have their *value* and can no longer be used to procure the necessities of life" (83; 1257b10; emphasis mine). Aristotle's internal contradiction is due to his limitation by the realm of the possible of οικονομια that forces him to define even in the context of χρηματιστικη the "value" of everything according to the criterion of οικονομια, as its ability to "procure the necessities of life." But according to his own overarching axiomatic premise of entelechy, which sees the value of everything in its proper or original purpose, just as the value of a shoe lies in wearing it on one's foot, the value of currency—something explicitly invented for the purpose of exchange—should be exchange itself, regardless of whether its effect is to procure the necessities of life or more currency. What forces Aristotle to contradict his own basic premise of entelechy is that even *it* is subjugated to a more fundamental axiom that defines his historical block: "nature's own equilibrium of self-sufficiency"—according to which "either the goods" required to satisfy the necessities of life "must be there to start with, or [the] technique of property-getting must see that they are provided," rather than letting exchange become, as in the case of trade, an end in itself, exchange for the sake of exchange (79; 1256b26). Aristotle himself is not blind to his own contradiction. "Trade," he writes:

> is thought to be concerned with coinage, because coinage both limits the exchange and is the unit of measurement by which it is performed; and there is indeed no limit to the amount of riches to be got from this mode of acquiring goods. (84; 1257b10)

It is no accident that Aristotle is willing to admit that the nature (entelechy) of exchanging coinage is to pose "no limit to the amount of riches" it obtains, at the very moment that he introduces the distinction between the "limits of exchange" and "the unit of measurement" employed in exchange. For these two terms provide a bridge toward his further distinction, through which he hopes to bypass his own contradiction, namely, the distinction between "means"—"unit of measurement"—and "end"—which he now defines neither as exchange itself nor as the "acquisition" of goods, but as the "use" of goods (84 and 77; 1257b25 and 1256a1). Thus:

> [T]here is no limit to the end which this kind of acquisition [trade or χρηματιστικη] has in view, because the end is wealth in that form, i.e., the possession of goods. The kind which is household-management [οικονομια], on the

other hand, does have a limit, since it is not the function of household-management to acquire goods [but to use them]. (84; 1257b25)

Even while recognizing that the entelechy of χρηματιστική is the limitless acquisition of wealth, including the limitless accumulation of profit, Aristotle is capable of condemning it by resorting to the end of οικονομια, as the "use" rather than the "acquisition of goods" (77; 1256a1). Once again, we see that the cause of χρηματιστική is not coinage (which may as well be employed in οικονομια, as long as it is exchanged for the goods used to satiate the needs of life), but its inherent absence of limit. This is why Aristotle feels compelled to conclude this chapter by distinguishing χρηματιστική, as the "unnecessary kind of acquisition," from οικονομια, as the "necessary" kind of acquisition, not by any reference to coinage but by stating that the latter differs from the former "in being concerned with household-management and food and in a way that accords with nature, and also in being limited as opposed to unlimited" (85; 1258a14). It is only the absence of this limit that renders "coinage" suitable for χρηματιστική, thereby letting it become, properly speaking, capital. While Aristotle's historical block allowed him to condemn χρηματιστική by providing him with the necessary axioms required to transcend his contradictions, Marx, writing within the historical block dominated by χρηματιστική itself, had little with which to defend the necessities of life against the assaults conferred to them by both the fact that "money as capital is an end in itself" and that the "movement of capital is . . . limitless" (Marx 1990, 253).

Nevertheless, even if by condemning it, Aristotle did grasp essential aspects of the logic of χρηματιστική, which is why Marx refers to him as "the great investigator who was the first to analyse the value-form," as well as "so many other forms of thought, society, and nature," including not least the necessary capitalist transformation of enjoyment into surplus-enjoyment (Marx 1990, 151). For, in Aristotle's words:

Some people . . . are eager for life but not for the good life; so, desire for life being unlimited, they desire also an unlimited amount of what enables it to go on. Others again, while aiming at the good life, seek what is conducive to the pleasure of the body. So, as this too appears to depend on the possession of property, their whole activity centers on business, and the second mode of acquiring goods [χρηματιστικη] owes its existence to this. For where enjoyment consists in excess, men look for that skill which produces the excess that is enjoyed. (85; 1257b40)

Χρηματιστικη introduces not only economic but also semantic disequilibrium, not only surplus-value but also a logical inconsistency regarding the truth-value of our acts: on the one hand, we engage in exchange in order to obtain what could offer us a good or pleasurable life; on the other hand, exchange becomes an autonomous subject whose end is itself. The sole way to overcome this inconsistency, Aristotle suggests, is to see good life itself in the excess accumulated through this limitless self-perpetuation of exchange. Once we've done so, we can find enjoyment no longer in a good life as defined by any standards of οικονομια but in pure excess. What is more, there we find not only the good and the pleasurable but even that which fulfills our "unlimited" "desire for life," that is, immortality—something that is crucial to biopolitics, as we shall see in part 2. And since excess is the source of both our enjoyment and our immortality, we invest out entire existence on developing the skills that produce this excess. There is no other purpose in our activities than producing excess, and this is so regardless of whether in their professions people directly engage in trade:

And if they cannot procure it [excess] through money-making they try to get it by some other means, using all their faculties for this purpose, which is contrary to nature: courage, for example, is to produce confidence, not goods; nor yet is it the job of military leadership and medicine to produce goods, but victory and health. But these people turn all skills into skills of acquiring goods, as though that were the end and everything had to serve that end. (85; 1257b40)

Aristotle grasped the fact that in capitalism the "end" of not only trade but of all life activities becomes the perpetual chase after ever more excess. The aspect that seems to have eluded him is the possibility that the illusion he describes—"as though that were the end and everything had to serve that end"—could obtain the status of a quasi-universal "objective truth." Aristotle could not grasp the possibility that excess

would enable what for him was a conspicuous contradiction or logical inconsistency—between exchange for the sake of a good life and
exchange for its own sake—to function as though it were the indubitable
end of human life and the sole path to both enjoyment and immortality. Furthermore, what remained inconceivable or beyond the realm of
the possible for Aristotle is that, in the domain of capital, while human
beings lose their ability to enjoy life by any standards of οικονομια and
are left only with enjoyment in excess (surplus-enjoyment), they nevertheless do enjoy insofar as they identify with the Master. The ultimate
enjoyment of the Master, now as then, remains to sustain his mastery as
an unquestionable authority—be it because he is the "natural master" or
the purveyor of some presumably "objective knowledge." All the better
when this knowledge is unquestionably respected in all its inconsistency,
since in this way it does not run the risk that some argument could
ever undermine it. (A glance at the rapid succession of vogues in dietary
and health prescriptions suffices to show their impotence in undermining the objective status of scientific knowledge.) Surplus-enjoyment is
that particular form of enjoyment that is accessible only to an invincible
Master, precisely because it is underpinned by conspicuous inconsistency.
And since surplus-enjoyment is equally and freely accessible to everyone,
everyone is an invincible Master.

Hegel, who is keenly aware that by his time there are no "natural
masters," writes that, although both the master and the slave or bondsman relate to the thing or the object of the bondsman's labor negatively,
"the bondman['s] . . . negating of it . . . cannot go the length of being
altogether done with it to the point of annihilation," for he "works on
it" and, hence desires it. Things look differently for the master, though:

> For the Lord, on the other hand, the immediate relation
> becomes through its mediation [via the bondsman] the
> sheer negation of the thing, or the enjoyment [*Genuß*] of
> it. What [the bondsman's] desire [*Begierde*] failed to achieve,
> he [the lord] succeeds in doing, viz. to have done with the
> thing altogether, and to achieve satisfaction in the enjoyment
> [*Genuß*] of it. Desire [*Begierde*] failed to do this because of
> the thing's independence; but the lord, who has interposed
> the bondsman between it and himself, takes to himself only
> the dependent aspect of the thing and has the pure enjoy-
> ment of it [*genießt es rein*]. The aspect of its independence

he leaves to the bondsman, who works on it. (Hegel 1977, 116; 1988, 133)

Here Hegel offers us the definitions of the modern or capitalist slave and master. Slave is that person who has an immediate relation to the thing, working on, and desiring, it, whereas master is whoever manages "to have done with the thing altogether," and it is this person alone who can "achieve satisfaction in the enjoyment of it." It follows that, having given up the enjoyment deriving from any things that satisfy life whatsoever for the sake of an enjoyment in sheer excess (surplus-enjoyment), any human being in capitalism is a master. Once again, the profound truth of the Hegelian dialectic regarding the illusions required for sustaining power in secular capitalist modernity is revealed. It is through work, Hegel argued and Alexandre Kojève stressed emphatically, that in the course of history the slave will show to the master his truth as the real master. Both thinkers turn out to have been right—as long as we understand that at stake is *work for the sake of excess*, both surplus-value and surplus-enjoyment. Or, as Lacan put it, the truth in what "Hegel *dixit*," namely, that "the slave will over time demonstrate his truth to [the master]," actually is what "Marx *dixit*," namely, that the slave "will have been occupied during all this time in fomenting his [the master's] surplus *jouissance*" (2007, 107). Taking 1917 as the year marking the attempt to actualize the Hegeliano-Marxist prophecy, it has taken almost a century of this demonstration for the dialectic to reach its apogee and reveal the truth of the Master globally.

Whence the Need for a
Meta-Phenomenological Ontology?

This part of the present work revisited Sartre's phenomenological ontology through the lenses of primarily Spinozian monism, Marx's analysis of capital and the commodity form, and Lacanian psychoanalysis, in order to formulate a monistic or meta-phenomenological theory of being *qua* surplus, as well as of time and history. Encountering this statement out of context one might justifiably object: But isn't phenomenology, at least Sartre's, an ontology that is also a theory of value, time, and history? Wasn't Sartre who said that being is value and that what we call time is the temporalization of the being-for-itself? And if this is so, what then was wrong with his phenomenology and why do we need a meta-phenomenological or monistic ontology? Although the present work has, at least obliquely, already addressed these questions in its ontological exposition, it seems fit here to reexamine the question directly on the level of phenomenology's overall epistemology and methodology.

In two words, the cardinal premises of Sartre's approach that account for the shortcomings of his ontology are *anthropomorphism* and *dialectics*.

To be sure, as far as the latter is concerned, there is arguably no more accurate structure of thought than the dialectics when it comes to grasping the mechanism of the imaginary. This is why throughout the present work dialectics has provided the matrix for accounting for all sorts of ideological illusions, including, as we just saw, the illusion of freedom and mastery that has increasingly dominated and facilitated the subjective and political constitution of secular capitalist modernity. As Lacan put it, Hegel's radical advance beyond "a certain religious individualism which grounds the existence of the individual in his unique tête-à-tête

73

with God," does not go beyond "showing that the reality . . . of each human being is in the being of the other," so that "in the last instance, Hegel leads us to" what for him is the ultimate and profoundest "one last division, one last separation, ontological, if I may say so, within man," the very reflection or internalization of "a reciprocal alienation" which "is irreducible, with no way out" (1991, 72). This "reciprocal alienation" is exactly what psychoanalysis designates as the imaginary relation, and insofar as the imaginary is indeed an inevitable constituent of human subjectivity, at least within secular modernity, in this historical block we will never "have gone beyond Hegel"—which is another way of saying, as Althusser did, that "ideology *has no outside*" (Lacan 1991, 71; Althusser 1971, 175). This, however does not mean that our ontologies, and for that matter even, if not above all, our analyses of ideology, should stop at the boundary of the imaginary—let us not forget that, nevertheless, "it is necessary to be outside ideology . . . to be able to say: I am in ideology" (Althusser 1971, 175).

It is no accident that in this context Lacan adds that pursuing the imaginary can at most bring us "at the limit of anthropology" (Lacan 1991, 72). This comment brings us to the second premise of phenomenology, anthropomorphism, which for Lacan is the prison house of not only Hegelian but all humanist thought. If "Freud got out of it" and "isn't a humanist" it is precisely because of his "discovery . . . that man isn't entirely in man" (72–73). Through the "metaphor of the human body as a machine"—what today we would call structure—Freud pointed to "the manifestation of a certain beyond of the inter-human reference" that is exhausted in the imaginary (76). Sartre, by contrast, seems to be confined within the limitations of anthropomorphic thought insofar as everything in his ontology emerges out of human consciousness.

The persistence with which Sartre reiterates throughout *Being and Nothingness* the primacy of consciousness is a direct reaction to Heidegger who, in Sartre's words, "completely avoided any appeal to consciousness in his description of *Dasein*" (134). If, as is the case in Heidegger, "the *Dasein* has from the start been deprived from the dimension of consciousness," Sartre maintains, "it can never regain this dimension" (120). Consequently, the fact that "Heidegger endows human reality with a self-understanding" is untenable for Sartre, for "how could there be an understanding which would not in itself be the consciousness (of) being understanding?" (120). One could say that Sartre's insistence on the primacy of consciousness is his way of responding to, if not altogether bypassing, what, as Joe Hughes reminds us, was "one of the fundamental problems of transcendental phenomenology as it manifested itself in France," namely, "to describe how meaning could be produced out of a completely meaningless corporeal experience" (44). Paul Ricoeur's "1965 interpretation of Freud in *Freud and Philosophy*" led to a revealing formulation of this question, here in Hughes's concise rendering:

> How does Freud's metapsychology, which explains psychic phenomena from the point of view of an economic, energetic, and therefore meaningless discourse, relate to Freud's more popular, interpretive approach in which successive meanings are uncovered by the analyst? What is the relation between a meaningless libidinal economy and a meaningful psychology? (45)

The question regarding the leap from "meaningless corporeal experience" to meaning reveals itself as one concerning the relation between the *corpus of a meaningless "economy" and meaning.* The real question, therefore, is: How does one go from meaningless economic structures to meaning, including empirical psychology with its interpretations? The present ontology indicates that what is presupposed for meaning is not consciousness but, as we have seen, pure signification, that is, a meaningless grid of relations transcendent to meaning, or, as Gilles Deleuze aptly put it: "One could not say more clearly that empirical psychology is not only founded on, but determined by, a transcendental topology" (2004,174). Deleuze is referring here to Lacan and his notorious reading of Edgar Allan Poe's "The Purloined Letter," in which he advanced the thesis that "it is not only the subject, but the subjects, grasped in their intersubjectivity, who line up" and "model their very being on the moment of the signifying chain which transverses them" (1988, 43). Both subject and intersubjectivity (which is always the encounter with, not the other but, the Other) are determined not only in terms of their identity, their self-understanding, and the meaning they make of the world, but up to the core of their "very being" by the meaningless "signifying chain which transverses them." Lacan's work made more conspicuous what Ricoeur had already argued about Freud, namely, that psychoanalysis is "not a reduction *to* consciousness but a reduction *of* consciousness" (Ricoeur, 424). This having happened, "everything that might be considered the stuff of psychology, kit and caboodle, will follow the path of the signifier" (Lacan 1988, 44). If Freud can speak of the human body, thought, and affects in economic terms, and if Lacan can replace these economic terms with the various topologies that articulate the chain of the signifier, it is only because being (body and thought, or being-in-itself-for-itself) is surplus, circulating in a concordant choreography in the values of economic and semantic exchanges.[1]

It is both this homology between economic and semantic systems of exchange and the primacy of the meaningless network of signification (material or unconscious thought), as the precondition for meaning and hence consciousness, that eludes Sartre's anthropomorphism. This anthropomorphism limits Sartre in his attempt to formulate an "existential psychoanalysis," just as it compromises his reading of Spinoza's monism and his apperception of Marx's commodity fetishism—the two key-theories, as we shall presently see more directly, that postulate the aforementioned homology and the non-primacy of consciousness.

It seems that it was Alfred Sohn-Rethel who first intuited the portentous significance of Marx's commodity fetishism by stating that the "formal analysis of the commodity holds the key not only to the critique of political economy, but also to the historical explanation of the abstract conceptual mode of thinking" (33). In Slavoj Žižek's paraphrase: "in the structure of the commodity-form it is possible to find . . . the network of transcendental categories which constitute the *a priori* frame of . . . knowledge . . . the apparatus of categories," in the "Kantian sense" (1989, 16–17). If the formal analysis of economy can reveal the *a priori* frame of knowledge, then there must be a homology between the two fields. The commodity can hold the key to the transcendental categories of thought only because the pantheism of value reigns on both levels, economic and semantic, or, external objective reality and thought. This also means that what idealist philosophy has traditionally supposed to be *a priori* (thought) coincides with the *a posteriori* (external reality). Žižek characterizes this overlap "a scandal, a nonsensical impossibility from the transcendental point of view," which demands that "the formal-transcendental *a priori* is by definition independent of all positive contents," that is, of all empirico-historical reality (17). Let us not forget, however, that this scandal, so "unbearable from the transcendental-philosophical perspective," was already expressed in Spinoza's God as the immanent cause of everything that exists: God, the presumed *a priori* cause of the world, is Itself an effect of Its own effects, that is, an effect of the *a posteriori* (world).

Žižek also points out that Marx's scandal "correspond[s] perfectly to the 'scandalous' character of the Freudian unconscious," and that consequently there is a "homology" between the "status" of what Sohn-Rethel calls "real abstraction"—"the act of abstraction at work at the very *effective* process of the exchange of commodities" as pure exchange-values without any "distinct, particular, qualitative determination"—and "that of the unconscious." "Before thought could arrive at pure *abstraction*"—at "the apparatus of categories presupposed . . . [for] the scientific procedure (that, of course of the Newtonian science of nature)"—the abstraction was "already at work in the social effectivity of the market," so that "*the 'real abstraction' is the unconscious of the transcendental subject, the support of objective-universal scientific knowledge*" (Žižek 1989, 17–18). In order for this thesis not to revert to a brutal materialism that would raise the "base" (economy) to the transitive cause of the "superstructure" (thought), economy or "social effectivity" and thought must be conceived as pertaining to the same ontological status, that is, as equal manifestations of a third—being, which is their own (unconscious) surplus. Žižek's invocation of the unconscious as the "real abstraction" underlying both economy and thought aims precisely at preventing transitive causality from creeping back into the relation between "base" and "superstructure." But we must also add that such a non-transitive relation between "base" and "superstructure" necessarily entails that "real abstraction"—something which takes place for the first time in the historical block of secular (and scientific) capitalist modernity—is itself a historical modulation of the third that is their cause and effect, their surplus.

Yet, one may still object, commodity fetishism may postulate the homology between semantic and economic systems of value, but why should this homology bear on being? To put it in Sohn-Rethel's terms, an apparently legitimate objection could be that the formal analysis of the commodity may hold the key to the historical explanation of the abstract conceptual mode of thinking, but this does not mean that it also holds the key to being, either in its historical or, even more so, in its transhistorical aspect. The response to the objection goes as follows. Once thought has become secular and, further, once ontology has reached its phenomenological point, that is, once it has transcended the opposition between being and appearance (*Sein und Schein*) and has arrived at the conclusion that being is that which appears and does not appear, then it becomes evident that *the status of being*, the ontological, is the *axiological*, in the literal sense of the word *axia* (Greek for "value"). For, in a world that allows no room for heavens, *only value is appearance and that which does not appear*, insofar as *it involves surplus*. To account now for both the transhistorical and the historical aspects of being, we need to make a further reference to the (non-)functional or (non-)operative character of that dimension of being that does not appear, as we have seen it in the comparison between the discourses of the Master and the University. It is, in fact, precisely because surplus is not operative in the discourse of the Master that, by structural necessity, it always requires heavens of some sort—what is generally referred to as the realm of the spirit, the omnipotent and transcendentalist function of which compensates for the inactivity of surplus *qua* immanent unconscious. The advent of secular capitalist modernity designates above all the shift from supreme spirit to operative surplus.

Returning to Žižek's words, we must say neither "before thought could arrive at pure *abstraction*, the abstraction was already at work in the social effectivity of the market," nor, inverting the order, that "before abstraction was at work in the social effectivity in the market, thought had already arrived at pure abstraction." Both realms, thought and market, are equally effects and causes of surplus, and therefore it cannot be said either that the Word became (binary) sign because first money had become capital (i.e., money that accrues surplus-value), or the inverse. There is no causal priority between the economic and the semantic fields of value precisely because both are caused, and are the causes of, one and the same substance, surplus.

A further, not objection but possible, question may concern the choice of "surplus" and "value," as the overarching terms designating both semantic and economic systems of exchange, rather than "sign." The latter is the choice, for instance, of Foucault who, in explaining the shift occurring in the first century of secular capitalism, writes that henceforth " '[m]oney does not draw its value from the material of which it is composed' " and instead begins to

> receive its value from its pure function as sign. . . . Things take on value, then, in relation to one another . . . but the true estimation of that value has its source in human judgment. . . . Wealth is wealth because we estimate it, just as our ideas are what they are because we represent them. Monetary or verbal signs are additional to this. (1970, 175–176; citing

Scipion de Grammont, *Le Denier royal, traité curieux de l'or et de l'argent* [Paris 1620, 48])

Indeed, "sign" and "value" function as interchangeable terms, and if I opt for "value," it is only because: first, our discourse is more used to associating this concept with surplus, while the fact that the sign always also involves a surplus (whether transcendentalist, as in theocracy's God, or immanent, as in capitalism's ideological fantasy) is lesser known; and, second, that, as one of the effects of the transcendentalist philosophical tradition, "sign" tends to evoke anthropomorphic associations, being linked to human thought and consciousness, as opposed to external reality. We have seen the effects of this tendency on Sartre's thought, and it also afflicts Foucault, for whom everything is reducible to "human judgment." Whenever being is conceived on the ground of human thought, consciousness, or judgment, a dualistic spell is inevitably cast on ontology. Monism, by contrast, is predicated on the principle that there are no two substances, human thought and its other, but one substance with two attributes, *cogitatio* and *extensio*, neither of which is the cause of the other. Ascribing primacy to one of the two attributes essentially amounts to raising the one to the status of substance and the other to a derivative, with the expectable dualist consequences for any ontological edifice. The dualism that starts with *cogitatio* as the primary substance invariably leads to anthropomorphic ontological schemes.

As we have seen, this is the fate of the Sartrean scenario with its two central ontological characters, being-in-itself (*extensio*) and being-for-itself (*cogitatio*), of which the latter stars as the protagonist. Actually, Sartre's admirable enterprise is handicapped by its commitment to an anthropomorphic conception not only of thought but of its true superstar: *lack*. For, as we shall presently see, it is through lack that Sartre eventually acknowledged the affinity of being to value, yet only by confining both within the realm of the human.

We recall that, to bypass the Kantian dualism between the thing-in-itself and appearance (consciousness), Sartre establishes from the outset that the being-in-itself cannot be conceived in terms of a hermetic closeness inaccessible to consciousness, for, in familiar Hegelian fashion: "If I conceive of a being entirely closed in on itself, this being in itself will be solely that which it is, and due to this fact there will be no room in it for either negation or knowledge" (245). The monist solution to this conundrum lies in presupposing thought in being itself, so that knowledge or consciousness is another thought that negates the thought of being as its unconscious thought, for, as we recall, in monism something can be negated only by something positive of the same nature. But Sartre opts for the Hegelian path and, thus, asserts that "every revelation of a positive characteristic of being is the counterpart of an ontological determination as pure negativity in the being of the for-itself" (248). The mere fact " 'that there is' being is not an inner determination of being—which is what it is [in its closedness]—but of negativity," that is, of knowledge or consciousness, which is itself defined as negativity: "a being such that in its being, its being is in question in so far as this being implies a being other than itself" (248 and 239). In other words, "consciousness" or the "for-itself is a being such that in its being, its being is in question in so far as this being is essentially a certain way of *not being* a being which it posits simultaneously as other than itself," that is, as the "being-in-itself" (242). This is why for Sartre, "the for-itself . . . is removed as far as possible from a substance and from the in-itself," which it posits as the negative of what it is (239). The initial intention was to "undertake[] the study of an ontological relation . . . which aims at establishing how in general an object can exist for consciousness," and the conclusion is that "it is impossible . . . for me to have an experience of an object as an object which is not me until I constitute it as an object" (244). The for-itself posits the in-itself of substance as its own negation, as that which it is not, while the in-itself is also constitutive of the for-itself, insofar as the "for-itself is outside itself in the in-itself since it causes itself to be defined by what it is not" (245). In short, the in-itself or substance, that which is supposed to be just by itself and not through an other, turns out to be an effect of consciousness; it is the *cogito* itself that entails that there is being-in-itself, thereby opening up the way to the outside of itself. In Sartre's words:

> The for-itself is perpetually determining itself *not to be* the in-itself. This means that it can establish itself only in terms of the in-itself and against the in-itself. Thus since the nihilation is the nihilation of being, it represents the original connection between the being of the for-itself and the being of the in-itself. The concrete, real in-itself is wholly present to the heart of consciousness as that which consciousness determines itself not to be. The *cogito* must necessarily lead us to discover

this total, out-of-reach presence of the in-itself. Of course the fact of this presence will be the very transcendence of the for-itself. But it is precisely the nihilation which is the origin of transcendence conceived as the original bond between the for-itself and the in-itself. Thus we catch a glimpse of a way of getting out of the *cogito* . . . . [I]ndeed . . . the profound meaning of the *cogito* is essentially to refer outside itself. (134)

Indeed, by now it is amply clear that, for Sartre, the essential function of the *cogito* is to refer outside itself, since *cogito* (consciousness) is that which determines itself *not to be* that against which it establishes itself, and which, therefore, is what the *cogito* (for-itself) is not: the in-itself. Sartre's reasoning pursues faithfully the dialectical fashion which, however, is not to be underestimated. Sartre's thesis seems to reconfirm Žižek's claim that the point of dialectics is not some synthesis of its opposing parties (such as the in-itself and for-itself), but their direct "*coincidentia oppositorum,*" "the immediate coincidence of the opposite poles," in which "each pole passes immediately into its opposite; each is already in itself its own opposite" (1989, 172). Thus, the in-itself or the (Kantian) "Thing-in-itself is effectively a pure 'Thing-of-Thought [*Gedankending*],' a pure form of Thought: the transcendence of the Thing-in-itself coincides immediately with the pure immanence of Thought" (172). The "Thing," Žižek continues, "is itself nothing but a lack, an empty place," insofar as "beyond the phenomenal appearance there is only a certain negative self-relationship because of which the positively given phenomenal world is perceived as 'mere appearance,'" that is, no longer as a *positively given* appearance but appearance insofar as it is *lacking* the essential thing, appearance as precisely *mere* appearance (193). If this is so, then, when Hegel infers that the Thing-in-itself or "the supersensible is therefore *appearance qua appearance,*" he does not mean an immediate coincidence of opposites—as in: the supersensible is the sensible appearance—but rather the equation of the supersensible with appearance *qua mere* appearance, with appearance insofar as it is lacking, and, finally, with the lack in the appearance (Hegel 1977, 89; §147). Hegel is emphatically explicit about this point:

We completely misunderstand this if we think that the supersensible world is *therefore* the sensuous world, or the world as it exists for immediate self-certainty and perception; for the world of [mere] appearance is, on the contrary, *not* the world of sense-knowledge and perception as a world that positively *is*, but this world posited as superseded, or as in truth an *inner world.* (89; §147)

Here Hegel, as the master of the imaginary relation, lays out the necessary link between the thing-in-itself *qua* mere appearance, and hence as "void," and the imaginary. For it is because the thing is "*empty in itself*" and nothing more than a "*complete void*" that "we must fill it up with reveries, *appearances*, produced by consciousness itself"—"since even reveries are better than its own emptiness"—so that the world of mere appearance or of the thing-in-itself is ultimately our "*inner world*" (88–89; §146).

In other words, the dialectic allows us to see that if, as Sartre argues, the *cogito* refers outside itself, *its referent is not the in-itself of facticity*—the being that is given in its own plenitude in the sensuous world—*but its lack.* This is why from the outset Sartre had told us that the essence of the appearance does not just coincide with the given appearance, but is rather *appearance and appearance-that-does-not-appear, appearance and what is lacked in the appearance*—that is, both appearance under a specific gaze *and* the infinity of all possible gazes that cannot appear and must therefore be filled in with the gaze of our inner world.

Thus Sartre has to bring to the stage the pinnacle of his *dramatis personae*, lack, and to do so he is forced to introduce a new division within the in-itself. Having concluded that "the for-itself can not sustain nihilation without determining itself as a *lack of being*," Sartre admits that nevertheless "this lack does not belong to the nature of the in-itself, which is all positivity" (134–135). Where does this lack come from then? Sartre retorts: "It appears in the world only with the upsurge of human reality" (135). Why? Evocatively, his response echoes more a relational structure rather than human reality *per se*:

A lack presupposes a trinity: that which is missing or the "lacking," that which misses what is lacking or the "existing," and a totality which has been broken by the lacking and which would be restored by the synthesis of the "lacking" and the "existing"—this is the "lacked." (135)

We cannot overlook that this passage offers a perfect description of the (impossible) totality of surplus, which in terms of surplus-value, involves the "lacking" as a finite amount of surplus-value, the "existing" as exchange-value, and the "lacked" as surplus-value it is totality. Even without having this in mind, Sartre rightly infers that, therefore, "lack is appearance on the ground of a totality," regardless of "whether this totality has been originally given and is now broken . . . or whether it has never yet been realized" (138). This is why, he continues, "we must not confuse this missing in-itself (the lacked) with that of facticity," since "the in-itself of facticity in its failure to found itself is reabsorbed in pure presence in the world on the part of the for-itself. The missing in-itself, on the other hand, is pure absence" (138). Henceforth, two distinct actors must be cast for the role of the in-itself which is now doubled: on the one hand, the in-itself of facticity (presence), and on the other hand, the in-itself of the "lacked" (absence). We had been told that the in-itself of facticity is posited by the for-itself insofar as the latter needs it in order to define itself against that which it is not, yet, now it turns out, that, after all, the for-itself could never do this since this in-itself is given to the for-itself as pure presence, and not as "absence" or lack. If the for-itself is capable of committing and sustaining nihilation in the first place it is not because of the in-itself of facticity but because of the "missing in-itself," the in-itself of the lacked. And the latter emerges not against anything that is given in its plenitude in nature and the sensuous world but against a "*totality*"—what, as both Kant and Sartre would agree, precisely *cannot* be given as appearance. At this point Sartre feels compelled to return to his reference to human reality:

> Human reality arises as such in the presence of its own totality or self as a lack of that totality. And this totality cannot be given by nature, since it combines in itself the incompatible characteristics of the in-itself and the for-itself. (140)

Indeed, if nature is defined as the in-itself of facticity, and totality requires both the in-itself and the for-itself, totality cannot arise from nature. But if we want to speak *truly* of human reality, the first thing we must recognize is that for humans nature is not, and has never been, a pure in-itself. For human reality, nature is always pantheist, that is, not just a mass given in its plenitude or a presence given in the sensuous world, but also a for-itself, be it, depending on the historical block, the thing's spirit or its exchange-value. This is why Marx can indentify totality just by looking at nature, even if not without being awe-stricken by its mysteries:

> It [value] is constantly changing from one form into the other, without becoming lost in its movement; it thus becomes transformed into an automatic subject. If we pin down the specific forms of appearance assumed in turn by self-valorizing value in the course of its life, we reach the following elucidation: capital is money, capital is commodities. In truth, however, value is here the subject. . . . By virtue of being value, it has acquired the occult ability to add value to itself. . . . As the dominant subject [*übergreifendes Subjekt*] of this process, in which it alternately assumes and loses the form of money and the form of commodities, but preserves and expands itself through all these changes, value requires above all an independent form by means of which its identity with itself may be asserted. . . . All commodities, however tattered they may look, or however badly they may smell, are in faith and in truth money . . . and, what is more, a wonderful means for making still more money out of money . . . money which begets more money . . . money which is worth more money, value which is greater than itself. (1990, 255–257)

This is why "the circulation of money is an end in itself" and the "movement of capital is therefore limitless"—its totality can never be given (1990, 253). And this movement is the movement of all nature, for what Marx is effectively telling us here, in Sartre's terms, is that in its facticity, in its "specific forms of appearance," capital is money (exchange-value, or being-for-itself), capital is commodities (use-value, or being-in-itself); in truth, however, the real "automatic subject" in this movement is capital as neither of its factual appearances but as "self-valorizing value," surplus-value, as the unlimited or infinite progression of its factual appearances, the totality or the "lacked" that will never appear.

Now, it is true that once Sartre arrives at the insight that totality is the "being of the self," he does conclude by stating: "Now we can ascertain more exactly what the being of the self is: it is value" (143). But then he turns to concrete examples, to reveal that the value he has in mind is exclusively *human moral* value. Still, if he nevertheless succeeds in linking value to totality it is precisely because he proceeds by rejecting the traditional conceptions of value offered by the "moralists" in general who "have very inadequately explained" it, and to offer a reading of moral value as surplus or lacked (143). Value, Sartre writes, has the "double characteristic . . . of both being unconditionally and not being." While, "for example," a specific noble act has the characteristic of being, "value is given as the beyond of the acts confronted, as the limit . . . of the infinite progression of noble acts" (143). *Qua* concrete act, nobility, or any other moral value, has being, whereas, *qua* ideal or the "limit" to which every actual noble act aspires, it has no being. In other words, "value has being, but this normative existent does not have to be precisely as reality," so that "its being is . . . not-to-be being." If one commits the error of taking value "precisely as reality," as facticity, then one "risks totally misunderstanding its unreality" and makes of it "a requirement of fact among other facts." On the other hand, "conversely, if one looks only at the ideality of values, one is going to extract being from them, and then for lack of being, they dissolve" (143). One should rather keep both aspects in mind, so that value is defined as surplus, that is, as that unique being that is unconditionally being (presence, value insofar as it is given, be it semantic, economic, or moral) and not being (the "unreality" of the limit of the infinite progression of all factual values).

Here we see the effects of commodity fetishism in action: if Sartre conceives of moral value and being as a lacking totality it is because value is structured also within the economic field as a lacking totality, as a "self-moving substance" that is always greater than itself. Such a conceptualization of value and being would have been impossible prior to the modern secular capitalist era because in any pre-capitalist economy, value was not a lacking totality, it always required in return its equivalent and nothing could ever be lacking or excessive except as the result of some injustice or fraud—for the rest, all surplus was relegated to the supernatural or the transcendental realm of divinity. Just as Aristotle's ethics could not have been conceived outside οικονομια, Sartre's account of moral value is possible only when surplus is operative in all actual fields of value, as the immanent transcendence of any appearance. As Sartre writes:

> Value taken in its origin, or the supreme value, is the beyond and the *for* of transcendence. It is the beyond which surpasses and which provides the foundation for all my surpassings but toward which I can never surpass myself, precisely because my surpassings presuppose it. (144)

It is impossible to surpass myself and become what myself presupposes, its transcendence or surplus, for the same reason that neither money nor the commodity, neither the for-itself nor the in-itself, can surpass itself and be one with the substance or "dominant subject [*übergreifendes Subjekt*]" of which they are the empirical modes. For surplus or immanent transcendence cannot coincide with the appearance that appears. If the for-itself (consciousness) attained this totality then "it would be its own foundation not as nothingness but as being and would preserve within it the necessary translucency of consciousness along with the coincidence with itself of being-in-itself" (Sartre, 140). We do have a name for this concept of realized totality, and a very old one at that: "God"; but now it must be understood, Sartre is cautious to add, that this "is not a transcendent God" but "only human reality itself as totality" (139). It is "an absolute transcendence in absolute immanence," insofar as it "points to consciousness as the meaning of its being and yet consciousness is no more conscious *of* it than *of* itself" (141). But, as we learn from Marx, there is no need for consciousness in order to have "an absolute transcendence in absolute immanence." There is no reason, therefore, to infer, as Sartre does, that:

> Value in its original upsurge is not *posited* by the for-itself;
> it is consubstantial with it—to such a degree that there is
> no consciousness which is not haunted by *its* value and that
> human-reality in the broad sense includes both the for-itself
> and value. (145)

Value, or, rather, surplus is "consubstantial" not just with the "for-itself" as human "consciousness" but also with all manifestations of the in-itself. It is undoubtedly only with human reality that value, economic or semantic, arrives in the world—but once it has arrived, it becomes an *autonomous substance*. It certainly takes human beings to exchange ideas, or money and commodities, and to even conceive of an "autonomous substance" or "structure," but this does not make ideas, structures, or that "self-moving substance . . . for which commodities and money are both mere forms" any less autonomous or more dependent on human consciousness (Marx 1990, 256). Each party, human consciousness and external reality or nature, are equally autonomous with relation to the other party—and, yet, they are not, because, being empirical manifestations of one and the same immanent transcendence, they share the same structures.

In short, commodity fetishism does not amount to the by-now trivial wisdom that thought is determined by its empirical reality and historical context. Rather, its point is that the empirico-historical reality and thought (unconscious and consciousness) are both empirical manifestations of surplus.

As I hope this chapter has shown, we need meta-phenomenology in order to explore the full import of the intertwining of Spinozian monism (beyond dialectics) and Marx's commodity fetishism (beyond anthropocentrism and anthropomorphism) for an ontology that can also account for historical reality.

Recapitulation in Other Words

The actualization of the historical block of secular capitalist modernity entailed and presupposed a shift in the modulation of surplus (the being-in-itself-for-itself) so that it ceased to enable equilibrium in the fields of economic and semantic exchange, and began to involve disequilibrium.

Another way of describing this historical revolution is as a shift from the distinction between matter and *spirit* or *soul* (which, albeit in starkly different ways, structured human consciousness from the days of tribal barter-centered communities to theocratic feudal organizations) to that between matter and *value*. As we have seen, neither matter and spirit nor matter and value are true opposites (in a dualistic sense), since they are the two empirical modes of surplus in its two overarching historical modulations, as inoperative and operative within the plane of immanence, respectively. In short, the shift in question can be described as the secularization (i.e., the inclusion within the plane of immanence) of transcendent spirit, in the form of self-valorizing value. Unlike the absolute transcendence of spirit, this value is an immanent transcendence because it emerges out of the differential relations of worldly things.

One might ask: Haven't people been exchanging objects of utility and thoughts since time immemorial? What is new and specifically modern about these human activities and the value that is thereby exchanged? As long as the purpose of exchange is the satisfaction of needs, money or whatever else serves as the means of exchange remains a *means*; but the moment the dominant objective or end of exchange becomes the accumulation of more money (surplus-value), the means itself becomes the end of exchange. At that instant, the external point of reference (need) is eliminated, and the system of exchange becomes self-referential: one exchanges the "means" in order to have more "means." It is precisely this *self-referentiality of the system of exchange that entails the accumulation of surplus-value.* In other words, the uniqueness of capitalist exchange that distinguishes it from all preceding modes of exchange is that in capitalism the *raison d'être* of things is their existence not as material objects (that satisfy needs) but as immaterial abstract values (that enable the accumulation of surplus-value).

The historical corollary of this economic shift on the level of human thought and consciousness is the moment in which the category of human *need* is superseded by *desire*, defined precisely, in Kojève's memorable commentary on Hegel's *Phenomenology*, as the instigation to "act not for the sake of subjugating a *thing*, but for the sake of subjugating another Desire (for the thing)" (Kojève, 40). Modern desire is not the "animal"-like appetite for any given thing that could satisfy a need but desire, insofar as, Kojève continues, it "is human—or, more exactly, 'humanizing,' 'anthropogentic,'" that is, "only provided that it is directed toward another *Desire* and an *other* Desire" (40). Of course, we cannot miss in Kojève's (Hegelian) account the discriminatory rhetoric that typically characterizes the differentiation of the "self" from its "other"—in this case, our block of secular capitalist modernity, as opposed to its past, which here appears to have been populated by animals. In truth, "animal" simply refers to that being that lives in an economy whose professed principle is the satisfaction of needs. A society of such an economy consists explicitly of masters and slaves, whatever their concrete titles may be. Once mastery and slavery are no longer given as natural states, and, recalling Marx, once "the concept of human equality had already acquired the permanence of a fixed popular opinion," then, returning to Kojève, "the man who desires a thing humanly acts not so much to possess the *thing* as to make another *recognize* his right . . . to that thing," and "—in the final analysis—in order to make the other recognize his *superiority* over the other" (Marx 1990, 152; Kojève, 40). Just as, with the shift from the discourse of the Master to that of the University, mastery becomes imbued with the imaginary function of the surplus (*object a*), human need, too, is permeated by the imaginary, and becomes the desire to have what someone else *desires*—not even what this person *has*, but something beyond (a surplus to) this. It is no longer mastery itself that is natural but, rather, the desire for mastery that is naturalized as the constitutive ontological criterion of humanity. Henceforth, along with surplus-value, the imaginary is the operative function of surplus that makes value specifically modern.

The obsoleteness of spirit, caused by the secular modulation of surplus as an operative function in value, entailed a radical reconfiguration of the relation between *being* and *representation*. For the most part, this shift has been described as the break of the organic link between representation and things, which in the past was upheld by the absolute transcendence of the spirit. For in the past, its absolute transcendence notwithstanding, the spirit had always populated the world, either because it directly inhabited being (as in the pan-spiritualism of archaic societies) or because it *was* the Word (as in monotheism), thereby guaranteeing the, greater or lesser, transparency of being through representation.[1] For centuries, secular modernity invested itself in self-representations around the pivotal chasm that was supposed to separate being from representation, and which was sanctioned by Kant in the Enlightenment. It remains to this day the dominant epistemological premise of secular thought, having survived through modernism, structuralism, and postmodernism, as is evidenced, with few exceptions, by both their adherents and critics who, time and again, attempt to bypass the "obstacle of representation." Such an obstacle is, however, a mirage produced due to the challenge posed to our historical block by the inherited split between immanence and transcendence, combined with the obsoleteness of spirit. But a truly secularized (i.e., immanent) transcendence entails that there is no severance between things and their representations not because either is inhered by spirit but because both are manifestations of the same being. For this being is the immanent transcendence that secularization is after: the totality of immanence itself. This totality remains transcendent only because it is not given either on the level of being or on the level of representation. If eventually phenomenology was able to define being in exclusive reference to representation—as that which *appears* and does not *appear*—it is because representation (semantic and economic) itself consists of that which appears and does not appear.

As the two modes of operative surplus, both external reality and representation are self-referential systems of value, which is why "matter" as an inanimate given mass in its plenitude—a notion supposed to be traditional, yet is retroactively constructed within secular modernity—increasingly reveals its untenability in all fields of knowledge.

In this regard, it is high time, more than a century later, we went beyond Georg Simmel, whose seminal observations on money as an abstract "symbol," a "numerical form" or "pure quantity," "regardless of" its material "specific qualities," linked capitalism to the possibility of modern sciences and generally abstract thought (148 and 150). It was not before mercantilism that values ceased to undergo physical decay, so that a coin retains the value inscribed on it regardless of any possible erosion of its actual metal, and as for paper money, its (symbolic) value is not effected by its worthless materially. Simmel pointed out the revolutionizing effect of this manifestation and conception of value as abstract symbol on both secular economy and thought. In his words:

> It may appear self-evident today that symbols should be created by segregating the quantitative aspects of things; but this is in fact an achievement of the human mind which has remarkable consequences. The institution of money depends upon it inasmuch as money represents pure quantity in a numerical form, regardless of all the specific qualities of a valued object. . . . The growth of intellectual abilities and of abstract thought characterizes the age in which money becomes more and more a mere symbol, neutral as regards its intrinsic value. (150 and 152)

The possibility of an economy based on "symbols" with no "intrinsic value" goes hand in hand with a mode of abstract science that regards only the "quantitative aspects of things." Thus, a phenomenon such as Newtonian physics became a possibility within the realm of knowledge, whereby objects began to be considered as abstract masses, their movements could be described purely quantitatively, and so on.

But Simmel's focus is limited to abstraction. Secular value is not only abstract but also *differential*. The fact that something like atomic theory or quantum physics eventually became also possible presupposes the ability to conceive of matter not only as an abstract quantity but also as *a system of differential relations*. Marx himself attempts to stress the point of the intrinsic relationality of value in the very passage that offers his definition of commodity fetishism, by juxtaposing value to vision as a neurophysiologic phenomenon:

> The mysterious character of the commodity-form consists therefore simply in the fact that the commodity reflects the social characteristics of men's own labour as . . . a social relation between objects, a relation which exists apart from and

outside the producers. Through this substitution, the products of labour become commodities, sensuous things which are at the same time suprasensible or social. In the same way, the impression made by a thing on the optic nerve is perceived not as a subjective excitation of that nerve but as the objective form of a thing outside the eye. In the act of seeing, of course, light is really transmitted from one thing, the external object, to another thing, the eye. It is a physical relation between physical things. As against this, the commodity form, and the value-relation of the products of labour within which it appears, have absolutely no connection with the physical nature of the commodity and the material (*dinglich*) relations arising out of this. It is nothing but the definite social relations between men themselves that assumes here, for them, the fantastic form of a relation between things. . . . I call this the fetishism which attaches itself to the products of labour as soon as they are produced as commodities, and is therefore inseparable from the production of commodities. (1990, 164–165)

As against vision, which is grounded on the "physical relation between physical things," value is the expression of purely "social relations"—in fact, the relations of humans themselves, which appears under the "fantastic form" of "a social relation between objects." In this astonishing passage we also evidence Marx's acute consciousness of the inseparability of the capitalist mode of production from the function of the imaginary ("fantastic"). In the face of this mystery, Marx is obliged to conclude that, "in order, therefore, to find an analogy we must take flight to the misty realm of religion," in which, again, "the products of the human brain appear as autonomous figures endowed with a life of their own." And just as the "life" of divine entities in truth expresses the relations of the lives of the humans whose brains produce them, "so it is in the world of commodities with the products of men's hands" (165).[2] Except that after the advent of structuralism and quantum physics, one need no longer necessarily take a flight into the "misty realm of religion," at least not rhetorically.

If, as Žižek writes, quantum physics exhibits "parallels [with] . . . Lacanian psychoanalysis," this is due to the "homologies between the quantum universe and the symbolic order," given the "purely 'differential' definition of the particle, which directly recalls the classic Saussurean definition of the signifier (a particle is nothing but the bundle of its interactions with other particles)" (1996, 282–283). In the fields of both particles and signifiers, to recall Saussure's words, "there are only differences without positive terms," with "both the signified and the signifier," or particles and waves, being "purely differential," for "in any semiological system," just as in any system of particles, "whatever distinguishes one sign [or particle] from the others constitutes it" (120–121).

And, yet, precisely because it is a purely differential system, the world of particles must also produce, as do the signifier and history, its own (meta-phenomenological) facts—beyond the phenomenological and contingent fact that, for instance, in front of me I see a wall (for other animals do not see the wall I see) and not the particles that constitute it. To make this point clear, let us follow Žižek's reading of the "double-slit experiment," in which electrons behave either as simple particles or as waves interfering with one another, depending not on the actual existence of a second emission of electrons through a second slit (which would interfere with a first emission through a first slit), but on whether a second slit is closed or open, so that a second emission of electrons *could* occur, even if it actually does not. In this case, as Žižek puts it:

> It is as if a single electron (a particle that, as such, must go through one of the two slits) "knows" whether the other slit is open and behaves accordingly; if the other slit is open, it behaves as a wave, if not, as an "ordinary" particle. (1996, 276)

In other words, "a single electron seems to 'know' if it is being observed or not" by the gaze not of an actual but of an imaginary electron, since the first electron behaves as a wave when the second slit is open, regardless of whether there is indeed an electron there (Žižek 1996, 276). This means that even when there is an actual electron in the second slit, the first electron is gazed not by this actual electron but by the electron the first electron imagines to be there by dint of the simple fact that the second slit is open—for whether or not there is an electron there, all it takes for the first electron to behave as being gazed by another is an open slit. The meta-phenomenological fact of particles is the gaze of another electron, which is lacking in itself and is imagined by the first electron in the field of the Other (in this case, the order of slits), thereby transforming the (lacking) gaze into a Master-Signifier that gives the electron its *telos*: to become a particle or a wave.

Quantum physics is a science that presupposes not only abstract thought and symbols but also that *matter is value* and, specifically, a value that involves disequilibrium, a *surplus or lacking gaze* that requires *fantasy in order for matter's vicissitudes to be determined*.

Of course, even as quantum physics as we know it today is a relatively recent development in the field of science, the possibility of conceiving of matter in terms of value was opened up since—when else?—the inception of secular capitalism. Already Roger Joseph Boscovich's (1711–1787) atomic theory, with its substitution of quasi-material point-centers of action (*puncta*) for the rigid units of matter, and its concomitant kinematics, which uses only two dimensions (length and time)—rather than, as in Newtonian dynamics, three (mass, length, and time)—had established particles as a system of elements whose identity is constituted purely differentially, without any regard to mass (an inherent quality of a physical object), even as an abstract quantity. And several philosophers, from Vico and Leibniz to Kant, also produced similar atomic theories. From Spinoza's philosophy to Marx's analysis of economy, and from Saussure's analysis of the sign to atomic and quantum physics, and Lacan's analysis of the human subject, the condition of their possibility remains one: the historical modulation of surplus as the specific value that involves disequilibrium. As we see here, the impact of this modulation far exceeds the fields of knowledge that canonically perceive themselves as epistemologically affected by the domains of either economy or ontology as a philosophical branch.

Last but not least among these fields is political theory, whose intrinsic relation to ontology has already been foregrounded by several theoreticians and philosophers. One of the hopes of this work—beyond enabling "a mode of thought" that, in Foucault's words cited in one of the epigraphs to this work, "will make it possible to reflect at the same time, without discontinuity or contradiction, upon man's being and the being of language"—is to contribute to the formulation of what Giorgio Agamben, in his epigraph here, refers to as "a new and coherent ontology of potentiality," as the precondition for also conceiving "a political theory freed from the aporias of sovereignty." What the full impact of this ontology of value or potentiality on political theory may be, and whether this impact might lie within or without the direction and boundaries of the intimations hinted to by Agamben's work, is something that is neither the object of the present work nor actually yet ripe for an answer (though biopolitics itself, if adequately conceived, might be what goes beyond the "aporias of sovereignty"). For what needs to be examined prior to beginning to approach such questions is the nature of power entailed in this ontology as the form of power specific to secular capitalist modernity. This is why the second part of the present work turns to biopolitics.

PART II

Bios: Biopolitics and Ethics

Bios in Extant Biopolitical Theories

The preceding ontology will help us fathom the exact nature of bios within the realm of being, which, in turn, will allow us to unravel the workings of biopolitics.

Although Aristotle used the term *bios* to designate the specifically human aspect of life as a social and political animal, as opposed to *zoe* (life in its physical or biological sense that characterizes all animals), the term "bios" reenters the contemporary theoretical discourse, through the neologisms "biopower" and "biopolitics," to designate the *political* control of life in its *biological* sense.

In the 1970s, Michel Foucault linked bios to political power to indicate a transformation in power's mechanisms beginning in the seventeenth century, in which political control over "juridical" matters extends to include and focus primarily on the "biological existence of a population." The old sovereignty as "the right of seizure of things, time, bodies, and ultimately life itself," gradually yielded to "the administration of bodies and the calculated management of life," with its various "disciplines of the body" and "the regulations of the population" as to its "propagation, births . . . mortality . . . health, life expectancy and longevity"—all of which are functions pertaining to a physical or biological body (1990, 136–140). The more recent shift from this "disciplinary society"—in which institutions did not yet completely permeate individual consciousness and bodies, so that the individual could still resist power—to the all-permeating biopolitics of the "society of control" simply denotes the increasing implication of individuals in power relations, as power structures are now inscribed in the habits and productive practices of these bodies.

In Foucault's aftermath, other thinkers adopted his terms into their own accounts of socio-political theories. Some saw in this development from disciplinary society to the society of control the sign that power has ceased to be unidimensional and is instead marked with multiplicity and counter-potentials. Thus, the cornerstone in Gilles Deleuze's and Félix Guattari's work on biopolitics becomes the tension between power's two tendencies: to enclose within itself every aspect of life, and to disclose, in the same movement, uncontainable potentialities and maximum plurality (see particularly Deleuze and Guattari 1987). The Deleuzean/Guattarian substitution of subjectivity for molar and molecular aggregates may be seen as an attempt to depart from anthropomorphism, but at the cost of becoming insentient to the imaginary distortions to which immanent transcendence lends itself.

In a more pessimistic tone, others discern in the same multidimensionality of power its voracious tendency to expand its control on all aspects of life. But they, too, embrace bios as the physical fact of the life. To stress this point, Giorgio Agamben returns to Aristotle and opts for the other Greek term, *zoe*, which indicates the undifferentiated, pre-symbolic or "bare life," as opposed to *bios* in the Aristotelian sense of organized political life. For Agamben, Foucault's hegemonic "liberal-democratic State" is destined since the politicization of "birth" (i.e., of "bare natural life as such")—evidenced in the first of the 1789 Declarations: "Men are born and remain free and equal in rights"—to become, through the logic of "blood and soil," totalitarian (Agamben 1998, 127–129). The Jews "were exterminated not in a mad and giant [sacrificial] holocaust but, exactly as Hitler had announced, 'as lice,' which is to say, as bare life," so that the "dimension in which the extermination took place is neither religion nor law, but biopolitics," a dimension in which life is bare, severed from the symbolic function of the signifier, and hence the law (114). Drawing on Hannah Arendt, Agamben argues that "Foucault never brought his insights to bear on . . . the exemplary place of modern biopolitics: the politics of the great totalitarian states of the twentieth century" and "the concentration camp," whose victims are not unlike the *homines sacri* (a concept introduced by Roman Law), insofar as both the victim of the Holocaust and the *homo sacer* are marked by "*the unpunishability of [their] killing and the ban on [their] sacrifice*" (124, 119, and 73). In the twentieth century, Agamben concludes, "the concentration camp" becomes "the new biopolitical *nomos* of the planet" (176).

Let us note here that, though it is true that Foucault has not focused as extensively as Agamben on the concentration camps and the rest of the politics of the totalitarian states of the twentieth century, he nevertheless elevates them to the blueprint according to which any biopolitical state must necessarily build and organize itself. There was "no State," according to Foucault, "in which the biological was so tightly, so insistently, regulated, as "Nazi society." "Controlling the random element inherent in biological processes"—through "control over the biological, of procreation and of heredity," among others—"was one of the regime's immediate objectives," because of which "disciplinary power and biopower . . . permeated, underpinned, Nazi society" (2003, 259). And even though "Nazism alone took the play between the sovereign right to kill and the mechanisms of biopower to this paroxysmal point . . . this play is in fact inscribed in the workings of all States," that is, "all modern States," "capitalist" and "socialist" alike, insofar as "socialism has made no critique of the theme of biopower," and both, capitalism and socialism, are always predicated on "a racist component" (260–261). For,

> ultimately, the idea that the essential function of society or the State, or whatever it is that must replace the State, is to take control of life, to manage it, to compensate for its aleatory nature, to explore and reduce biological accidents and possibilities . . . it seems to me that socialism takes this over wholesale. And the result is that we immediately find ourselves in a socialist State which must exercise the right to kill or the right to eliminate, or the right to disqualify. And so, quite naturally, we find that racism—not a truly ethnic racism, but racism of the evolutionist kind, biological racism—is fully operational in the way socialist States (of the Soviet Union type) deal with the mentally ill, criminals, political adversaries, and so on. (261–262)

Foucault, therefore, would not in principle disagree with Agamben that the concentration camp, as the ultimate, most unabashed manifestation of racism, is the "biopolitical *nomos*" of modern society. Eventually, we shall address the issue of racism and its biopolitical mutation.

Returning for now to Agamben, our current conjuncture is marked by the ubiquitous invocation of human rights, because of which our life is supposed to be "unsacrificeable," and the fact that, as is evidenced by phenomena ranging from innumerous traffic accidents to the abundance of technological means of massive destruction, this same life "has nevertheless become capable of being killed" with impunity "to an unprecedented degree." Therefore, we should perhaps conclude, Agamben suggests, that "we are all virtually *homines sacri*" (1998, 114–115). Whether one would tend to side with Deleuze and Guattari's or Agamben's accounts of the workings of biopower, the point is that both approach bios or *zoe qua* biological or natural life.[1]

On the other, optimistic, extreme of the spectrum of possible accounts of biopolitics, Michael Hardt and Antonio Negri launch a duel between biopolitics and biopower, as fatal opponents. Having introduced in *Empire* this distinction between "biopower" and "biopolitics" or "biopolitical production," Hardt and Negri identify in *Multitude* the former as "security" or "police action" that manifests itself as "absolute," "global," and "ontological" war—insofar as "genocide and atomic weapons put life itself on center stage"—as well as "individual violence," in all its forms of "torture" (2004, 18–22). Biopower is Empire's "current war regime [that] not only threatens us with death but also rules over life" by exercising what should more accurately be called, to use Agamben's term, "thanatopolitics [death-politics]" (2004, 94; Agamben 1998, 123). Opposite to this "transcendent" and "corrupted" lethal biopower, which "stands above society . . . as a sovereign authority" that "imposes its order," Hardt and Negri place the "immanent" "immaterial labor and biopolitical production," whose products, whether directly "immaterial" (e.g., information) or "life forms" (e.g., biogenetic products, bacteria, seeds, the OncoMouse, etc.), are always the product of "immaterial labor," insofar as they "do not belong to nature" but "are the result of human labor," "produced specifically, as knowledge, information, or code" (2004, 94–95 and 181–185). In this battle between transcendent, oppressive Imperial biopower and immanent, revolutionary, and spontaneous force of the multitude and its biopolitical production, even as the liberating "rising biopolitical productivity of the multitude is being undercut and blocked by the process of private appropriation" imposed by biopower, the former is nevertheless determined, by historical necessity, to triumph over the latter because the multitude's "*telos*" ("communism"), as we already know from *Empire*, is "*theurgical*" (2004, 186; 2000, 396). One might wonder how a professedly Spinozist approach to society and history can be reconciled with such a (Hegelian) teleological conception of historical time.[2] But what is of more importance in the present context is the distinction itself between the two presumed opponents of our current historical struggle: biopower and biopolitics. Commenting on this distinction, Hardt and Negri write:

> Both of them engage social life in its entirety—hence the common prefix *bio*—but they do so in very different ways. Biopower stands above society, transcendent, as a sovereign authority and imposes its order. Biopolitical production, in contrast, is immanent to society and creates social relationships and forms through collaborative forms of labor. (2004, 94–95)

A reader of Spinozian sensibilities might again be annoyed by this reference to a transcendence (biopower) that "stands above" society, and whose attributes rather than manifesting themselves in the modes of immanence (biopolitical production) are supposed to oppress and hinder this immanence from its full realization. Nevertheless, let us proceed to examine wherein actually consists Hardt and Negri's distinction between transcendence and immanence. The distinction in question concerns two kinds of production: the one produces dead bodies, while the other involves immaterial products (information, knowledge, codes, etc.) produced through immaterial labor (services, entertainment, education, etc.). In other words, contrary to the other aforementioned commentators of biopolitics, for Hardt and Negri biopolitics concerns only immaterial (and hence immortal) life, while physiological or biological (and hence mortal) life is exiled to the oppressive and fatal realm of a transcendent biopower.

Thus, Hardt and Negri seem to introduce an innovation into the standard accounts of biopower and biopolitics, by conceiving of life as both biological (the object of biopolitics) and immaterial (the object of biopower). In this regard, their theory presupposes a conception of life and being that may appear to come closer to the ontology presented in the first part of the present work than the other accounts of biopolitics we saw earlier, for which bios is taken exclusively in its physical or material aspect. This is, however, not the case, and actually for two reasons. First, Hardt and Negri's use of the terms "material" and "immaterial" is predicated on physico-chemical criteria or on the distinction natural versus human-made, and not on the distinction between in-itself or use-value and for-itself or exchange-value, as specified here, in the chapter "Matter" in part 1. We recall that according to that definition, information, for instance, taken in its aspect as a use-value, counts as matter (in-itself). Second, whereas, according to my ontological argument, however matter and the immaterial may be defined, they are both immanent manifestations of a third transcendental function (surplus), Hardt and Negri operate within a dualism that attributes biological life to transcendence and immaterial life to immanence, thereby producing the further political dualism between the subjection of the material aspects of life to an oppressive power (biopower), and the attribution of revolutionary potential (biopolitics) to the immanent and immaterial aspect of life. I do not believe that this convenient distinction between oppressive transcendence and revolutionary immanence can help us grasp the actual workings of the politics of biopower (or the power of biopolitics), not least because it preempts the very thrust of Foucault's interlacing of bios and political power, as the control that relies not just on the sovereign right to kill (Hardt and Negri's "biopower"), but on the interplay between this right and the management, regulation, protection, and sustenance of life, whose mechanisms are also operative in peaceful, creative, and spontaneous production (Hardt and Negri's "biopolitical production").[3]

Other differences notwithstanding, all of the aforementioned biopolitical theories either treat bios as a physico-biological given entity or split it according to the dualism of the classical conceptions of matter and the immaterial, attributing, in the fashion of the theurgical tradition, all redemptive power to the latter.

It is apparent that none of these models of extant conceptions of bios and biopolitics is in sync with the meta-phenomenological ontology presented here. In beginning to approach bios according to the present theory, the question arising first concerns the historical specificity and the transhistorical aspect of bios. While Foucault argues that biopolitics is a phenomenon specific to secular capitalist modernity, gradually taking shape since the seventeenth century, Agamben argues, through the figure of the *homo sacer* and, further back, through Aristotle, that biopolitics is consubstantial with the emergence of the law and sovereignty in antiquity. It is evident that the present ontology entails that, in a sense, biopolitics is transhistorical—as are, for instance, the unconscious and surplus—but, in another sense, that is, as an operative function within the field of political immanence, it is not.[4] In the following I will be concerned exclusively with the historical specificity of bios and biopolitics as operative functions within the historical block of secular capitalist modernity.

Bios

Surplus qua Labor-Power

At stake, therefore, is the modern bios that emerges at the moment at which surplus takes on that specific modulation that involves disequilibrium in all systems of value that constitute the plane of immanence.

The generalized "fixed" idea that, with capitalism, economy is no longer dependent on slavery but on "free" laborers introduced an unforeseen transformation in the nature of labor. As Marx writes in the *Grundrisse*, labor-power is "the use-value which the worker has to offer to the capitalist, which he has to offer to others in general, [and which] is not materialized in a product, does not exist apart from him at all, thus exists not really, but only in potentiality" (Marx 1993, 267). Since the inception of capitalism with its "free" workers, labor-power, whether it produces boots, linen, coats, or information, is sheer "potentiality." As Paolo Virno astutely remarks, biopolitics "is merely an effect . . . or . . . one articulation of that primary fact—both historical and philosophical—which consists of the commerce of potential as potential," that is, the commerce of labor-power (84). For, "where something which exists only as *possibility* is bought and sold," Virno continues, "this something is not separable from the *living person* of the seller," the "living body of the worker," which "is the substratum of that labor-power which, in itself, has no existence" (82). The body and life, Virno continues, understood as "pure and simple *bios*, acquires a specific importance in as much as it is the tabernacle of *dynamis*, of mere potential," and it is "for this reason, and this reason alone, [that] it is legitimate to talk about 'bio-politics'" (82). If in capitalist modernity we can legitimately talk of biopolitics—defined as a *mode of politics that is concerned with the commerce of the potential as potential*—it is because, through the commodification of

105

labor-power in this historical block, "mere potential" becomes a commodity. Biopolitics means that intrinsically entangled with the system of relations that constitute and sustain power is not simply biological life (the physical body of the laborer) but, due to the commodification of labor-power's potential to actualize itself, also *potentiality*.

Virno's remarks foreground the historico-philosophical revolution in the capitalist commodification of labor-power. For the first time in history, what is bought and sold is labor-power, that is, pure potentiality, the power of self-actualization—in one word, being or surplus itself. Unlike any other commodity, which in its aspect as use-value is an in-itself, *the use-value of labor-power is being-for-itself-in-itself*, the potential (for-itself) of labor to actualize (in-itself) itself. *The specific object of biopolitics in the block of capitalist modernity*, therefore, is neither biological life nor the immaterial labor and products of informatized capital, but *bios qua surplus*. The body as the object of biopolitics is the tabernacle of surplus, the potentiality of being to actualize itself in the form of "labour-power . . . as a *capacity* of the living individual" (Marx 1990, 274; emphasis mine).

If this historical philosophic-economic revolution has begun to occur already since the advent of capitalism, why is it first the postmodern or late capitalist discourse that becomes conscious of biopolitics or biopower, so as to render it an explicit object of analysis? Because, as we saw in the chapter "Historiographical Project" in part 2, if there is any teleology in the stages of a given historical block, this is the tendency to actualize in its fullest the potential of the formal structure of the block to which they belong.[1] This is why, as Foucault has rightly argued, and both Marx and Virno reaffirm, our discussion of biopolitics must retroactively presuppose an indissoluble link between bios and political power in all secular capitalist modernity.

The following is a close examination of bios *qua* labor-power against the background of the ontology presented in the first part of this work, which will eventually lead us to unraveling at least some aspects of the logic and workings of biopolitics.

Double Representation of Bios

Darstellung and Vertretung

Bios or "the capacity of labour (*Arbeitsvermögen*)" or "labour-power (*Arbeitskraft*)" is unique in that, unlike all other commodities, it is an in-itself-for-itself or, in Marx's words, it is "a commodity whose use-value possesses the peculiar property of being a source of value, whose actual consumption is therefore itself an objectification (*Vergegenständlichung*) of labour, hence a creation of value" (Marx 1990, 270). As we saw in the chapter "Historical Time" in part 1, labor is a unique commodity in that it is represented in two different ways, as the *exchange-value* of the *"congealed" labor* embodied in the commodity, and as the *cost* ("wages") at which the same labor is purchased from the laborer as *labor-power*. The former is determined synchronically within the sphere of circulation-time, the latter diachronically within the sphere of production-time. This is why "labour does not receive a double representation" within circulation, as the other commodities (i.e., the *products* of labor) do, which are represented as both M and M′, the exchange-value in which they are bought and that in which they are sold—*both of which*, M and M′, *are arbitrarily and differentially determined exchange-values* within circulation-time. Labor "is not represented [*stellt sich nicht dar*] both in the value of the commodity [M] and in an excess quantity over and above that value [M′], it is not represented in a price of 10 which is simultaneously a price of 11, i.e., in a value which is greater than itself" (1990, 268; 2009, 167). Rather, labor receives *two different kinds of representation*. On the one hand, "outside circulation, the commodity-owner only stands in relation to his own commodity," and it to him, so that instead of obtaining a value through differential relations with other values, its value is determined by the fact that "the commodity contains

107

a quantity of his own labour which is measured according to definite social laws" (1990, 268). On the other hand, the same commodity as the embodiment of his *congealed* labor is represented as exchange-value within circulation, where it receives a representation that is always greater than itself, as "a price of 10 which is simultaneously a price of 11." As congealed labor, the commodity receives, through differential relations with other commodities that also embody certain amounts of congealed labor, values that are always greater than themselves, but as labor-power it has a cost which is not an exchange-value but an idiosyncratic "value" defined by diachronic "historical" and "moral" factors. The commodity itself, however, is always bought and sold within circulation and thus, never at the cost of the labor-power that produced it; it is only labor-power itself that is bought at that cost. "In other words, the value [cost] of labour-power *is* [*ist*] the value of the means of subsistence necessary for the maintenance of its owner" (Marx, 1990, 274; emphasis mine; 2009, 172). While *all commodities receive a double representation within circulation, labor receives in addition to this another kind of representation: as congealed labor* (i.e., as a commodity other than labor-power) *it receives a double representation within circulation-time, but as labor-power it also receives another representation outside circulation, in the realm of production-time.* This is why, "when we speak of capacity for labour, we do not abstract from the necessary means of subsistence"; "on the contrary, their value is expressed [*ist ausgedrückt*] in its value," that is, the cost of labor-power is expressed in the value of all of the laborer's "so-called necessary requirements" (277; 175). Or again, "the value of labour-power can be resolved [*löst sich auf*] into the value of a definite quantity of the means of subsistence" (276; 173), which is why, unlike exchange-value which is defined arbitrarily through purely differential or systemic relations, the cost of labor-power is determined by external factors. For

> the ultimate or minimum limit of the value of labour-power is formed [*wird gebildet*] by the value of the commodities which have to be supplied every day to the bearer of labour-power, the man, so that he can renew his life-process. That is to say, the limit is formed by the value of the physically indispensable means of subsistence. (1990, 276–277; 2009, 174)

And such limits

are themselves products of history, and depend therefore to a great extent on the level of civilization attained by a country; in particular they depend on the conditions in which, and consequently on the habits and expectations with which, the class of free workers has been formed. (1990, 277 and 275; 2009, 175).

In short, the representation of the cost of labor-power is of a radically different kind than the representation [*Darstellung*] of the value of the commodity through its exchange-value, for—recalling Saussure's distinction between synchronic (universal) laws and diachronic (imperative) forces—the cost of labor-power is determined also by diachronic factors that force themselves upon it without being universal, whereas exchange-value is determined through the synchronic differential relations of the exchange-values of all commodities. While the exchange-value of any other commodity is arbitrary and can vary in any possible way depending on the fluctuations of the market, labor-power is organically linked to its cost, since any change of this cost is possible only if "the conditions . . . the habits and expectations" that form "the class of free workers" change first.

This means that, in the context of labor, Marx refers to *two distinct systems of representation*, whose unsurpassable difference he had extensively stressed over a decade prior to the publication of *Capital*, in *The Eighteenth Brumaire of Louis Bonaparte*. This is a difference that can easily be obfuscated in English, while in German it is expressed through two distinct linguistic values—*Darstellung* and *Vertretung*—both of which are translated in English as "representation." Labor-power's cost is *vertreten*, while its exchange-value (the value of the labor objectified in its product) is *dargestellt*. To clarify this distinction, we turn once again to Karatani, who scrutinized Marx's following observation in *The Eighteenth Brumaire of Louis Bonaparte*:

> in the parliamentary system based upon universal suffrage, the representative system is thoroughly "fictitious" as compared to the *Ständeversammlung*—an assembly of different castes/ professions from preindustrial Europe, as Hans Kelsen later claimed. (Karatani 2003, 144)

Karatani refers to Kelsen's observation that "der Gedanke, daß das Parlament nur Stellvertreter des Volks sei [the thought that the parliament is simply the representative (proxy or placeholder) of the people]" is "die Fiktion der Repräsentation [the fiction of representation]" since "die Abgeordneten von ihren Wählern keine bindenden Instruktionen anzunehmen haben [the appointed members of the parliament are not obliged to follow any binding instructions from their voters]," so that "das Parlament in seiner Funktion vom Volke rechtlich unabhängig ist [in its function, the parliament is legally independent from the people]," in opposition to the "alten Ständeversammlung . . . deren Mitglieder bekanntlich durch imperative Mandate ihrer Wählergruppen gebunden und diesen verantwortlich waren [old *Ständeversammlung* . . . whose members, as is known, were bound by the imperative mandates of their voter groups, toward whom they were held responsible]" (30; translation mine). The advent of the parliamentary system replaced in politics *Vertretung*—as was practiced in the *Ständeversammlungen*, in which the representers (*Stellvertreter*) were bound to reflect the interests of the caste or profession of their voters—with *Darstellung*. The latter is a representation in which "the relationship between the *political* and the *literary representatives* of a class and the class they represent" or between the "spokesmen and scribes of the bourgeoisie . . . the ideologists of the bourgeoisie and the bourgeoisie itself, the representatives and the represented," is such that the two sides "faced one another in estrangement and no longer understood one another" (Marx 1998, 51 and 103). Whereas *Vertretung* involved an organic link between represented and their representatives, *Darstellung* is an arbitrary system of representation, because represented and representatives understand each other no more than a potato (taken as in-itself) can understand the value for which it is exchanged—even as, and in spite of the fact that, matter thinks. This alienation between in-itself and for itself is the rupture in being (being-in-itself-for-itself) introduced by the political and economic secular capitalist modes of representation.

And this break in communication is also true of the two modes of representation of labor, as *Vertretung* and *Darstellung*. Whereas the representation (*Vertretung*) of the cost of labor-power is based on an *organic link*—labor-power's remuneration is determined by its specific kind and the specific cultural and "moral" norms of the society in which it is performed—its representation (*Darstellung*) as congealed labor in the form of exchange-value is purely "fictitious," that is, it involves, to use Karatani's formulation, "no apodictic rapport between the representer [exchange-value] and the represented [congealed labor]" (2003, 144).

It follows that *Vertretung* is a presecular mode of representation, as was, at least conceptually and structurally, also the *Ständeversammlung*. For *Vertretung* is based on ternary signs: the thing (labor-power), the mark (cost, i.e., remunerating money), and the similitude ("moral" and other historically determined judgments) that provides the "organic" bond between the mark and the thing. By contrast, *Darstellung* is a secular system of representation, for it consists of binary, differential signs: the thing ("congealed" labor) and the mark (exchange-value), with no "apodictic rapport" or "organic" bond but only an "arbitrary" or "fictitious" connection between them. Like the representational system of the secular binary sign, labor's *Darstellung* as exchange-value is a "system [that] exists autonomously," in its own synchronic differentiality and in no communication with its representation (*Vertretung*) as cost, which is defined within the diachrony of production-time (Karatani 2003, 144–145).

Only in the realm of *Darstellung* is the self-valorization of labor, as congealed labor, possible, while within *Vertretung* labor-power behaves like precapitalist goods whose value remains stagnant as long as no further labor is added to it. In Marx's words:

> The commodity-owner can create value by his labour, but he cannot create values which can valorize themselves. He can increase the value of his commodity by adding fresh labour, and therefore more value, to the value in hand, by making leather into boots, for instance. . . . It is therefore impossible that, outside of the sphere of circulation, a producer of commodities can, without coming into contact with other commodity-owners, valorize value, and consequently transform money or commodities into capital. (1990, 268)

Because labor can be valorized only within the "sphere of circulation," which it enters as already congealed labor and, hence, as exchange-value, it does not receive the *quantitatively* double representation within *Darstellung* that all other commodities receive (as both M and M'); rather, labor receives a *qualitatively* double representation: *Vertretung* (which represents the cost of its remuneration, outside circulation, in production-time), and *Darstellung* (its exchange-value within circulation, as M, which, to be sure, will become M', but this bears only on the value of the congealed labor, not of the labor-power).

Of course, any other commodity, too, cannot increase its value outside circulation and without being exchanged with the commodities of the "other commodity-owners." Outside circulation, the leather cannot increase its value unless it becomes, through "fresh labour," boots. Every commodity, therefore, behaves outside circulation (in production-time) like static precapitalist money, and is consequently, like labor, *vertreten*. In short, whether labor or other commodities, use-values are *vertreten* within production-time, while exchange-values are *dargestellt* within circulation. The crucial difference, however, is that there is no reason to speak of the *Vertretung* of the other commodities, since they are both purchased and sold within circulation, as exchange-values. *Only labor is that peculiar commodity that is purchased outside the circulation of exchange-values, in the realm of production-time, where its cost is defined by diachronic factors.* If the laborer decided to sell the piece of leather at the price that it costs him to buy it, adding just the cost of the labor he invested on it, he would make no surplus-value and, hence, he would be selling the leather at a price defined by *Vertretung*, within production-time. This would be a precapitalist mode of exchange, which is why Marx is not concerned with it. Only *labor's Vertretung* is a requirement for capitalism to work, and, being a precapitalist mode of exchange and representation, *Vertretung* is *a scandal* within the realm of capitalist value.

While in the realm of secular modern politics the *Ständeversammlung* has, through parliamentarism, become obsolete, *Vertretung* continues to thrive in capitalist economy, where it finds its *exclusive manifestation in the remuneration of the exceptional commodity, labor-power*. Given that on the semantic level, as Karatani puts it, "classes come into consciousness only via this system" of fictitious or autonomous "*Darstellung*," constituted by the parliamentary representatives and their ideology, *Vertretung* is that paradoxical system of representation that is never represented—it constitutes an illegitimate (presecular) mode of representation that exists only as *the repressed underside of Darstellung* (2003, 144–145).

Similarly, on the economic level, use-value—the underside of exchange-value, which exists only in production-time where it can only be *vertreten* (and cannot valorize itself)—exists only as the repressed of capitalist circulation. This is the point of Marx's "general formula of capital." In the process of buying and selling a commodity (C) for more money (M), that is, capital (M—C—M′), specific objects of utility are necessary as the intermediary stage between "money" (M) and "more money" (M'). Yet, an object of utility and capital face one another in estrangement; if they succeed in communicating with (exchanging) one another, it is because the sole available language (representation) in circulation is that of exchange-value: *Darstellung*. No sooner does the commodity appear in the formula "M—C—M'" than it is already an exchange-value, and not at all an object of utility, which is why it can in the first place be exchanged with capital. It follows, Marx concludes, that

> circulation . . . presents itself in abridged form, in its final
> result and without any intermediate stage, in a concise style,
> so to speak, as M—M', i.e., money which is worth more
> money, value which is greater than itself. (1990, 255–257)

In other words, one of the empirical modes of substance, exchange-value, monopolizes the attributes of the modulation of surplus as surplus-value, and presents itself as if it were self-valorizable, whereas in truth, it is only surplus-value that valorizes itself, and can do so under the precondition that it manifests itself empirically as both exchange-value and as an object of utility. There is no surplus-value without both *Vertretung* and *Darstellung*, for, recalling Marx's words, value has its "origin" in both universes, "in circulation and not in circulation," that is, in circulation and in production, or in *Darstellung* and in *Vertretung* (1990, 268). Yet, as Marx's "abridged" formula indicates, equally imperative for capitalism is that *Vertretung* remains its repressed.[1]

Now we are in the position of specifying a distinctive symptom that marks the specific historical modulation of surplus as *surplus-value* and differentiates it from surplus as the transhistorical *being-in-itself-for-itself*. *Surplus-value* is the historical modulation of surplus by means of which *the in-itself aspect of surplus* is *repressed, so that the plane of immanence appears to consist only of the for-itself*. To say that the abridged formula of capital appears as M-M', without the mediation of objects of utility (C), or that the *Vertretung* of labor-power is never represented, is to offer two different expressions to the single historico-philosophical fact that through surplus-value the materiality of surplus is repressed. This is the secular version of the monotheist/Christian idealization of the spirit and debasement of the flesh, and it explains the dominant philosophical tendency toward idealism and the overall preponderance of consciousness.

A preliminary conclusion regarding biopolitics is that its function concerns the concealment or revelation of the fact that, while our labor is *sold as congealed labor for capital, our labor-power is bought with money* (in the precapitalist sense of the word). Or, in other words, biopolitical mechanisms involve arrangements and administrations of representation in such ways that the persistent perpetuation of *Vertretung* within secular capitalist modernity is hidden, so that everything appears as abstract, immortal, differential, arbitrary, and autonomous value—as if there were no bodies whose labor-power bears an organic link with the money that remunerates it. Of course, given that representation could be administered in other ways that would reveal *Vertretung*, the question becomes: What is the purpose that requires the concealment of *Vertretung*?—a question to which we shall return later. If the concern with concealing representational aspects becomes central to modern biopolitics it is because labor, as it is reconfigured in the capitalist mode of production, is that which intertwines indissolubly these two distinct modes of representation. To clarify this point, let us approach once again the uniqueness of labor-power as use-value.

Capital does not ever come in contact with the use-values (materialized products) of labor; no sooner does capital buy or sell a product than the latter is no longer a use-value but an exchange-value—hence Marx's formula M—M′. The accumulation of surplus-value presupposes the total repression or exclusion of the in-itself in circulation. On the other hand, the "mysterious" character of labor lies in the fact that it encounters capital only in the form of labor congealed in the commodity, and, as such, as exchange-value (within circulation), while in its other form, as labor-power, the pure potential of the laborer to labor, it has a cost that is defined diachronically (in production-time) by historical conventions, and is thus paid not in capital but in money. *The sole transaction in which capital abandons the sphere of circulation* (of exchange-values that procure surplus-value) *and reemerges in the sphere of production-time as precapitalist money is the purchase of the unique use-value we call labor-power.* This is why *Vertretung* must not be taken as the type of representation of the realm of production in general, but only as the mode that represents the cost of labor-power. To do so, capital must exit circulation and enter the realm of cost (a value that is not exchange-value) and momentarily behave as precapitalist money—even as this is a precondition for it to continue to be capital within circulation, where the labor-power it bought through money will be sold as congealed labor against capital. In fact, it is precisely because its cost is represented through *Vertretung*, while it is exchanged in circulation in the mode of *Darstellung*, that "free" labor produces surplus-value. The question here is: how is it possible that capital, which turns everything it touches into exchange-value—which is why commodities can enter circulation not as use-values but only as (relative) exchange-values (looking for their equivalent exchange-values)—exits its realm of circulation and enters the realm of production that is populated by use-values?

This is possible precisely because, as we have seen, the true magnificence of the "mystery" of labor-power consists in the fact that it is the unique use-value that "exists not really" but only "in potentiality." That is, unlike both use-value or the in-itself that exists really, and exchange-value that, as the for-itself which is determined to be what it is not and to not be what it is, is determined never to exist really, *labor-power is the potentiality of the for-itself to be the in-itself, it is the being-in-itself-for-itself.* Labor-power, therefore, has access to both worlds, the world of the in-itself—which is why it lives in production time—and the world of the for-itself—which is why, nevertheless, it can be exchanged for capital, even if not without causing this capital to behave in this particular interaction as (precapitalist) money. *Labor-power, therefore, is the instance that both engenders and reveals the necessary intercourse between the world of production-time and that of circulation-time*—the very intercourse that the formula of capital, M—M′, endeavors to conceal.

Modal Aspects of the Unconscious

Conscious Darstellung and Repressed Vertretung

Vertretung, the peculiar representation of labor-power, amounts to the paradoxical secular manifestation of the presecular mode of representation, which makes its appearance only after "free" laborers emerge and offer their labor-power against a certain cost. In the presecular mode of representation, as Foucault reminds us, "language" is "a thing in nature" whose "words offer themselves to men as things to be deciphered," for, due to their divine organic links, there is a continuity between words and things, so that words are concept-things, just as things are thing-concepts (Foucault 1970, 35).[1] *Vertretung* is such a language-thing, except that, unlike in the past, now it emerges against the background of sheer *Darstellung*, a world that is represented through binary signs that are determined in purely arbitrary differential and synchronic relations. Thus, the similitudes that bind the word to the thing in *Vertretung* are no longer guaranteed by divinity but by that which transcends synchronicity: history insofar as it transcends systematicity and its laws. It is such contingent moral, cultural, and other historical judgments that bind organically or apodictically the thing-concept of labor-power to its cost, which, thus, is a not an arbitrary sign but a Mark (with capital letter, by analogy to the Word). *Vertretung bestows on labor-power the Mark of its remuneration, which is organically bound to it and, thus, redoubles its nature as an in-itself-for-itself: labor-power is a concept-thing because it bears on itself its organic Mark* and *because, as the power of its self-actualization, it is a concept that is itself the thing for which it stands.*

Nevertheless, the contingent character of the similitudes does not in the list diminish the absolute (divine) authority of the bond between labor-power and its Mark, for their combination constitutes, recalling

117

Sartre, "the impossible synthesis of the for-itself [potential] and the in-itself [actual]," which "preserve[s] within it the necessary translucency of consciousness [concept] along with the coincidence with itself of being-in-itself [thing]"—in short, "God" (140 and 139). In other words, like surplus-value, labor-power is a historical modulation of the attributes of substance or surplus within capitalism—God, understood as "human reality itself as totality" (Sartre, 139). There would be no friction between these two modulations of surplus—surplus-value and labor-power—no rift in its unity, if it were not for their difference in kinds of representation. For the entire universe of the empirical manifestations of surplus-value, including its two temporalities of production and circulation, is represented through *Darstellung*—the secular system of representation with its binary sign—while labor-power is represented through *Vertretung*—a presecular system of representation in the midst of a secular universe. *It is for this reason that biopolitics is constituted as the tension between the expression of Vertretung, required by labor-power, and its suppression, demanded by surplus-value.* The interests, so to speak, of the two capitalist modulations of surplus collide, and their battlefield is biopolitics.

A further distinction between surplus-value and labor-power can now become clear. True, they are both modulations of surplus, but in essentially different ways. Surplus-value is a modulation of the attributes of substance (in-itself and for-itself) insofar as it is the cause and effect of both; labor-power, by contrast, is a modulation of the attributes of substance because it is the potential of the for-itself to actualize itself as in-itself. Surplus-value is self-caused insofar as it is the cause (and effect) of what it presupposes (use-values and exchange-values); labor-power is self-caused because it is the direct power of its self-actualization, without the mediation of any presupposition, not even presuppositions of which it itself is the cause. In short, it can be said that surplus-value is a potentiality, but only *quantitatively*: the potentiality of the for-itself to generate more of itself as, again and again, for-itself—which is why, even though it presupposes the in-itself, it ends up repressing it. Labor-power, on the other hand is *qualitatively potential*: the potential of the ontological leap from the for-itself to the in-itself—which is why it requires the expression of both attributes.

This does not automatically entail that labor-power is a modulation of surplus better or closer to it than surplus-value is. Why should quality be better, or closer to substance, than quantity? This is why it is *not* the case that the distinction between *Darstellung* and *Vertretung*, and, as I have argued elsewhere, the distinction between their Spino-zian homologues, *potestas* and *potentia*, or in Hardt's translation, "Power and power[,]" reveals an opposition between metaphysics and history" (Hardt, xiv).[2] Both *Darstellung and Vertretung, potestas* and *potentia*, are modal manifestations of the attributes of substance and, as such, per-tain to history, even as—following Spinoza's dictum that "truth is the standard of both itself and of the false"—the repressed (*Vertretung*) may be privileged as being the "itself," and not "the false" (*Darstellung*), of that which is the standard of both (Spinoza 1985, 479; *Ethics*, part II, prop. 43, schol.). As we shall see in more detail in the next chapters, the unconscious *qua* repressed is *not* the metaphysical; the metaphysical—if by this we mean that which pertains directly to the attributes—is the unconscious *qua* standard both of the repressed and of the non-repressed (consciousness). Just as (metaphysical) truth is the standard of both of its modal manifestations, itself and the false, (metaphysical) *potentia* is the standard of both (historical) *potentia* and *potestas*, none of which is transcendent to the other. The function of repression represents not a relation of transcendence but a relation of representational effacement, which in political terms amounts to oppression. This is also the reason why the tendency of labor-power to express *Vertretung* and the tendency of surplus-value to repress it and to represent everything through *Darstel-lung* do not correspond to the two sides of the opposition between biopower and biopolitics, *as proposed by* Hardt and Negri. Or, again, one can term them biopower and biopolitics if by this one means the intrinsic interrelation of subordination of the repressed under the unre-pressed manifestations of the attributes of surplus.

Lacan's notorious statement that "the unconscious is structured like language" pertains to the metaphysical unconscious (1981, 149). We can, therefore, now spell it out in the statement: *the unconscious is struc-tured like* Darstellung *and* Vertretung. The attributes of the unconscious, *Darstellung* and *Vertretung*, manifest themselves modally or empirically as consciousness and the (unconscious *qua*) repressed. And the repressed consists of the Marks of *Vertretung*.

Let us examine now the function of the repressed in consciousness, that is, the function of the Marks of *Vertretung* in the binary signifiers of *Darstellung*. Their relation is indicated in the Lacanian relation between speech and the network of the signifier.

As we saw in the chapter "Historical and Transhistorical Aspects of Being," the unconscious as something that has an operative function in the sustenance of knowledge and truth is a specifically secular category, pertaining not to the discourse of the Master but to that of the University, whose knowledge is presented as "objective."[3] And being secular, this "objective knowledge" is *Darstellung*, a system of arbitrary binary signs that relate to one another differentially within their synchronic logical (as opposed to diachronic or chronological) interrelations, while aiming at presenting themselves as (if they constituted) linear deduction. The latter illusion is facilitated by dint of an unconscious fantasy (surplus-enjoyment) which makes the inconsistent Other (*Darstellung*) appear as (if it were) consistent ("objective knowledge"). Let us also recall our distinction between the gaze, as the infinity of all possible points of view from which one could perceive the Other or *Darstellung*, and which does not and cannot appear empirically—"there is no gaze of the Other," to repeat Lacan's words—and the Master-Signifier, as the specific finite gaze from which each of us nevertheless perceives *Darstellung*, thereby assuming it to be the gaze of the Other—again repeating Lacan's words: "the gaze I encounter . . . is not a seen gaze, but a gaze imagined by me in the field of the Other." The Master-Signifier, that is, not the real but the gaze that I imagine in the Other, determines the aspects (*Abschattungen*) of *Darstellung* that will henceforth constitute for me a consistent system of knowledge and truths. In other words, if God is the gaze as the infinity of all possible empirical gazes, the Master-Signifier is the specific God I imagine in the field of the Other, through whose gaze *Darstellung* becomes for me consistent.

Now, "consistency" is a concept that moves in two directions, which need to be spelled out. The Latin root of the word is "*com + sistere*," to stop or stand still together, and even to take a stand together. The question then is what are the parts that come together in this halt?

Firstly, they are the two elements that constitute the binary sign of *Darstellung*: the signifier and the signified. To say that, through (the imagined gaze of) God, the Other becomes consistent amounts to saying that the God in question provides what is lacking in *Darstellung*, the third element of the divine links or "similitudes" because of which the arbitrary bond between signifier and signified becomes (i.e., is imagined as) organic. In other words, the first function of the Master-Signifier is to supplement *Darstellung* with *Vertretung*, as its surplus presupposition: the God under whose gaze the claims of *Darstellung* become consistent in the sense of being accepted not as arbitrary but as absolute truth. And, beyond truth, *Vertretung* entails the continuum between the sign and the thing, so that the parts that actually come to stand together through an organic bond are in total three: signifier, signified, and the thing. So, the first mechanism of *Vertretung* consists in its intervention into *Darstellung* in order to provide the latter's signifiers with a bond to signifieds and, further, to things, which appears to be organic, necessary rather than arbitrary.

This first sense of "consistency" and the corollary function of the Master-Signifier explain why "repression . . . is structured like a linguistic phenomenon" in which "the symptom is in itself, through and through, signification, that is to say, truth, truth taking shape" (Lacan 1993, 63; 1991a, 320). The psychoanalytic symptom is not signification in the sense of *Darstellung*, whose arbitrary differentiality and binary signs cannot allow truth to take shape. Rather, the symptom is signification in the sense of a *Vertretungs*-Mark, a mark with an organic bond to a concept-body, which is why it is capable of manifesting itself not only on the level of speech but also as a bodily mark (e.g., hysteric paralysis), offered to be deciphered. "The unconscious," as Lacan says, "is constituted by the effects of speech on the subject, it is the dimension in which the subject is determined in the effects of speech," and these effects of speech (*Darstellung*) are organic, not arbitrary, bonds, *Vertretungs*-Marks between signifiers and the body (Lacan 1981, 149). It is through the intervention of *Vertretung* that *Darstellung*, the system of arbitrary signifiers, becomes meaningful speech capable of representing reality not as a chimera but as truth.

While signifiers circulate arbitrarily in *Darstellung*, the Master-Signifier (the imagined gaze of God) provides the similitudes that suture them to some signified and to the subject's organs, so that they come to form bodily Marks, organ-concepts. Whatever the arbitrary circulation of semantic value within *Darstellung*, these Marks remain fixed as long as the surplus presupposition of the circulation of value remains the same (imagined) divine gaze. For the sutures of *Vertretung* to be reconstituted, the circulation of values must be thus restructured as to posit another gaze as its own presupposed transcendental surplus (God). Which is why psychoanalytic therapy does not work, the symptom does not disappear, unless "free association" (*Darstellung*) manages to bring about *Vertretung* to the point of introducing a new gaze that can restructure the bonds between signifiers, signifieds, and body.

Secondly, and concomitantly to the first mechanism of the unconscious, the term "consistency" refers to the coming together of truth and desire, thereby assigning the meaning and, hence, purpose or *telos* of life. For, however true the statements of the Other may appear to me, the question remains: "*He is saying this to me, but what does he want?*"—what does he want me, what am I supposed, to be or do knowing this truth? (Lacan 1981, 214). There are certainly truths in just about everything, from how to prepare a good meal to how to make a lavish profit out of a given business, but this does not necessarily entail that I see cooking as a meaningful expenditure of my time today, let alone that I see either cooking or profit-making as the purpose animating my entire life. To do so, I must sense that my meaning and purpose in life *is* cooking or profit-making. To put it intentionally in terms that smack of presecular discourse, to a lesser or greater extent, I must perceive myself as *made* (by God or Nature) to be a cook or a capitalist, at least for as long as I am doing it, if I am to do it well. God, as the unconscious or gaze in-itself (i.e., the infinity of all possible empirical gazes) is, recalling Sartre, this coincidence of "the self-as-being-in-itself" which, although it "is what human reality lacks," is also "what makes its [human reality's] meaning" at the very moment I imagine a gaze in the Other, my Master-Signifier (Sartre, 138). So, the further effect of the *Vertretung*'s intervention into *Darstellung* is the constitution of the subject's desire, as that which gives its life meaning and purpose.

It is this intervention of *Vertretung* into *Darstellung* that allows the latter to emerge as "the capital Other (*le grand Autre*), the locus of speech and, potentially, the locus of truth" (Lacan 1981, 129). The truth concerns nothing but the subject's desire, which, as we know, is "the desire of the Other," that is, the "gaze imagined by me in the field of the Other," which is both why "the gaze intervenes . . . only in as much as it is . . . the subject sustaining himself in a function of desire," and why "of all the objects in which the subject may recognize his dependence in the register of desire, the gaze is specified as unapprehensible," that is, "more than any other object," the gaze is "misunderstood (*méconnu*)," allowing for "the illusion of the consciousness of *seeing oneself see oneself*, in which the gaze is elided" (235, 84–85, and 83).

The second sense of "consistency" makes clear that, unlike *Darstellung*, which is a purely synchronic and arbitrary system that, as such, cannot give life its meaning and, hence, a direction in linear time, *Vertretung* introduces a diachronic (imaginary) teleology. This is why, as we saw in the chapter "Meta-Phenomenological Fact," the Master-Signifier—the imaginary gaze that confers a specific desire or intention on otherwise non-directional truths—is that meta-phenomenological specific gaze that makes the contingent phenomenological facts appear as (if they were) necessary in diachrony, that is, as either necessarily caused by their past or as necessarily following the present.

Discourse, or the Symptom of the Repressed, and Language

Therefore, *Vertretung*, the function that transforms *Darstellung* or the network of the signifier into speech, relates to what Lacan calls "discourse," as opposed to "language." As Lacan puts it, drawing on Saussure:

> Firstly, there is a synchronic whole, which is language as a simultaneous system of structured groups of opposition, then there is what occurs diachronically, over time, and which is discourse. One cannot but give discourse a certain direction in time, a direction that is defined in a linear manner. . . . It is basically true that there is no discourse without a certain temporal order, and consequently without a certain concrete succession, even if it is a virtual one. . . . But it is not quite exact to say that it is a simple line, it is more probably a set of several lines, a stave. It is in this diachronism that discourse is set up. (1993, 54)

Beyond the synchronic system of language, in which signs constitute themselves in their differential relations ("groups of opposition") to one another, there is the "diachronism" of discourse, which, albeit "linear," should be conceived not as "a simple line" but as "several lines," insofar as even the most determinist conception of historical causation or genealogy is always much more complicated of, say, the behaviorist model of stimulus and response. To return to our example from the chapter "Historical Time" in part 1, even the most traditional historian (i.e., one who takes historical genealogy at face value) would not reduce the cause of Nazism to any single past event in German or world history—be it the failure of the 1848 revolution, the late formation of the German nation-state in 1871, the failure of the First World War, or what have you—and would admit that each such event in itself could have propelled a different course of history if it had not been accompanied by other events, whose overall combination alone could produce the circumstances that eventually led to Nazism.

It is, therefore discourse (*Vertretung*), and not language (*Darstellung*), that bestows meaning to historical events (this meaning being, of course, always imaginary/ideological). In Lacan's words: "There is indeed a relationship between meaning and the signifier, it is what the structure of discourse supplies" (1993, 155). Moreover, "meaning is by nature imaginary," and, yet, "real," insofar as by the latter we mean, as we said about the meta-phenomenological fact of the (ideological) Master-Signifier, something "impossible," yet necessary in order to account for its effects that are real (1993, 54; 1981, 111).[1]

Here we have arrived at an insight that will eventually turn out to be crucial to the mechanisms of biopolitics. We recall that the potentiality of labor-power is represented by *Vertretung*, yet *Vertretung*—this interpolation of money into the world of capital, as the remuneration of labor-power—is what *Darstellung*, the dominant mode of representation in capitalist modernity, perpetually represses. What emerges in the place of the repressed *Vertretung* is *discourse* itself, that is, the official representation of history *qua* diachrony (the very temporality that is inscribed in *Vertretung*), but a diachrony divested of its contingent forces and masqueraded as teleology or finality. *The teleological representation of history (discourse) is the symptom of the repression of the proper representation of the remuneration of labor-power (Vertretung). Discourse is the symptom of repressed Vertretung.*

Similarly, as we shall presently see, *Darstellung* is the other, corollary, symptom of the repression of *Vertretung*. To clarify this point, let us turn to Lacan's attempt to formulate a theory of ethics in his seventh seminar. In his extensive reading of Sophocles' *Antigone* offered at that seminar, Lacan takes recourse to the distinction between discourse and language in order to differentiate King Creon's (and the city's) position from Antigone's, who persists, against Creon's decree, on burying her brother, Polynices, regardless of the fact that he has committed treason and fratricide. Recall, on the one hand, that Antigone and Polynices, as well as his brother and victim, Eteocles, and their sister, Ismene, are the children of Oedipus, as well as, on the other hand, that the actions of the characters, as in any Greek tragedy, are motivated not by the qualities of some interior subjectivity but by their *moira* which, more often than not, is determined by a curse for some ancestral crime, as in this case the curse on the house of Labdacides, which beyond Oedipus goes back through his father, Laius, and his father, Labdacus, to the latter's father, Cadmus, the founder of the city of Thebes. In his commentary, Lacan positions Creon "outside of language," in the realm of discourse, in whose diachrony Polynices cannot be detached from his past acts, for there, "the being of him who has lived cannot be detached from all he bears with him in the nature of good and evil, of destiny, of consequences for others, or of feelings for himself." By contrast, the "unique value involved" in Antigone's ethical stance "is essentially that of language," that is, "that purity, that separation of being from the characteristics of the historical drama he [Polynices] has lived through, [which] is precisely the limit or the *ex nihilo* to which Antigone is attached" (Lacan 1992, 279). The ethical act presupposes a detachment from discourse, the "historical drama" and its "consequences," along with the historical moral norms (*Vertretung*) that define "good and evil" and reward the former while punishing the latter. It would seem, then, that Lacan is arguing here that the ethical dimension can be accessed only through an at least momentary seclusion within *Darstellung* or, in his words, "language," understood as a realm of (morally) value-free differential relations that suspend the historical norms of *Vertretung* and, thus, render impossible the distinction between good and evil. For good and evil are cultural constructs, each time defined according to the given historical concepts of morality, which are themselves predicated on the interests (*telos*) of the given historical society; ethics, by contrast, cannot be motivated by any interests, whether one's own or the others'. Rather, as several Lacanian and other theoreticians have argued, the effect of the successful ethical act (i.e., the act that is retroactively acknowledged as ethical by the society that emerges as its effect) is the radical restructuring of the discourse and *Vertretung* of the society against whose background it occurs, since the act in question could be recognized as ethical only from the perspective of a set of norms other than that which condemned it (in this case, Creon's). In our terms, *the ethical act leads to a new Master-Signifier that reconstitutes the Marks of* Vertretung *and, by extension, the discourse.*

This thesis on ethics concurs with the function and task of the analytical situation, which for Lacan is compromised (reduced to a normalizing, assimilating function, as evidenced in ego psychology and other forms of talk therapy) unless it constitutes precisely an ethical act—hence the title of his seventh seminar: *The Ethics of Psychoanalysis*. The analytic situation *qua* ethical act can then be described as follows: insofar as it is structured as *Vertretung*, the unconscious *qua* repressed consists of Marks (organic bonds) that cannot be undone unless the interaction between the analysand's "free association" (*Darstellung*) and the analyst manages to introduce a new Master-Signifier that effects a restructuring of *Vertretung* by suturing new Marks. As Bruce Fink puts it: "the analyst sets the patient to work, to associate, and the product of that laborious association is a new master signifier" (135). The analytic situation represents for Lacan the matrix of any ethical act, however greater in effects than it the latter may be.

However, this is not all. This description makes the ethical act look like a random shuffling of signifiers (the elements of *Darstellung*) in which the outcome (new Master-Signifier and *Vertretungs*-Marks) is entirely arbitrary and haphazard. This description is predicated on the assumption that the sole principle governing *Darstellung*, the set of synchronic differential signifiers, is pure chance. And this assumption, in turn, is nothing but the effect of the repression of *Vertretung*, the very state that the psychoanalytic situation is supposed to undermine. In the capitalist modulation of surplus as surplus-value, *Darstellung* is reduced to this synchronic game of chance only because *Vertretung* is repressed. That *Darstellung* (consciousness) and *Vertretung* (the repressed) are the modal manifestations of the (metaphysical or attributive) unconscious means precisely that the two are always intertwined, that there is no pure *Darstellung* or pure *Vertretung*. To be sure, that there is no telos in *Darstellung* means that everything there happens by chance, but one must not forget, Lacan cautions already in his second seminar, that "there is a close relation between the existence of chance and the basis of determinism" (1991, 295). For, "when we say that something happens by chance," we "may mean one of two things . . . either that there is no intention or that there is a law"—but these two things, although it appears that they "may be very different," are exactly the same. As "the determinist theory" teaches us, the idea of "chance as the absence of intention" goes hand in hand with "the very idea of determinism [which] is that law is without intention." In short, "nothing happens without a cause, determinism tells us, but it is a cause without an intention," whether we call it "chance" or "law" (295). To approach *Darstellung* ("language") from the metaphysical point of view means precisely to grasp the overlap of chance and law, since they are both devoid of intention or *telos, which* is the exclusive prerogative of *Vertretung*. In other words, the chance-game of *Darstellung* is always determined by the inexorable law of the Marks of *Vertretung*, but devoid of the intentionality that *Vertretung* bestows on them.

Returning to *Antigone*, this means that for Antigone Polynices is certainly not that being characterized by the "historical drama" of his life because of which the polis condemns him, but also not just any random "replaceable" being: "this brother is something unique" for her (Lacan 1992, 279). Beyond the torrent of all possible transformations that a human being may undergo in its itinerary both in the historical discourse and in the defiles of the signifier there remains a limit—"*Atè*," as both Sophocles and Lacan persistently keep repeating—because of which the being is fixed to its Marks. Outside of discourse, in the realm of language, these Marks operate autonomously, without serving or being governed by any intention, as the law of chance or the chance of law. This is the very aspect of *Darstellung* that the biopolitical repression of *Vertretung* aims at obscuring. And it is this aspect of language that Lacan strives to bring to the light, at the same time as he unmitigatedly condemns the teleological fixations of Creon's discourse. In his words:

> Antigone invokes no other right than . . . a right that emerges in the language of the ineffaceable character of what is—ineffaceable, that is, from the moment when the emergent signifier freezes it like a fixed object in spite of the flood of possible transformations. What is, is, and it is to this, to this surface, that the unshakeable, unyielding position of Antigone is fixed.
>   . . . It is nothing more than the break that the very presence of language inaugurates in the life of man.
>   That break is manifested at every moment in the fact that language punctuates everything that occurs in the movement of life. Αυτονομος is the word the Chorus uses to situate Antigone. (1992, 279)

As a "fixed object," beyond his historical drama, that results from the "ineffaceable character" with which the signifiers of language mark the human being, Polynices *is* what he is, which for Antigone is nothing less than a unique opening, a "question of going εκτος ατας, of going beyond the limit of *Atè*" imposed on her house ever since the "crimes" of her father, Oedipus (Lacan 1992, 264). For, after all, "the μεριμνα of the Labdacides is that which drives Antigone to the border of *Atè*" (264). By demanding to treat Polynices as if the fatal curse on the Labdacides family had never been pronounced so as to freeze Oedipus's descendants in the fixed position of the cursed, she "violates the limits of *Atè* through her desire" and, as "the Chorus emphasizes," she goes "in search for her *Atè*," disregarding the limits imposed by both gods and the city (Creon) (277). This is why when "the Coryphaeus sings her praise" he says: "You then are half-goddess." Antigone does not accept this characterization, but "the striking thing about Antigone is that she undergoes a misfortune that is equal to that of all those who are caught up in the cruel sport of the gods" (281–281; citing *Antigone*, line 840). The transgression of the limit of *Atè* "concern[s] the relationship of mortals to the gods" because "*Atè* concerns the Other, the field of the Other, and it doesn't belong to Creon" or, for that matter, to any mortal, that is, to anyone within diachronic finite time (282). Antigone, therefore, acts from within another temporal dimension, not the temporality of mortal life but the temporality of, to recall Lacan's phrase, "the *ex nihilo*," in which there is nothing other than the potential of the new—the new discourse, the new Master-Signifier, the new Marks of *Vertretung*—to actualize itself.

In other words, *the ethical dimension and labor-power share the same time: the temporality of potentiality.* This is the temporality of semi-gods, that is, humans who are their own cause, humans as the potentiality of actualizing themselves. It is time, therefore, to approach closely the temporality of potentiality.

Attributive Aspect of the Unconscious

The Temporality of Potentiality and Ethics

Another notorious Lacanian thesis about the unconscious, in its metaphysical aspect, is that "the status of the unconscious is ethical, and not ontic" (1981, 34). Lacan's statement is double: not only the unconscious, but also the ethical does not pertain to the ontic (empirical) level. This means that the ethical dimension cannot emerge out of either ontic mode of being, the diachronic in-itself or the synchronic for-itself. Rather, it pertains to the non-ontic aspect of being, the metaphysical. In the ethical dimension, therefore, at stake is the temporality of surplus *as attribute*, not as empirical modes. The question is then: what is the temporal attribute of surplus, of which diachrony and synchrony are the concrete manifestations in the historical block of secular capitalist modernity? The same question applies to the unconscious, which cannot be formulated in its metaphysical dimension until the attribute has been revealed, of which *Vertretung* will turn out to be a modal manifestation.

The attributive temporality of surplus is itself transhistorical and capable of accounting for any empirical modes of temporality throughout history. It is the time that, whatever the given times, flows *sub specie aeternitatis*. Let us approach it more closely.

As if in an attempt to express its temporality, Lacan locates the ethical in the realm "between two deaths," that is, that "point of view" from which "life can only be approached, can only be lived or thought about, from the place of that limit where . . . life is already lost" (Lacan 1992, 270 and 280). Antigone exemplifies literally the realm "between two deaths," being already symbolically dead—both in the sense of having acted outside the lawful limit of the *Atè* designated by both the city

131

and gods, and in the sense of being, as a consequence, literally excommunicated from the city—and awaiting her imminent physical death in the tomb where she has been confined alive and left to die. After Antigone's biological death (which actually turns out to occur as a forced suicide, as she ultimately prefers to kill herself rather than awaiting to die slowly in her tomb, and which is also followed by the suicide of Creon's son, Haemon, and wife, Eurydice), Creon repents and intimates the need for the reconstitution of the symbolic order of the city—concretely, the political transition from clan-based government to the democratic city-state—by acknowledging his "guilt" for all the disasters he has caused, admitting: "Ah yes, I have learnt, I know my wretchedness" (Sophocles, 50 and 48). Thus, in truth, the two deaths framing the ethical act are, on the one side, the symbolic death of whomever chooses to cross the limit of *Atè*, and, on the other hand, the death of the Other, the reconstitution of the discourse as a response to the ethical act—otherwise the act will not be recognized as ethical.

In other words, the forced (physical) death of the transgressor, however inevitable it may often be whether dramaturgically or practically, is not structurally necessary for an act to obtain the status of the ethical. In the ethical act, it is not physical death that is sought or required; rather, what is required is that the transgression "pushes to the limit the realization of something that might be called the pure and simple desire of death as such" (Lacan, 1992, 282). It is "an illustration of the death instinct [that] we find" in *Antigone*, whose protagonist "incarnates that desire," as she has "been telling us for a long time that she is in the kingdom of the dead," so that what "takes on an outward form"—when Creon declares that "her punishment will consist in her being shut up or suspended in the zone between life and death," so that while "she is not yet dead, she is eliminated from the world of the living"—is only the official confirmation of what she has always already affirmed herself to be, it is the point at which her own "idea is consecrated" (Lacan 1992, 280–281). It is only from this position of "the pure and simple desire of death as such" that life can "be lived or thought about" as "already lost," and it is only then, when life is lived and thought about as already lost, that the human being is capable of the ethical act. For, by definition, the ethical act is sustained not by the pleasure principle—one's concern with, as Alain Badiou puts it, "the pursuit of [one's] interest, or the conservation of the self"—but by its *beyond*, the death drive (46). The death drive or the beyond the pleasure principle that Freud discovers in his eponymous book is, as Lacan puts it, "an incontestably metaphysical category . . . outside of the limits of the domain of the human in the organic sense of the word . . . it is a category of thought, to which," nevertheless, "every experience of the concrete subject cannot but refer" (1991a, 79). It is not the dead but only the concrete living subject that can refer to the death drive, just as it is only the actual living human body that can refer to the potentiality of labor-power. And though both, labor-power and the death drive, are "incontestably metaphysical" categories of "thought," they become in secular capitalist modernity part of the experience of the concrete subject, covering the entirety of the plane of immanence, both the socio-pragmatic and the ethical. The ethical dimension pertains to the temporality of the death drive for only there can human life be experienced as the potentiality of actualizing itself as a new life, in a new discourse and *Vertretung*. This is why, to invoke Deleuze's words, "there is no analytic difference between Eros and Thanatos" (1994, 113).[1]

This "incontestably metaphysical" dimension of the ethical, "outside of the limits of the domain of the human in the organic sense of the word," is the ultimate object of Spinoza's *Ethics*, and makes its appearance under the name of the "third kind of knowledge." This Spinoza defines as a "kind of knowledge [that] proceeds from an adequate idea of the formal essence of certain attributes of God to the adequate knowledge of the [NS: formal] essence of things" (1985, 478; *Ethics*, part II, prop. 40, schol. 2).[2] The use of the word "formal" here stresses that the object of the third kind of knowledge does not concern contingent particular accidents (in the Aristotelian sense of the word) but the immutable and universal forms constituting the essence of the things examined. Moreover, Spinoza's statement indicates that it is by obtaining an adequate idea of the formal essence of the attributes of substance that we can arrive at an adequate knowledge of the *essence* of things, beyond their ontic determinations, organic or otherwise.

To specify further the third kind of knowledge, we must juxtapose it to the two other kinds from which Spinoza distinguishes it. The "first kind of knowledge" is derived "from random experience" or "from signs, e.g., from the fact that, having heard or read certain words, we recollect things, and form certain ideas of them, which are like them, and through which we imagine the things," so that this kind of knowledge amounts to nothing more than "opinion or imagination" (1985, 477–478; part II, prop. 40, schol. 2). The "second kind of knowledge" consists of our "common notions and adequate ideas of the properties of things" (478; part II, prop. 40, schol. 2). While the first kind of knowledge pertains to imagination and "*is the only cause of falsity,*" "*knowledge of the second and third kind is necessarily true,*" with the second pertaining to reason, and the third forming what Spinoza calls "intuitive knowledge" (478; part II, prop. 41 and prop. 40, schol. 2). Even though both are necessarily true, what differentiates "intuitive knowledge" or the "*third kind of knowledge*" from the second is that the former "*depends on the Mind, as on a formal cause, insofar as the Mind itself is eternal*" (610; part V, prop. 31). Here Spinoza has in mind the crucial distinction between "duration" and the "species of eternity," or what, in our terms, the distinction between diachrony and the temporality of potentiality: "*Whatever the Mind understands under a species of eternity, it understands not from the fact that it conceives the Body's present actual existence, but from the fact that it conceives the Body's essence under a species of eternity*" (609; part. V, prop. 29). For:

> Insofar as the Mind conceives the present existence of its Body, it conceives duration, which can be determined by time, and to that extent it has only the power of conceiving things in relation to time. . . . But eternity cannot be explained by duration. (609; part V, prop. 29, dem.)

Here Spinoza draws the preliminary conclusion that: "Therefore, to that extent the Mind does not have the power of conceiving things under a species of eternity" (609; part V, prop. 29, dem.). But in the second part of the *Ethics*, he had already argued that—given that God is Nature, that is, everything existent, including the Mind—"the very necessity of God's eternal nature" entails that it "is of the nature of Reason to perceive of things under a certain species of eternity," and, hence, "to regard things as necessary, not as contingent." This also means that "the foundations of Reason are notions . . . which explain those things that are common to all, and which . . . do not explain the essence of any singular thing" but of the universal, which therefore "must be conceived without any relation to time, but under a certain species of eternity" (481; part II, prop. 44, cor. 2, and dem.). And this, returning now to the fifth part, forces him to revise his preliminary conclusion that the Mind can conceive the Body only in time, and to infer:

> But because it is of the nature of reason to conceive things under a species of eternity . . . and it also pertains to the nature of the Mind to conceive the Body's essence under a species of eternity . . . and beyond these two, nothing else pertains to the Mind's essence . . . this power of conceiving things under a species of eternity pertains to the Mind only insofar as it conceives the Body's essence under a species of eternity. (609–610; part V, prop. 29, dem.).

The third kind of knowledge is concerned only with the universal under "a species of eternity," wherein there is no time (in the sense of "duration" or diachrony) and the Mind conceives the Body as eternal. The third kind of knowledge, therefore, addresses neither organic life nor life as a "historical drama," both of which take place within "duration," but life under the species of eternity. It follows that the third kind of knowledge can manifest itself in neither of the two empirical modes of temporality—neither in the realm of *Vertretung* or discourse nor in that of *Darstellung* and its synchrony (and we shall see more closely the difference between eternity and synchrony in the next chapter)—but only on the metaphysical level, where alone things can be considered under the species of eternity.

What is more, Spinoza continues: "*whatever we understand by the third kind of knowledge we take pleasure in.*" For if, as we have seen, the Mind's essence is to think in terms of the third kind of knowledge, then "from this kind of knowledge there arises the greatest satisfaction of Mind there can be . . . Joy" (1985, 611; part V, prop. 32 and dem.). This explains how it is possible, as in the case of Antigone, to experience the threat of death as lesser evil, in fact, as the sole possible Joy, if all other alternatives oppose one's nature: "death is less harmful to us, the greater the Mind's clear and distinct knowledge" (613; part V, prop. 38, schol.). It is to this metaphysical pleasure or joy, deriving from the third kind of knowledge, that Lacan refers to with the term *jouissance* (enjoyment), the very concept he introduces in his attempt to formulate a theory of ethics that goes beyond the dominant tradition since "the origin of moral philosophy," according to which "all meditation on man's good has taken place as a function of the index of pleasure . . . along the paths of an essentially hedonistic problematic" (Lacan 1992, 221). Spinoza's ethics is clearly an exception to this tradition, placing at the center of his investigation metaphysical Joy, a pleasure beyond the pleasure principle, that is, beyond any pleasure or concern the Mind and the Body may have as physical objects within time. If, as Spinoza argues, *"there is nothing in nature which is contrary to this intellectual Love"* that accompanies Joy *"or which can take it away,"* it is because even death— as a temporal conclusion—cannot conquer that which exists *sub specie aeternitatis* (1985, 613; part V, prop. 37).

Spinoza explicitly subordinates pleasure to Joy also in the context of concrete examples of ethical attitude. For instance: "What if a man could save himself from the present danger of death by treachery? Would not the principle of preserving his own being recommend, without qualification, that he be treacherous?" (587; part IV, prop. 72, schol.). Spinoza's negative response is unambiguous:

> If reason should recommend that, it would recommend it to all men. And so reason would recommend, without qualification, that men make agreements, join forces, and have common rights only by deception—i.e., that really they have no common rights. This is absurd. (587; part IV, prop. 72, schol.)

In the first part of the *Ethics* Spinoza had introduced God's own pleasure as a radically indifferent will: "this opinion, which subjects all things to a certain indifferent will of God, and makes all things depend on his good pleasure, is nearer the truth than that of those who maintain that God does all things for the sake of the good" (438; part I, prop. 33, schol. 2). In other words, God's pleasure has nothing to do with our historically defined conceptions of good and evil. Which is why God or Nature "has no end set before it, and . . . all final causes are nothing but human fictions," determined by our constructed notions of what is supposed to be good and what evil (442; part I, prop. 36, appendix). In the fifth part we come to understand that God's pleasure is the very pleasure or Joy we experience through the third kind of knowledge, which is why *"our pleasure is accompanied by the idea of God as a cause."* This has as its corollary that:

> From the third kind of knowledge, there necessarily arises an intellectual Love of God. For from this kind of knowledge there arises . . . Joy, accompanied by the idea of God as its cause, i.e., Love of God, not insofar as we imagine him as

present . . . but insofar as we understand God to be eternal. And this is what I call intellectual love of God. (611; part V, prop. 32, dem. and cor.).

Here we obtain the definition of God as rendered through the third kind of knowledge: God is not that which we imagine to be present but that which we understand to be eternal. Through Lacan's ultimate secular definition of God as the unconscious, we understand that in the attributive temporality of the unconscious everything is taken *sub specie aeternitatis*—and it is in this properly metaphysical dimension that the status of the unconscious is ethical. This is the unconscious *qua* God, that is, to recall Sartre's definition of God, the unconscious as "its own foundation not as nothingness but as being" that "would preserve within it the necessary translucency of consciousness along with the coincidence with itself of being-in-itself" (140). It is the unconscious or God directly as surplus or being-in-itself-for-itself, and not the historico-empirical manifestation of surplus as the split between the repressed *Vertretung* of the in-itself (diachrony) and the conscious *Darstellung* of the for-itself (synchrony), which are the two empirical manifestations of the species of eternity and, thus, pertain to the ontic, not the ethical, status.

Let us conclude this chapter on ethics with a note about its necessity in the present context. Within traditional philosophy one tended to take as given the separation between the ontological and the ethical domains because of the standard conception of being as the in-itself, that is, as Sartre puts it, "precisely as reality" or "facticity." And "to take" the ethical "as being [in-itself] is to risk totally misunderstanding its unreality and to make of it, as sociologists do, a requirement of fact among other facts" (143). In the present ontology, however, being is conceived not as reality or facticity but as the in-itself-for-itself, and hence as both reality and its presupposed transcendental or metaphysical unreality. In other words, if this discussion of ethics is inevitable in the context of a theory of being, it is because the ontological includes within itself both the ontic (historical/modal) and the metaphysical (transhistorical/attributive) aspects of being.

As for biopolitics, as we shall presently see, its dimension lies in the passage from the metaphysical to the ontic, where what comes in as attribute evolves into modes.

From Eternity (Attribute) to Immortality (Mode)

What remains conspicuously unaddressed so far are two intertwined questions: (a) How is it possible that the temporal attribute of surplus—eternity—manifests itself empirically in these two modes—diachrony and synchrony; and (b), while it is evident that diachrony is distinct from eternity, how is it distinct from synchrony?

To address these questions I'll take a short detour through Deleuze's presentation of the species of eternity as what he calls the "third synthesis of time." There Deleuze shows that what is at stake in the passage from attribute to mode is the unfolding of what is conceptual or formal unto linear time. The diachronic sequence that we call "past, present, and future" or "before, during, and after" can be represented as a purely spatial configuration or "rigorous formal and static order," as in the conception of the narcissistic ego, out of whose shattering emerges the split between subject and object (external reality). In Deleuze's words:

> The narcissistic ego repeats once in the form of the before or lack, in the form if the *Id* (this action is too big for me); a second time in the form of an infinite becoming-equal appropriate to the *ego ideal*; a third time, in the form of the after which realizes the prediction of the *superego* (the id and the ego, the condition and the agent, will themselves be annihilated)! (1994, 110–111)

These three scansions can assume the form of linear time only because they are the three dimensions of the "symbol" (Deleuze, 1994, 89), that is, to put it in economic terms, the symbol (value) in its secular/capitalist

139

modulation as self-valorizing value: M—C—M′. As a value, in "effect, there is always a time at which the imagined act"—the act of accruing more value, of becoming more than myself—"is supposed to be 'too big for me,'" and this supposition "defines *a priori* the past or the before" (89). "The second time . . . is thus the present of metamorphosis, a becoming equal to the act and a doubling of the self, and a projection of an ideal self in the image of the act"—so that "C," as use-value, doubles or projects itself as its ideal self as exchange-value, and thus enters the equation (89). And because "what the self [use-value] has become equal to is the unequal in itself [exchange-value]," in "the third time in which the future appears . . . the event and the act . . . turn back against the self which has become their equal and smash it to pieces," so that all that remains is pure difference (M′) (89–90).

But, crucially, once we leave aside the specific contingent modulation of surplus as surplus-value, we understand that the product of the formal order of surplus does not need to be the "same difference" of surplus-value, but can be "the repetition of the future, as eternal return" of surplus, that is, as the power of the self-referential being to actualize itself eternally, always as "complete novelty" (Deleuze 1994, 90). It is not the recurrence of ever more, yet the same thing (surplus-value), but a complete novelty, the product of the *ex nihilo*, which Antigone produces when, in her moment of "the before or lack" and in the face of the excruciatingly intimidating curse of her *Atè* ("this action is too big for me"), she proceeds, in the second time of the present of the entire tragedy, to "an infinite becoming-equal" with the gods or the Other—or whatever it is that one should call that which announces the *Atè* of an individual, of a family, a clan, or a whole country or society—to realize in the "third time" of "the after" what she always already knew ("the prediction"), whereby both her *Atè* and the Other (along with her, since she has become Its equal) are themselves annihilated.

Under the species of eternity, being is difference—in all its possible variants: lack, equality, or excess—which is why it can manifest itself empirically as much in the sequential order of past, present, and future, as in the synchrony of differential relations. Thus, *sub specie aeternitatis*,

> it matters little whether or not the event itself occurs, or whether the act has been performed or not: past, present, and future are not distributed according to this temporal criterion. Oedipus has already carried out the act, Hamlet has not yet

> done so, but in either case the first part of the symbol is lived in the past, they are in the past and live themselves as such as long as they experience the image of the act as too big for them. (Deleuze, 1994, 89)

But, unlike in sheer synchronicity, under the species of eternity it does matter that the "too big for them" manifests itself diachronically as the past, the equal as the present, and the realization of the "too big" as the future. *This is what distinguishes eternity from synchronic differentiality.*

Recapitulating, *eternity is the attribute of substance* (surplus or the unconscious), whereas *synchronicity* and *diachrony*, as well as *Darstellung* and *Vertretung*, are the *empirical modes* in which this attribute manifests itself precisely because it is at once a conceptual or formal static order and the succession of before, during, and after. The Mind's essence, which gives it its greatest Joy, is to conceive of everything neither synchronically nor diachronically but *sub specie aeternitatis.* The species of eternity enables being to enter its ethical dimension, that is, to live beyond the pleasure principle and all the concerns of self-interest, for *sub specie aeternitatis* life and death do not form an opposition, and questions regarding survival, mortality, and immortality cannot even be raised. Such concepts presuppose change—whether affirmatively (from life to death) or as its negation (immortality)—whereas the *sub specie aeternitatis* conceives of the body as eternal, in its *unchangeable difference,* as *potentiality.* For potentiality alone cannot pertain to time or be subject to change, since it is itself permanent change—the "eternal recurrence" of the possibility of the virtual to become actual, without this difference between the two poles, the virtual and the actual, ever changing into anything else. This is why the ethical act is ephemeral—once it has been accomplished, once the new discourse (which recognizes it as an ethical act in the first place) has been actualized, everything resumes again ontic dimensions. The birth of the ethical act is its death. In the ethical dimension, therefore, the distinction between death and life does not apply, and all change, up to and including mortality and immortality, pertains exclusively to the ontic level. (This explains the tendency in fiction to intertwine the ethical with physical death.)

Thus, while on the metaphysical and ethical level of eternity being is surplus or pure difference, on the ontic level pure difference manifests itself as immortality in circulation-time or synchrony—the realm of the for-itself: exchange-value and the signifier—and as mortality in production-time and diachrony—the realm of the in-itself: use-value and meaning. While the phenomenological in-itself and for-itself are one another's negation, meta-phenomenologically both are the eternal difference that constitutes the being-in-itself-for-itself.

In other words, in the passage from the metaphysical or ethical to the ontic level, there is a slippage from eternity to the dualism between immortality and mortality. It is in the interstice of this passage, which is also the passage from monism to dualism, that the biopolitical mechanism is played out. Once eternity splits itself into mortality and immortality, the repression of *Vertretung* amounts to the repression of mortality, thereby allowing immortality to appropriate the temporality of consciousness. Thus—following once again the fetishistic logic, according to which knowledge, not belief, is unconscious (repressed)—although the human subject knows very well (unconsciously) that it is mortal, it believes (consciously) that it is immortal. In its ontic, non-ethical, dimension, the subject of secular capitalist modernity is doomed to mistake eternity for immortality.

Nowhere else is this slippage from the metaphysical to the ontic as the precondition for the production of the illusion of immortality depicted more transparently than in Kant's admirable discussion of permanence—a text that functions as a veritable *symptom* of biopolitics, insofar as it both commits the slippage and reveals the structure because of which dualist thought cannot avoid it. Given that Kant's premise is the dualism between (ontic) appearance and (in his terminology, ontological or transcendent) substance or the thing-in-itself, substance remains always outside the reach of knowledge. Thus, Kant proceeds by arguing first that:

> Pure reason requires us to seek for every predicate of a thing its own subject, and for this subject, which is itself necessarily nothing but a predicate, its subject, and so on indefinitely (or as far as we can reach). But hence it follows that we must not hold anything at which we can arrive to be an ultimate subject, and that substance itself never can be thought by our understanding. (1977, 75; §46)

Given that, for Kant, the ultimate subject or substance cannot be thought by our understanding, its attributes also cannot be known. What philosophers and others present as attributes of the substance, for Kant, concerns only the ontic level, so that the concepts representing these presumed attributes can have any validity only within the ontic level. Thus, regarding the attribute in question Kant infers that: "permanence can never be proved of the concept of a substance as a thing in itself, but only for the purposes of experience" (1977, 76; §47). Turning then to the "soul" as the name of the permanent substance, Kant concludes that:

> If, therefore, from the concept of the soul as a substance we would infer its permanence, this can hold good as regards possible experience only, not of the soul as a thing in itself and beyond all possible experience; consequently we can only infer the permanence of the soul in life, for the death of man is the end of all the experience that concerns the soul as an object of experience, except the contrary be proved—which is the very question in hand. The permanence of the soul can therefore only be proved (and no one cares for that) during the life of man, but not, as we desire to do, after death. (76; §48)

Here Kant shows us that once the concept of permanence is applied to the ontic level ("possible experience"), it is inevitably transformed into the concept of immortality, since, "except the contrary be proved," death is the end of all possible experience. But what makes this passage even more astonishing is the fact that it simultaneously proves that immortality pertains exclusively to the ontic level, it is an illusion that emerges with logical necessity—which is why it can "be proved"—only once permanence is examined "for the purposes of experience," and applies only to experience, "during the life of man." Not only cannot permanence enter the ontic level as anything other than immortality, but it enters it to prove that *we are immortal only as long as we are alive*, not "after death." Kant misfires here with regard to only one, yet crucial, assumption, namely, that: "no one cares for" immortality "during the life of man."

Quite the contrary, *secular* immortality *is immortality "during the life of man"* and does not in the least concern afterlife. Biopolitics does not rely on, nor does it foster, the presecular assumption of the immortal soul. Secular immortality is facilitated by the subject's conscious identification with *Darstellung* and the repression of *Vertretung*, whereby the subject experiences itself exclusively as the for-itself (exchange-value or signifier), and hence as immortal, precisely while it lives. It is the immortality of the subject *qua* arbitrary synchronic value that constitutes the basis of biopolitics, and this remains so regardless of whether certain secular subjects may also believe in immortality in the sense of afterlife. The latter is as irrelevant to the mechanisms of biopolitics as the fact that many secular subjects believe in God is to the premise of the secular historical block that "God is unconscious." To refer to an almost trite example, Einstein may have believed in God, but what matters is that he could not invoke God as the guarantor of the truth of the theory of relativity. The point is not what individual people believe in but what the epistemology of a given historical block acknowledges, whether explicitly or not, as the legitimate ground of truth. And the immortality that is legitimate in the secular capitalist block is premised not in afterlife but, tacitly or not, in differential synchronic value.

Correlatively, the eternity in question, albeit the temporal attribute of substance and, hence, transhistorical, does not evade the effects of the secular modulation of surplus as an operative function in the plane of immanence. It is only because of this modulation that eternity becomes the temporal dimension of the ethical, as the beyond of any good and evil that is defined within the domain of the pleasure principle. Such a conception of ethics was impossible for both antiquity and monotheism, throughout which ethics remained tied to one or the other "hedonistic" principle—ranging from any earthly to any heavenly reward—for the simple reason that eternity was relegated to absolute transcendence, that is, to a domain inaccessible to humans.

Battlefield of Biopolitics

Gazes of Immortality and Lethal Certainty

We are in the position to condense our investigation regarding biopolitics to the following: the proper object of biopolitics is bios or the body in its triple quality: (first), as *potentiality sub specie aeternitatis*, which manifests itself on the ontic level in (second) the mode of a mortal physical body and (third) in the mode of an immortal value.

Like the unconscious, the gaze, and surplus-value, bios is one of the modulations of surplus within secular capitalist modernity, which, too, manifests itself on the ontic level always in two modes—which, depending on the context, can be labeled as use-value and exchange-value, *Vertretung* and *Darstellung*, and so forth—and in their corresponding temporalities—the two modal manifestations of eternity—diachrony and synchrony, and, hence, mortality and immortality.

Two questions regarding biopolitics arise here. First: How is the subject constituted in secular capitalist modernity, in which bios as potentiality emerges, so that it experiences itself as a mortal body and as an immortal value? And, second: How do these two modes of experience of the secular subject relate to the same subject in its metaphysical or ethical dimension, where it is potentiality *sub specie aeternitatis*? Responding to these questions is the task of this chapter.

We have already established that the body or bios is potentiality, and this by dint of two major functions of secular capitalist modernity—labor-power and the gaze—both of which are the potentiality of self-actualization. And we have also recurrently indicated that potentiality—the power of self-actualization—is Spinoza's substance. In "Nature," Spinoza writes, "there is only one substance," which is "the cause of itself," so that substance is "God, *or* Nature," as "*the immanent, not the transitive, cause of all things,*" that is, as precisely the effect that is the cause of its own cause (1985, 420, 412, 544, and 428; *Ethics*, part I, prop. 14, cor. 1 and prop. 7, dem., part IV, preface, and part I, prop. 18). And the temporality of substance or power of self-actualization that we call the body or the gaze, in its attributive dimension, is eternity, or, in Spinoza's own words, the "eternal nature" of substance, which is "necessary and not . . . contingent," exists "under [the] species of eternity [*sub specie aeternitatis*]" (481; *Ethics*, part II, prop. 44, cor. 2, dem.). More precisely, Spinoza's, and our, species of eternity is the secular transmutation of eternity, which since the inception of capital and secular thought designates the temporality of potentiality—a potentiality that is part of the plane of immanence (as opposed to the presecular absolutely transcendent potentiality of self-actualization that was attributed exclusively to an equally transcendent, and creationist, divinity).

Now, although, as we have also seen, there is a kind of knowledge in which human thought can "perceive of things under a certain species of eternity" and "conceive[] the Body's essence under a species of eternity," human beings would be incapable of functioning without their ability to operate outside the sphere of eternity and self-referential potentiality, in that quite more familiar territory where everything appears as a multitude of distinct objects in distinct moments in time (481 and 609; *Ethics*, part II, prop. 44, cor. 2, and part V, prop. 29). As both, Spinoza writes, in our everyday life we employ, depending on the clarity of our distinctions, two other kinds of knowledge, "imagination" and "reason" (478; *Ethics*, part II, pro. 40, schol. 2). And, as Lacan tells us, "in order to constitute itself" as a consciousness that operates on the basis of imagination and reason, "the subject . . . has separated itself off" from, nothing less than, the "gaze"—that is, the self-referentiality of the body that pertains to eternity (1981, 103).[1] Inevitably, this separation entails a "lack" which, albeit constitutive (without it the subject could not constitute itself as a conscious being), does not prevent the subject from seeking ways to compensate for it. Just as, although it "is no longer anything for" the infant that can feed itself without breastfeeding, the "object of weaning may come to function . . . as privation," weaning from eternity may likewise generate its own search for surrogates (104). The separation of the subject from the self-referential gaze leaves behind it a yearning for eternity. As is entailed in my connection of Spinoza's Joy, derived from knowledge under the species of eternity, and (Lacanian) ethics, *it is this yearning that instigates humans to act ethically.* And *it is precisely on this level that biopolitics intervenes.* Reformulating once again our definition, *the object of biopolitics is the subject's relation to eternity and to its surrogates.*

The modulation of value *qua* surplus-value and the concomitant emergence of labor-power have had the same effect on the body as did the secular gradual extinction of the absolutely transcendent gaze of God, the creator (i.e., the first, transitive cause). During the last three centuries, this plodding but steady elimination of an avowedly unfathomable yet secure gaze—which is the parallel inverse process of the often subliminal yet inevitable constitution of immanent causality and the launching of potentiality into the plane of immanence—has entailed the gradual permeation of life with self-referentiality, as a result of which there remains eventually no anchoring point to ground and fix any empirical gaze.[2]

The moment at which there is no divine gaze, and beyond appearances there is only the gaze as the infinity of all possible empirical gazes, the subject can experience as real the world realized under its gaze only insofar as it imagines that only one gaze among the infinity of the gazes is *the* gaze. (Two or three, occasionally even more, can be the case—this is why we have the gamut of experience that ranges from ambivalence and doubt to paranoia—but under no circumstances can one deal with an infinity of gazes. And to proceed to any action, including deciding for non-action, all extant gazes must ultimately be subordinated to one.) It is, again, no accident that Descartes' primary problem was to find a guarantee that he is not deceived in assuming that what he sees is real and not an illusion; and the sole way out of his predicament was to "prove" not only that beyond his gaze there is another gaze, but also that this gaze is the gaze of a benevolent God, for if the gaze belonged to a *"genius malignus,"* then this might want to deceive him.[3] Being deceived would mean that this body that I take for mine might not exist. In other words, alongside labor-power, the gaze, too, "calls into question the repository from which it is indistinguishable, that is, the living body" (Virno, 83). It follows that the secular body shares the same fate as the binary sign: Like the link between thing and word, the link between empirical gaze (body) and transcendental gaze (which for us, moderns, is nothing more or less than the gaze we must imagine in the place of the infinity of gazes) ceases to be organic and becomes arbitrary.

This means, recalling Saussure, that now both body and (imagined) gaze "are purely differential and negative," *yet* this is true only "when considered separately," for "their combination is a positive fact," an organic, non-arbitrary bond. Once the transcendental gaze has been imagined, the arbitrary differentiality of the signs of *Darstellung* produces as its own precondition the Marks of *Vertretung*, which render the link between the body and the gaze organic, since they are not just signs but concept-bodies. And, inversely, the transcendental gaze can be imagined in the first place only insofar as the Marks of *Vertretung* have rendered the link between the body and *a* gaze organic, so that it appears as the transcendental gaze. This particular link between the body and the gaze we can call, by analogy to the Master-Signifier, the *Master*-Vertretungs-*Mark*, and it *is that which determines the formation of all other* Vertretungs-*Marks*.[4] By making the link between body and gaze organic, the *Master*-Vertretungs-*Mark* actualizes the body as a thing made of flesh and bones—that is, as an in-itself—and thereby renders it a mortal body in time. Without this organic link the body would experience itself only as self-referential potentiality under the species of eternity. In other words, the *Master*-Vertretungs-*Mark* is the other side of the separation of the subject from the gaze as an "organ" (Lacan 1981, 103). *In order to constitute itself, the subject gives up one organ, the gaze as the self-referentiality of the body that pertains to eternity, and attaches itself instead to the concept-organ of the Master-*Vertretungs-*Mark.*

It follows that if there is a Master-*Vertretungs*-Mark, there is *Vertretung*, and then the potentiality of the body *sub specie aeternitatis* manifests itself as a mortal body, which is further endowed with consciousness (*Darstellung*). If there is no Master-*Vertretungs*-Mark, then there is only *Darstellung*, and the potentiality of the body *sub specie aeternitatis* manifests itself as immortal value. We call biopolitics, therefore, the production, management, administration, and control of *the presence or absence of gazes that allow the subject to experience itself as mortal or immortal.*[5]

Consciously, within *Darstellung*, we *believe* that we are immortal, while it is only unconsciously, in the system of (repressed) *Vertretung*, that we *know* that we are mortal. The anxiety of modern secular subjectivity stems from this conflict between the conscious belief in immortality and unconscious knowledge of our mortality. A central task, therefore, of the biopolitical mechanisms lies in domesticating the radical anxiety of an unrepresentable death by vicariously including it in representations of immortality or, as we shall see in the chapter "Postmodern Bioracism: Exporting Mortality," by representing it as something that cannot ever happen to "us." Moreover, since it is now evident that bios designates not the physical or organic body but the *body-gaze* cluster, biopolitics concerns not the control of given physical bodies but *the materialization of immaterial bodies by providing specific gazes*, and, conversely—since, anyway, gazes (like labor-power) do not exist without their material tabernacles, bodies—*the dematerialization of material bodies, the disembodiment of embodied gazes*, which facilitates the illusion of immortality.

Regardless of any biopolitical intervention, the subject of secular capitalist modernity is both mortal and immortal because it partakes in both *Vertretung* and *Darstellung*, the two ontic modes of the attributive temporality of surplus, eternity. At the same time, the ethical or metaphysical vocation of the subject of capitalist secular modernity is to be able to conceive of its body *sub specie aeternitatis*, that is, under the species of unchangeable difference, in which life as duration or "historical drama" is already lost. Only this dimension confers on the subject its dignity. Entrance to this dimension, we recall, presupposes a detachment from discourse, along with the historical moral norms (*Vertretung*) that define good and evil. But, as we saw in the chapter "Discourse, or the Symptom of the Repressed, and Language," this detachment is only the necessary but not the sufficient condition for obtaining the ethical dimension. Once detached from discourse, one *must inhabit Darstellung from the metaphysical point of view*, that is, in full consciousness of the fact that the chance-game of *Darstellung* is always determined by the inexorable law of the Marks of *Vertretung* devoid of their intentionality. This attitude amounts to the radical coincidence of relativism and what I would call not essentialism but organicism—an attitude in which one does not detach the apparently arbitrary constructedness of all values, from moral and cultural to economic, from the marks that underpin them. We have seen how easy it is to assume that detachment from the discourse, with its values and teleologies, amounts to nothing more than seclusion within *Darstellung* as the unlimited play of value-free differential relations, in which "everything goes." This amounts to a seclusion within radical relativism, which is required for the subject's identification with purely differential value and, hence, for experiencing oneself as immortal. Thus, thanks to the illusory slippage that occurs in the transition from the metaphysical to the ontic level, in which eternity appears as (if it were) immortality, *Darstellung* can offer a surrogate experience of eternity. The temptation of this abundant surrogate instigates the subject to abandon its ethical dimension in order to live under the illusion of immortality, even as it (unconsciously) knows that it is mortal. And if this "immortal" subject could speak the truth, it would say what commodities in circulation would say, which, in Marx's ventriloquism, is the following:

> if commodities could speak, they would say this: our use-value may interest men, but it does not belong to us as objects. What does belong to us as objects, however, is our value. Our own intercourse as commodities proves it. We relate to each other merely as exchange-values. (1990, 176–177)

In *Darstellung* there are neither use-values nor "men," only pure immortal values. Advanced capitalist countries are countries in which *Darstellung*, as both economic circulation and relativism, prevails over *Vertretung*, as both production and (more) organicist modes of thought. It is in these regions of the world that this secular administration of the illusion of immortality—a kind of Faustian pact in which subjects give up their ethical dimension in exchange for immortality—is a central biopolitical mechanism.

The present situation is a replication, albeit with a whimsical twist, of the conflict to which Hans Blumenberg largely attributed the shift from the presecular to the secular era, namely: the inconsistency between the Gnostic conclusion that the destruction of the world is the sole salvation and the fact that the world continued to exist. In Hans Blumenberg's recapitulation, Gnosticism concluded that if the universe was, according to Christian Neoplatonism, divided into two parts (ideal heavens and inferior earthly simulacrum), then divinity must also be divided into two entities: the redeemer who "has never had anything to do with this world," and the demiurge or creator of the earthly world. The demiurge thereby became "the principle of badness, the opponent of the transcendent God of salvation," just as the demiurge's creation, the "cosmos," became "the system of a fall." As a result, Blumenberg concludes, "the downfall of the world becomes the critical process of final salvation, the dissolution of the demiurge's illegitimate creation" (128–129). The destruction of the world became the logical require-ment of Neoplatonic theodicy. Ignoring Neoplatonism, however, the world stubbornly continued to exist, and the sole way to negotiate this inconsistency was to attribute the world's continuing existence to a delay of the Last Judgment as the manifestation of a merciful God-Redeemer who was willing to satisfy the human prayer for postponement of the destruction of the world. The difference between the presecular and the secular conceptions of the Last Judgment, Blumenberg concludes, lies in the shift of historical consciousness from "prayer . . . for the early coming of the Lord" to prayer "for postponement of the end" (131). Today, too, contrary to the epistemological mandates of *Darstellung* (the purveyor of redemption), bodies stubbornly continue to die. To negotiate this inconsistency, biopolitics must find a culprit: it must effect a shift in historical consciousness, such that its "prayer" explains why bodies continue to die. Once again, the sin befalls on us. *Darstellung* lets us continue to die because we pray for access to the in-itself. A cursory glance at contemporary art, particularly the specifically postmodern genre of performance art, suffices to evidence an obsession with the physicality of the body, including its abject or painful aspects. But, incomparably more ubiquitous is the highly popularized art of tattooing, the literal experience and visualization of the *Vertretungs*-Mark. In short, in spite of the promises of *Darstellung*, we keep dying because we pray for *Vertretung* (the demiurge's omen), that is, for what we (unconsciously) know will *certainly* occur, our inevitable death. This certainty itself is the ultimate sin that deprives our bodies from their immortality—for any certainty, beyond and above any doubt, simply resurrects what the entirety of secular thought and life aimed at exterminating: an absolute gaze. Any specific gaze suffices to render the body material and, hence, mortal, so that the culprit is ultimately *certainty* tout court.

To "pray" for *Vertretung* is to "pray" for the return of the repressed, that which the capitalist ideological fantasy wants to keep hidden, and is therefore forbidden. And since *liberal (non-coercive) coercion* postulates that ideally nothing be forbidden, biopolitics must present *Vertretung* and its linear temporality as *impossible*. Thus, death itself becomes impossible, and the certainty thereof a transgression of the biopolitical postulates.

Therefore, the dominant biopolitical gaze *par excellence* is *uncertainty*. While the ethical gaze approaches the infinity of all possible gazes *sub specie aeternitatis*, uncertainty involves an indefinite sliding of gazes—under, of course, the aegis of the exceptional gaze of uncertainty itself, which here becomes absolute—in which one gaze substitutes for another, reducing the values of *Darstellung* to an incessant race of pure differentiality that nothing can stop and can lead only to a haze of confusion. Put slightly differently, while the ethical dimension involves the infinity of gazes, which to the ontic eye appears as the absence of any gaze whatsoever, the biopolitical degradation of the subject from the ethical dimension to the illusion of immortality involves the specific gaze of radical uncertainty, because of which the subject is hystericized, that is, doomed both to search for the right gaze and to reject any given gaze as wrong, indefinitely.[6]

Enjoyment (*Jouissance*) and Utilitarianism

Prior to examining further the biopolitical administration of the gaze and certainty, we have to return once more to the intellectual Love of God or enjoyment (*jouissance*), the greatest Joy of the mind, accessible to it only in its capacity of perceiving the body *sub specie aeternitatis*. For there remain two questions: What exactly is the nature of this enjoyment, and what becomes of this enjoyment when the subject gives up its ethical dimension in exchange for immortality?

Whenever the question of enjoyment is raised, sexuality offers itself as the most obvious place to look for it. Indeed, sexuality figures in Foucault's work as a major object of biopolitical control. Returning to a point made in an endnote in the previous chapter on his by now notorious refutation of the "repressive hypothesis," Foucault argued that "rather than a massive censorship" or a "uniform concern to hide sex" and a "general prudishness of language," what in truth "distinguishes these last three centuries is the variety, the wide dispersion of devices that were invented for speaking about [sex]" (1990, 34). Following the psychoanalytic principle that there is no repressed prior to its return, sexuality as we know it (which includes that it is a subject to be hidden) emerged precisely through its return, as a subject that must be spoken about, in the most possible fields of knowledge. The injunction since the "seventeenth century" has been that "one ha[s] to speak of it as of a thing to be not simply condemned or tolerated but managed, inserted into systems of utility, regulated for the greater good of all, made to function according to an optimum" (17 and 24). Since the advent of modernity, sexuality became "a thing one administered," destined to develop "in the eighteenth century" into "a 'police' matter," by which is meant "not the rigor of a taboo, but the necessity of regulating sex through useful and public discourses" (24–25). As Foucault's choice of terms—management, administration, systems of utility, a useful public regulation and optimal function for the greater good of all—emphatically indicate, biopolitics is based on a subjugation of sexuality to the pragmatist principle of *utilitarianism*. The primary shift taking place in the seventeenth century concerns the gradual domination of the discourse by the utilitarian principle, of which the administration of sexuality could be seen as just one department among others.

Yet, if "sexuality become[s] a field of vital strategic importance" for biopolitics and cannot be reduced to just one department of regulations, it is because, by having "procreative effects, sexuality is also inscribed, takes effect, in broad biological processes that concern not [only] the bodies of individuals but . . . the multiple unity of the population"; in short, the subjection of sexuality to the utilitarian principle amounts to the subjection of everything to this principle because "sexuality exists at the point where body and population meet" (Foucault 2003, 251–252). In other words, as Freud already knew, everything is about sex because "sex" designates not just itself but also everything else. The agenda of utilitarianism is to eliminate waste in general, to transform everything into something that has a use and serves a purpose, however vaguely the latter might be conceived, as the humanitarian invocation of the "good of all" makes clear. The *compulsion to usefulness* is the *motor of biopolitics*.

What allowed utilitarianism to become the principle of the new, secular and capitalist, episteme? The elimination of the presecular *a priori* organic link between body and God's gaze entailed also a shift from the theocratic conception of earthly life as human suffering for the sake of afterlife enjoyment to the secular conception of earthly life as a source of enjoyment *hic et nunc*. The contrast between the two conceptions is amusingly, and stunningly, represented throughout Federico Fellini's film *8½* (1963), which stresses the incommunicability between the doctrine of the Catholic church and the modern, bourgeois male individual, with his neuroses, ennui, and, nevertheless, the undying aspiration to enjoy life. The conflict is illustrated at its most condensed in one scene in particular, in which the protagonist, Guido (Marcello Mastroianni), is received by the cardinal (Tito Masini) for a hearing, while the latter is taking a bath, assisted by three other clerical men, in a steamy room. As the camera, representing Guido's point of view, enters the room from a slowly opening window located at the lowest level of the room's wall, we hear Guido say: "Eminence, I am not happy." This is Guido's last line in this scene. From then on, we hear only the cardinal who—alternatively appearing as a "real person" or as a shadow, as the other men are at times concealing him from view with a large white sheet, and at other times revealing him from behind it—retorts: "Why should you be? This isn't your job. Who told you we come into the world to be happy?" As if to raise to the superlative the discrepancy between the languages and perspectives of the church and contemporary life, Fellini has the cardinal respond to his own question with a tediously repetitive monologue, both in Latin and in translation into modern Italian:

> Extra Ecclesiam nulla salus. There is no salvation outside the church. Extra Ecclesiam, nemo salvatur. No one will meet salvation outside the church. Salus extra Ecclesiam non est. There is no salvation outside the church. Civitas dei. He who isn't in the *City of God* belongs to the City of Devil.

Whereupon the camera (Guido) begins to withdraw from the room through the same aperture, which then closes again. The dreamy, ethereal, yet austere, atmosphere of this scene is subsequently followed by an opulent outdoor patio in bright day light, in which a distinctly, or, rather—in Fellinesque fashion—grotesquely bourgeois audience is listening to the soothing music emanating from a live orchestra, to yield to a further scene of a street busy with, again, an almost caricature-like bourgeois crowd, where eventually the protagonist will spot and speak to his wife for the first time since the beginning of the film. But before he sees her, while he is still walking aimlessly amid the crowd, we hear very clearly the following words, which are the first since the cardinal's reference to the City of Devil:

> 20,000 . . . 22,000 . . . 23,000 . . . and the lady in the back? 25,000? Very well, the bid is 24,000. Do I hear 30,000? Splendid. 35,000 . . . 40,000. Going, going . . . One more offer? 50,000 . . . the bid is 50,000.

The cardinal's chant is replaced, in a stark contrast, with the equally tedious substitution of numbers in the speech of, as the camera has meanwhile revealed to us, an auctioneer in a crowded antique store. Exchange-value substitutes for Latin phrases conveying the divine dogma which, anyway, the bourgeoisie treats not much unlike the other antiques in the store that can be bought and sold.[1] And no communication between the two worlds can in all this occur. *Darstellung* may be able to communicate with *Vertretung*, but not with the presecular Word (whether in Latin or in translation), for which happiness and enjoyment (let alone in the specific forms accommodated by consumerism) is not in the least assumed to be our job in the world.

Whatever our individual modes of enjoyment may be, enjoyment, as the film amply indicates and as we know from our experience, has come to be considered our inalienable, most natural right. And therein lies the problem: enjoyment has become a *right*, that is, something that is intrinsically intertwined with the *law*. As Lacan points out with regard to the "right-to-jouissance": "right (*droit*) is not duty. Nobody forces anyone to enjoy (*jouir*) except the superego. The superego is the imperative to jouissance—Enjoy!" (1998, 3). The problem is that the "superego" comes in various guises, so that it is almost impossible to tell whether you enjoy because it is its imperative or because you just do, given that you also have the right to do so if you so wish.

This interlacing of right and duty relates to the following ambivalence characterizing the vicissitudes of enjoyment within the secular capitalist block. Enjoyment involves the paradox of both being represented by labor-power itself and constituting its antipodean. For, to return to Marx's words, and place this time the emphasis elsewhere, there is a difference between the labor-power "which the worker has to offer to the capitalist" and the labor-power "which he has to offer to others in general," up to and including himself. Labor-power, as the potential or *dynamis* of the living body, may be channeled into all possible activities one may want to perform for the enjoyment of oneself or others, but it may also be the labor one is forced to sell, whether one wants to or not, in order to survive. The latter is the labor sold by the "worker" who is "free in the double sense that as a free individual he can dispose of his labour-power as his own commodity, and that, on the other hand, he has no other commodity for sale," which means both that "he is rid of them, he is free of all the objects needed for the realization [*Verwirklichung*] of his labour-power," and that "instead of being able to sell commodities in which his labour has been objectified, [he] must rather be compelled to offer for sale as a commodity that very labour-power which exists only in his living body" (Marx 1990, 272–273). By contrast, the labor-power expended for the laborer's own pure enjoyment or offered to others just out of the laborer's pure enjoyment and for their enjoyment, presupposes a worker not "free," evidently in the second sense of the word, but, as we shall presently see, also not "free" in the first sense of the word. Here is Marx's passage describing the conditions under which labour-power offers itself for purchase:

> Labour-power can appear on the market as a commodity only if, and in so far as, its possessor, the individual whose labour it is, offers it for sale or sells it as a commodity. In order that its possessor may sell it as a commodity, he must have at his disposal, he must be the free proprietor of his own labour-capacity, hence of his person. He and the owner of money meet in the market, and enter into relations with each other on a footing of equality as owners of commodities, with the sole difference that the one is a buyer, the other the seller; both are therefore equal in the eyes of the law. (1990, 271)

First, let us remark that the "market" Marx refers to here is not to be confused with the circulation of the differentially defined exchange-values, since labor-power is sold to the buyer at a cost defined not differentially but according to historical "moral" standards. The aforementioned scene is staged in the realm of *Vertretung*, in production-time. Now, the selling and buying of labor-power, Marx argues, presupposes that both the seller and the buyer enter this market on equal footing, as "equal in the eyes of the law." A universal equality among buyers and sellers is presupposed for the buying and selling of labor-power. There can be no buying and selling of labor-power, and, for that matter, no capital, without the universal law of the equality of people as owners of commodities, even as some are owners of capital and others owners of only one commodity, their labor-power. As Marx puts it:

> The historical conditions of [capital's] existence are by no means given with the mere circulation of money and commodities. It arises only when the owner of the means of production and subsistence finds the free worker available, on the market, as the seller of his own labour-power. (1990, 274)

In other words, the emergence of capital presupposes the *unnatural* imposition of the law of universal equality within the realm of *Vertretung*.

For in the realm of *Vertretung*, as we have seen, laws *cannot be universal*, they are only imperative. The moment *Vertretung* is colonized by this universal law is the moment at which enjoyment itself is subjected to the law, whereby the right to enjoy is always the duty to enjoy, insofar as, to repeat: "the possessor of labour-power, instead of being able to sell commodities in which his labour has been objectified, must rather be compelled to offer for sale as a commodity that very labour-power which exists only in his living body." *To subscribe enjoyment to the law, to make of it a right, amounts to reducing it to a duty—the duty to Enjoy!* For the laborer to be able to derive real enjoyment from his labor-power, the latter must not enter the realm of *Vertretung*, that is, it must not be sold as a commodity that is use-value. Once this has happened, the laborer can only be obliged to enjoy, which is to say, he cannot really enjoy.

Marx alludes to real enjoyment as something that was possible only in precapitalist societies, where the "product" of labor was not a "commodity" but "the immediate means of subsistence of the producer himself" (1990, 273). Once "labour-power, in the eyes of the worker himself, takes on the form of a commodity which is his property" and "his labour consequently takes on the form of wage-labour . . . from this moment [on] . . . the commodity-form of the products of labour becomes universal," which is why: "Capital, therefore, announces from the outset a new epoch in the process of social production," and with it, a new epoch in the history of enjoyment (274 and 274n4). Having understood however, that the "past" of capitalism is the in-itself of its present for-itself and contemporaneous with it, we must examine the subjection of enjoyment to the law and its transformation into a duty against the background of a *real enjoyment* conceived not as something past and gone but as something *presupposed, by the present*, for its present adulteration or alienation. The conception of a labor-power that is not put to the service of capital is possible only within capitalism itself. "Indeed, were the Law to give the order, *'Jouis!'* [Enjoy! Or "Come!"], the subject could only reply *'J'ouis'* ["I hear"], in which the jouissance would no longer be anything but understood," or, rather, implied "*sous-entendue,*" (Lacan 2002, 306).[2] It is by implication, through its prohibition by the Law, that *jouissance* emerges in the first place.[3]

Be this as it may, there is no enjoying worker in Marx's account of the present of secular capitalism, whose universe is populated either by "free" workers or non-working capitalists. For Marx, there are two kinds of labor, one defined quantitatively, and another qualitatively, but both are parts of the capitalist mode of production. The one is "abstract, human labour that . . . forms the value of commodities," while the other is labor "in a particular form and with a definite aim, and it is in this quality of being concrete useful labour that it produces use-values" (1990, 137). Engels thought he could make this distinction clearer by adding a footnote to the fourth German edition: "The English language has the advantage of possessing two separate words for these two different aspects of labour. Labour which creates use-values and is qualitatively determined is called 'work' as opposed to 'labour'; labour which creates value and is only measured quantitatively is called 'labour,' as opposed to 'work'" (Marx 1990, 138n16). If, as Ben Fowkes, the translator of the Penguin edition of *Capital*, Volume 1, notes, "unfortunately, English usage does not always correspond to Engels' distinction" (Marx 1990, 138, translator's note), this is so because both terms correspond to two aspects of one and the same labor, for it is this same concrete labor that produces use-values that is also the abstract labor embodied in the commodities during circulation as exchange-value. The laborer does not labor twice, once in order to produce use-value, and once more in order to produce exchange-value. A really distinct labor that does not partake in the capitalist mode of production would have to produce use-values that are inassimilable by exchange-value, and, by the same token, from the perspective of capital, useless use-values. The labor-power that is assimilated by capital always, in both its qualitative and its quantitative aspects, serves a purpose that is linked to needs and necessity—for the worker, the need to survive; for capital, the need to be exchanged with commodities in order to fulfill its destiny as capital, that is, to increase; for the others, the need to find in the market the products required for their own sustenance. Labor-power *qua* "[j]ouissance" proper, by contrast, "is what serves no purpose" (Lacan 1998, 3).

How is this distinction tenable, when, as we know all too well, everything serves a purpose, as the expression, "for the purpose of sheer pleasure," amply makes clear? The distinction in question is one between "purpose" as a goal in general and "purpose" defined in specifically utilitarian terms—a distinction of which Marx was clearly aware. When a certain amount of material goods, education, leisure, entertainment, and means to facilitate procreation, is seen as a prerequisite for the laborer to recover so that he is able to return and labor productively, then all these things fulfill a purpose *necessary* for the sustenance of capital (see Marx 1990, 274–277). Thus, far from being a useless excess or wasted surplus in the proper sense, everything, including sex and leisure, becomes the prerequisite for that which is not wasted surplus but surplus-value. This is why Hardt and Negri, among others, are right in describing capitalism as a system in which the proletariat (i.e., all of us) labors all day, as a result of which it would indeed be fair that we are paid for every single moment of our existence (see Hardt and Negri 2000, 401–403). Through the introduction of utilitarianism, all forms of enjoyment are subsumed under the yoke of utility and need, and should therefore be remunerated. What thereby falls entirely out of the picture, however, is precisely labor-power as one's enjoyment. One exists only in the service of capital and need/necessity, without any room for "useless" enjoyment.

Sexuality offers indeed a conspicuous example of the malleable and polymorphous reincarnations of "enjoyment" under the process of the utilitarian transformation, taking at times, as it used to do, the form of a means of reproduction, and at others, as in our days, in addition to that form, the form of an activity, among others, conducive to good health and well-being. Thereby, sexuality is transformed into necessity and duty, no less than are nowadays our dietary, hygienic, and athletic habits. The ultimate consequence of utilitarianism is the subjection of all life to the totalitarianism of need and necessity.

However, although this conclusion is true it is an error to mistake it for the ultimate principle of biopolitics. Admittedly, just as capital stands for exchangeability itself, and body for potentiality itself, utilitarianism stands for gaze-ability itself. That is, any object can exist insofar as it can be exchanged with capital; any body can be immortal insofar as it is the substratum of some commodifiable labor-power; and any gaze can survey the world insofar as it is itself supervised by the gaze of utilitarianism. The notorious tolerance of capitalist liberalism occurs only under the totalitarian auspices of utilitarianism, the ultimate, omni-seeing gaze of capitalist secular "objective knowledge." Yet, the fundamental inconsistency of this "objective knowledge" becomes evident in the inability to respond to the question: "What purpose does utility serve?" (Lacan 1998, 3). *The basic principle of biopolitics, therefore, is not utilitarianism but the fact that utilitarianism as a principle of life is inconsistent.* The effect of utilitarianism is not limited to rendering that which *would* be the subject's enjoyment (an enjoyment that serves no "purpose") impossible, but, because of its inconsistency, it also includes the fact that what emerges in the place of the subject's incapacitated enjoyment is the potent enjoyment of the (utilitarian) Other—the enjoyment utilitarianism derives from the fact that it is being sustained in spite of its inconsistency.

This transformation of enjoyment proper to the Other's enjoyment is already entailed in the concept of "usufruct" (from the Latin *usus* and *fructus*, which mean "use" and "enjoyment," respectively), "that is, a legal notion," introduced around 1630 to indicate the right to use and enjoy the profits of something belonging to another. Specifically, Lacan continues, to "have the usufruct of an inheritance" means that "you can enjoy the inheritance (*en jouir*) as long as you do not use up too much of it," that you "can enjoy (*jouir de*) your means, but must not waste them" (Lacan 1998, 3).[4] Through usufruct, the law's task becomes to constrain enjoyment within the boundaries of the useful, to make sure that it is not wasted. The "essence of law" in utilitarianism is "to divide up, distribute, or reattribute everything that counts as jouissance," so that the latter "is forbidden to him who speaks, as such," since "to speak" presupposes that the subject is subjected to the Law, and "the Law is grounded in this very prohibition" of "jouissance" (1998, 3; 1977, 319).

Enjoyment and Uncertainty

There is more to be said about enjoyment. For, in order to articulate in its entirety the homology between economic and semantic value within secular capitalism, we must map our central economic categories—surplus-value and labor-power, exchange-value and use-value—onto their equivalent set of concepts on the level of the signifier and the subject, as the "subject of the signifier" (Lacan 1981, 67). The latter is the cluster of enjoyment: surplus-enjoyment (*plus-de-jouir*), enjoyment-of-sense (*jouis-sens*), and enjoyment (*jouissance*).

Just as surplus-value is a specific historical modulation of surplus or being-in-itself-for-itself that manifests itself empirically as exchange-value and use-value, surplus-enjoyment, too, is a specific historical modulation of surplus that, as we shall presently see, manifests itself empirically in two modes. In its metaphysical dimension, as the specific historical modulation of surplus, surplus-enjoyment—as we have seen in the chapters "Historical and Transhistorical Aspects of Being" and "Aristotle's Discourses: Οικονομια versus Χρηματιστικη"—is the pure negativity of the Other's inconsistency, the gap because of which "objective knowledge" falls apart as inconsistent (in the first sense of the word, as lacking the ground that would make it appear as necessary rather than arbitrary). In this dimension, surplus-enjoyment corresponds to the gaze as the infinity of all possible points of view, under which ontic experience cannot decide what the Other wants, so that the Other remains inconsistent (also in the second sense of the word).[1] On the ontic level, surplus-enjoyment manifests itself as the specific gaze, fantasy, or Master-Signifier that is required for "objective knowledge" (*Darstellung*) to appear as (if it were) consistent. To return to our earlier example, the narrative of "primitive accumulation" can appear as a consistent diachronic genealogy of capitalism only insofar as there is in place a fantasy that

163

from the outset presupposes capitalism as the *telos* of history, or at least the *telos* of history thus far.

Through this fantasy, the circular logic of "primitive accumulation" appears as a consistent (diachronic) narrative, thereby offering the subject enjoyment-of-sense, in a double sense. First, the subject enjoys the meaningfulness of life, the impression that everything in life, and hence history, has a meaning and a *telos*—here the subject enjoys *sense* in the sense of *meaning*. Second, given that the subject is split and (unconsciously) knows that in truth life is meaningless (i.e., the Other is inconsistent), it devotes itself to the Other's "objective knowledge" not because it is indeed consistent but unconditionally, the same way a religious believer devotes herself to her faith. Here the subject enjoys not sense *qua* meaning (the Other remains inconsistent) but *sense* qua *bodily sensation*: the subject devotes itself to the narratives of the Other not because they make sense but because she feels organically linked to them, above and beyond reason and its arguments. In other words, *enjoyment-of-sense is the bridge that allows for the passage from significatory sense (*Darstellung*) to sensation, from the sign to the body (*Vertretung*), which is thereby constituted.*

The result is the enjoyment (*jouissance*) of the Other, which it derives from its appearance as consistent, or, what amounts to the same, from the fact that it sustains itself in spite of its inconsistency, since the subject is unconditionally devoted to it.

Enjoyment-of-sense (*jouis-sens*) and enjoyment (*jouissance*) are the two ontic modes in which surplus-enjoyment (*plus-de-jouir*) manifests itself empirically. Within the enjoyment-of-sense itself, its aspect of meaning corresponds to exchange-value—just as surplus-value must adjoin itself to exchange-value in order for money to become capital, the surplus of fantasy must adjoin itself to the arbitrary signs of *Darstellung* so that they appear consistent. In its aspect as sensation, enjoyment-of-sense is the bridge that links the arbitrary sign to the body, whereby the sign ceases to be arbitrary and obtains an organic link, which supplements *Darstellung* with *Vertretung*, thereby offering enjoyment to the Other by sustaining it. Because they involve and constitute the body, this aspect of enjoyment-of-sense and the enjoyment of the Other are the semantic homologues of use-value.

If Lacan calls "surplus-enjoyment" "*plus-de-jouir*," and not "*plus-jouissance*," which would be the exact correspondent to "*plus-value*" (surplus-value), it is in order to indicate—through the double meaning of "*plus-de-jouir*" as both "surplus-enjoyment" and "no more enjoyment"—that surplus-enjoyment (what Aristotle called enjoyment in excess) amounts to no enjoyment as far as the subject is concerned. Rather, it is the subject's sacrificial offering of enjoyment to the Other. The only enjoyment left to the subject is enjoyment-of-sense, the enjoyment in believing that the Other is consistent, coupled with the enjoyment in its sacrificial devotion to the Other, even as the subject (unconsciously) knows that the latter is inconsistent. As Lacan puts it: "The master [Other] in all this makes a small effort to make everything work, in other words, he gives an order. Simply by fulfilling his function as master he loses something," namely, as Aristotle teaches us, his dignity, since "a master's knowledge consists in knowing how to put his slaves to *use*" and "the use of slaves is not a form of knowledge that has any great importance or dignity" (Aristotle, 75; 1255b30). "It's at least through this something lost," Lacan continues, "that something of *jouissance* has to be rendered to him [Other]—specifically, surplus-*jouissance*" (2007, 107).

While, ontically, enjoyment-of-sense is the semantic homolog of exchange- and use-value, metaphysically it is the semantic equivalent of labor, insofar as both function as the bridge between *Darstellung* and *Vertretung*. On the one hand, labor is labor-power, which is *vertreten* (remunerated) at a price that is organically linked to it by "moral" standards of a society, and, on the other hand, labor is congealed labor, which is *dargestellt* (exchanged) at a price differentially and arbitrarily determined within circulation. Similarly, enjoyment-of-sense is, on the one hand, *vertreten* as the subject's "organic" link (unconditional devotion) to the Other, in spite of the latter's inconsistency, and, on the other hand, it is *dargestellt* as the Other's inconsistent "objective knowledge," which functions as (if it were) consistent precisely because of the above organic link, so that it is the Other that in the last analysis derives enjoyment from its being sustained as if it were consistent.

Labor and enjoyment-of-sense are the bridges, economic and semantic, respectively, through which value slides between *Darstellung* and *Vertretung*, taking the forms of both an arbitrary and fictional binary sign or value and of an organic link between a mark and a concept-thing, or, rather, a concept-body.

The *ethical* dimension is the suspension of the subject's sacrificial offering of its surplus-enjoyment to the Other, an act through which the inconsistency of the Other is revealed on the ontic level, whereby the subject refuses to continue to derive enjoyment-of-sense, and the Other can no longer enjoy its being sustained as if it were consistent. It is only on this dimension that the subject can gain his/her dignity and experience the enjoyment of the intellectual love of God, an enjoyment that neither serves the sustenance of the Other nor is of any use for the subject in its ontic dimensions, which are governed by the pleasure principle. While in its ethical dimension the subject assumes the gaze (all possible points of view under the species of eternity), *biopolitics*, as we have seen, offers a surrogate experience by offering in the place of this gaze the Master-Signifier of the specific gaze of uncertainty (which generates the sliding of gazes in diachrony). *By emulating the eternity of the gaze as an infinite series of gazes in diachrony, the Master-Signifier of uncertainty is mistaken for the gaze,* for the same reasons that eternity is mistaken for immortality, namely, the impossibility of the species of eternity to manifest itself as such on the ontic level.

The *uniqueness of the specific gaze* (Master-Signifier) *of uncertainty,* as opposed to all other specific gazes, lies in its ability to organize *Vertretung* in such a way that, even as its Marks entail as such a mortal body, they also allow for an indefinite sliding of gazes (*Darstellung*) under the auspices of the overseeing gaze of uncertainty, in the web of which the subject is caught, forgetting the presupposed specific gaze of uncertainty that enables the sliding of gazes in the first place. The Master-*Vertretungs*-Mark of the gaze of uncertainty is the specific primary repression that allows for all other (secondary) repressions by means of which the subject comes to identify itself as purely exchange-value or binary sign, and which, thus, foster the illusion of immortality. Being *certain* of its uncertainty, the gaze of *uncertainty* is conspicuously inconsistent. Yet, its inconsistency "does not show," as its greatest sleight-of-hand consists in *presenting certainty as an impossibility*: we live in an era in which claims to truth, to the extent that they dare at all to be raised, can legitimately be voiced only in the humble aura of historico-cultural relativism, in all oblivion of the haughty certainty of this relativism itself. Any other appearance of truth is perceived as an arrogant and preposterous eruption of something past (not only passé but regressive or primitive) into the present—a fact which, of course, does not prevent this past from being projected onto any present place on the globe (something to which we shall return in the last chapter of the present work). The sublimity of uncertainty lies in *halting the self-referentiality of being*, that is, in closing the not-all set of being by posing an exception: Everything is uncertain only under the precondition of one exception—the absolute certainty that everything is uncertain.[2] This applies also to the gazes of all cognates of uncertainty, such as radical doubt, relativism, pluralism, insofar as they can admit any specific gaze except the one for which not anything is relative, doubtable, and ultimately deconstructible (i.e., reducible to anything beyond the signifier). This interpretation of Jacques Derrida's famous "there is nothing outside of the text [there is no outside-text; *il n'y a pas de hors-texte*]" ends up assuming that there is no outside-*Darstellung*, no *Vertretung*, and hence no death (158). This is why we should be reminded that, to recall Lacan's words, "if beyond appearance there is nothing in itself, there is the gaze," that is, the infinity of all possible gazes because of which being is a self-referential not-all that cannot be reduced to a closed set, at least not with impunity (1981, 103). While being is self-referential, the fundamental matrix of uncertainty and all its cognates is a *distortion of the not-all* that transmogrifies the *infinity of all possible gazes sub specie aeternitatis* into an ontic *indefinite diachronic sliding of gazes*.

All other known ontic gazes are not structured in the fashion of the gaze of radical uncertainty. This is true not only of radical certainty (say, fanaticism) but also of partial certainty, as in the gaze under which some things are certain and others are not. That is, such gazes are not based on the structure of the closed set that presupposes an exception that contradicts them. (If these gazes are inconsistent, they are so not on the level of their precondition.) But it is precisely because of its blatant inconsistency that the gaze of uncertainty constitutes the ideal gaze under which subjects are enticed to offer their surplus-enjoyment to the Other, in order to sustain it as (if it were) consistent. *Uncertainty is the discourse par excellence of secular capitalist modernity.*

The centrality of uncertainty in secular capitalist modernity is not irrelevant to the fact that secular philosophy was inaugurated by *Descartes' method of "radical doubt."* Its epitome, as we have seen, is the inevitable anxiety that a malign spirit might deceive us into believing that all things we perceive in the world exist, when in truth they may be sheer illusion. The moment thought takes the leap to the secular mode, that is, the moment it decides to ground the existent not on an absolutely transcendent God but on immanence, it cannot avoid raising the question as to whether it is deceived in accepting what perception offers it. This inevitable secular suspicion of a deceiving malign spirit is the cause of, in Lacan's words: "the social dialectic that structures human knowledge as paranoiac" (1977, 3). By "paranoiac" is, of course, meant here not a clinically pathological state but a structure marking "normal" secular subjectivity, such as when one cannot be certain whether one's interlocutor is telling the truth or attempting to deceive—a question that, after God's secular "death," extends itself to the Other, in the metaphysical sense. Which is why in order to prove that his perceptions are not deceiving him, Descartes had eventually to reintroduce God through the back door, as it were. If I am deceivable and, hence, imperfect, in order not to be deceived there must be some other perfect being that shows me truth and not illusion, therefore, God must exist, for only God "cannot be a deceiver," since "He" alone is perfect, and "the natural light teaches us that deceit stems from some defect" (Descartes, 131; "Third Meditation"). We are in the realm of *logos*: Descartes' reasoning is secular precisely because it is circular, presupposing what it purports to prove: "I can be certain only if there is God; therefore, beyond my imperfection, there must be perfection; therefore there is God, q. e. d."

The "extraordinary consequences," as Lacan puts it, "that have stemmed from this handing back of truth into the hands of the other, in this instance, the perfect God," become evident only once reason becomes, in the next, Spinozian, step, fully secular, that is, once this "perfect God" is no longer the creator but the immanent cause of the world (1981, 36). At that point—which constitutes a veritable historical shift—God becomes the unconscious of secular reason. For how could secular reason ever find certainty as to whether or not the Other wants to deceive us unless it presupposes a guarantee beyond and above all linear deduction? The difference between presecular and secular thought lies not in the elimination of the function of God but in its transformation from an *a priori* conscious assumption to a retroactive unconscious presupposition. The immediate consequence in the latter case is that, no longer being the biblical Creator, the "perfect God, whose truth is the nub of the matter," can allow anything to pass as truth, "since, whatever he might have meant, would always be *the* truth—even if he had said that two and two make five, it would have been true" (Lacan 1981, 36). That truth becomes arbitrary means that any gaze can appropriate the function of the gaze of the Other, thereby inaugurating the era of secular biopolitics. While the presecular God guarantees the actual existence of anything perceived, including the body, secular bodies are doomed to uncertainty as to whether they are illusory or actually existing—unless they are offered a gaze that gives them certainty as to their existence.

But, conversely, they remain illusory if what is offered them is not the gaze of the perfect, non-deceiving God, but that of the malign spirit that condemns us to radical uncertainty. In the secular ironic twist, *God's certainty is also the certainty of actual, physical, existence and, hence, of mortality.* The heaven of *secular immortality*, therefore, *can be reached only in the absence of a perfect God, in radical uncertainty.*

Part III

Biocinema and Bioracism

Biocinema

A Drop in Total Recall

It would perhaps be impossible to produce an exhaustive list of concrete biopolitical mechanisms that permeate our culture and life. In the following I will try to present just one example that is by no means either comprehensive or even necessarily the most representative, but at least indicative of possible concrete ways in which the biopolitical cultivation of uncertainty, as the guarantor of immortality, can take place through the medium of film. Postmodern films (and literature) are more often than not renditions of the Cartesian doubt as to whether reality exists as we perceive it or our perception thereof is an illusion. Think of Hollywood blockbusters such as *Blade Runner* (1982) (and, of course, generally Philip K. Dick's novels, whose *A Scanner Darkly* also became a film, in 2006), *Lost Highway* (1997), *The Matrix* (1999) and its sequels, *Fight Club* (1999), *Being John Malkovich* (1999), *Memento* (2000), *Mulholland Drive* (2001), *The Final Cut* (2004), *Inland Empire* (2006), and more recently, *Inception* (2010). As a rule, through the devices of amnesia, memory or dream implants, alter egos, among others, these films pivot around an unresolved uncertainty as to whether what is presented to us as reality or as a certain character is indeed what we take them to be. To be sure, moments of certainty abound in these films, but only momentarily, as they are always taken back for the sake of another possible certainty, and the substitutions could theoretically go on *ad infinitum*. *Blade Runner*'s subtle finale with its lingering insinuation that the replicants' terminator (significantly named "Deckard," [Harrison Ford]) might himself be a replicant is a representative example. And, as the following example will show, the divine gaze required for the status of reality to be bestowed, however transiently, on the objects of perception no longer needs to emanate from the heavens, as was the case in Descartes' time. Rather, it may as well make its surreptitious entry through the lowly earthly human body, including its secretions.

To exemplify this point I turn to one scene from Paul Verhoeven's *Total Recall* (1990), whose plot up until that scene can be summarized as follows. Quaid (Arnold Schwarzenegger), a construction worker, goes to "Total Recall," a company that transplants memories, so that, as the film has it, one can have the memory of a vacation on a planet other than Earth without the hassles involved in real transportation and vacations. After Quaid has undergone a memory transplant of a vacation on Mars, both he and the audience are uncertain as to whether what happens in the rest of the film takes place within this imaginary vacation or in Quaid's real life. Both he and we gradually understand that in his past he had been Hauser, the leader of the revolution on Mars against its exploitative tyrant, Cohegan—but both he and we remain uncertain as to whether or not this past identity, fully erased from Quaid's present memory, yet fully reconfirmed by characters whom Quaid encounters on Mars, is also part of the "Total Recall" transplant.

At that point, a psychiatrist from "Total Recall" shows up in Quaid's hotel room on Mars, to try to convince him that he is Quaid, still "strapped on a transplant chair" at "Total Recall" on earth, "dreaming" all this adventure on Mars—including the psychiatrist who, according to himself, is "artificially implanted as an emergency measure" in order to help Quaid overcome his "free-form delusion"—and not "an invincible secret agent from Mars who is the victim of an interplanetary conspiracy to make him think that he is a lowly construction worker," as the psychiatrist sarcastically puts it. The psychiatrist delivers his lines under the threat of Quaid's gun pressed against his head, and as Quaid (and presumably the spectator) is gradually leaning toward believing the psychiatrist, the camera, slowly but dramatically, zooms on a drop of sweat on the psychiatrist's forehead. This minute, yet cinematographically magnified, drop provides Quaid with the absolute certainty that he is not dreaming, and thus allows him to escape his Cartesian radical doubt with a gesture that might lack the philosophical subtleties of a Descartes but not the resolute determination worthy of both specifically Schwarzenegger's cinematographic persona and generally the contemporary renditions of the Sci-Fi action genre: the close-up is abruptly cut by a shot of Quaid shooting the psychiatrist in his forehead.

Crucially, if this drop of sweat functions as the gaze providing Quaid with his longed-for certainty that he is not dreaming this is due to the fact that its function as evidence of reality is utterly ungrounded or arbitrary. Given that life in "memory transplants," as "Total Recall" advertisements reassure us throughout the film, is indistinguishable from real life, shouldn't the psychiatrist sweat under the pressure of an Arnold-held gun on his forehead, regardless of whether they both are transplants or real? In truth, the secretion of the drop proves nothing, which is why we, the audience, are simply shocked by Quaid's shot at the moment of its occurrence, and can only retroactively, after the shot, and due to the editing sequence, see in the drop of sweat the source of Quaid's certainty. *If* we accept it as a proof of reality it is not because of its consistency but because our identification with Quaid, who has accepted it as (if it were) an undeniable (consistent) proof of reality, invites us to offer to the narrative of the film our surplus-enjoyment: the fantasy that only a "real" man could sweat and not a man as he appears in his own "fantasy" under the influence of a memory transplant.

The film needs no surplus-enjoyment, however, in order to convince us that the proverbial "God is in the details," such as a tiny drop, is true. The jacket of the film's Artisan Home Entertainment videotape stresses the point: "The attention to detail paid off and the film won the Academy Award for Special Achievement in Visual Effects." By contrast, the organ whose attachment to or detachment from Quaid determines whether the objects of his (and our) perception are gazed by a benevolent or malign spirit, is represented in the film by nothing smaller than Arnold's entire body. If his experience as a revolutionary leader in a hotel room on Mars is, as the psychiatrist argues, a sheer illusion caused by a memory transplant, then the self who lives this experience is totally disembodied, since his body is actually not in that room but in the "transplant chair" of Total Recall. At the moment the psychiatrist's drop of sweat becomes for Quaid the proof that his experience in the hotel room is not an illusion, Quaid's body is transplanted from the Earth to Mars. While in uncertainty, Quaid's body in the hotel room on Mars may be not a mortal body but, as the psychiatrist argues, a technological product: an immortal image, artificially generated by a memory transplant. By contrast, the moment certainty is established through the psychiatrist's drop of sweat, mortality is suddenly introduced in Quaid's universe, as the immediate subsequent death of the psychiatrist startlingly foregrounds.

This gaze, according to which only "real" people sweat while the disembodied images of their bodies do not, administers the organic links that constitute the Marks of the system of *Vertretung* within the filmic universe, and which allow for the sliding from *Darstellung*'s domain of meaning to the sensuous realm of *Vertretung*, required for our unconditional commitment to its "objective knowledge." Cardinal in *Total Recall* feature two Marks: on the one hand, the organic link between technology and uncertainty (and hence immortality), and, on the other, (inappropriate) bodily secretion and certainty (and hence mortality). Thus the film enacts the following biopolitical configuration of enjoyment-of-sense: an unconditional commitment to technology and uncertainty, as the guarantor of immortality, and the corollary abjection of bodily secretion and certainty, as fatal indexes of mortality.

Although secular reason remains throughout Cartesian with regard to its paranoiac character, biopolitics is post-Cartesian, as it were, with regard to its treatment of the relation between (mortal) body and (immortal) soul. To safeguard immortality, Descartes had to separate the body from the soul and to align the latter with God as the guarantor of both certainty and immortality. Once the historical block of disequilibrium has however been fully established through both a (Spinozian) non-creationist conception of God, as the immanent cause of the world, and the population of the market by the "free" sellers of labor-power, the questions of certainty and (im)mortality begin to play out along the lines of the following arrangement: on the one hand, there is the negative, dematerialized, technological body, which is an immortal image that remains such as long as it is not attached with certainty to any self or identity (soul); and, on the other hand, there is the certain, organic link between this self or identity (soul) and a body which thereby becomes material and, hence, mortal. The *Cartesian dualism between body and soul* is presupposed as much for Descartes as for biopolitics, but now *the self or soul*, the certainty of identity, *becomes the very enemy of the body as the tabernacle of immortality.*

The fact that the body itself, once separated from its self, becomes the site of immortality is particularly apparent in the scene in which Arnold-*qua*-Hauser (the past self) addresses Arnold-*qua*-Quaid (the present self) through a laptop screen, directing him to extricate from his skull the "bug" through which Cohegan and his cronies trace him. As Quaid, in apparent pain, pulls a disproportionately huge bug out of his nostril,

Hauser's recorded voice tenderly cautions him: "Be careful! . . . It's my head too." Quaid's self presupposes the death of Hauser's self, but the "head" survives this death and becomes an immutable substance claimed by both selves. The self must split itself into at least two selves for the body to remain non-material, immortal. *The illusion of immortality in the secular capitalist block presupposes, in addition to the dualism of body and soul, the multiple splitting of the soul itself.*

The celebrated postmodern fragmented subjectivity is part and parcel of the biopolitical promise of immortality. Having replaced traditional conceptions of immortality—as the transmigration of an eternal soul to either another world or from one body to another—with the *transmigration of an eternal body from one identity (soul) to another*, the film reinforces the secular capitalist fantasy of the body as *an immortal negativity that must frantically keep hopping from identity to identity* in order to sustain its status as such. *Identity or the soul is thereby reduced to sheer exchange-value.* It is for this reason that, in its relatively short life, secular epistemology had gradually to demote Truth from the level of absoluteness to that of relativism, where there is only a *multiplicity of exchangeable truths,* each sharing the same "rights" as any other. The empire of the value that involves disequilibrium is also the reign of the commodification of truth. As Karatani succinctly puts it: "capitalism itself is deconstructive" (1995, 71). This means not simply that, as Derrida reminds us, "the movements of deconstruction do not destroy structures *from the outside*," but that the movements of deconstruction do not destroy structures *tout court* (24). Deconstruction only destroys the imaginary stuff that fills in the sites within a structure.

This illusion of the immortality of the body through its reincarnations under theoretically infinite identities (exchange-values) is further intensified through the star system itself, with its interfilmic reappearance of one and the same, ideally immutable (fit), body that always comes back under different identities. To repeat, although the present work is not the place to examine them, there are innumerable mechanisms that foster the illusion of the immortality of the body within postmodernity, covering a wide spectrum from all forms of pop culture and everyday practices (with the fitness industry and medicine, cosmetic and not, in their center) to "high" literature and theory, up to and including science, whose vernacular representations often offer the promise of immortality as the bait for obtaining unconditional devotion.[1] This is becoming increasingly true of the mainstream representations of biogenetic DNA reproduction, with Roger Spottiswoode's *The 6th Day* (2000) (another Schwarzenegger film) being one of its most pronounced filmic examples.

Let us recapitulate the logic of secular immortality, including in its relation to the transhistorical aspects of immortality. Immortality is transhistorically predicated on a split between body and soul or self (which is why, as an aside, Spinoza's radical repudiation of this split had to meet such a vehement resistance from both Christian and Jewish institutions). The creationist conception of God allows for the certainty of the immortal soul. Once God becomes a gaze that must emanate from earthly immanence, the body itself becomes the tabernacle of immortality, under the condition that it does not fix itself to an unsubstitutable soul. Thereby, mortality is relegated to *Vertretung*, where "God's" gaze guarantees the certainty of the organic bond between body and soul. To sustain the illusion of immortality, therefore, biopolitics must prevent any gaze from fixing itself as the gaze of the "perfect God," something which would establish the certainty of such organic bonds. Gazes must keep circulating, so that souls can also circulate through a body that thus becomes immortal. *Biopolitics makes use of the fact that the God who is unconscious is the imperfect God of uncertainty.*

Because uncertainty must have the ultimate word beyond and above any momentary certainty offered to the film viewers, a new kind of popular denouement had eventually to be invented in our historical block. *Blade Runner's* ultimate uncertainty about Deckard's nature as a human or not is structurally not different than the doubt introduced at the very end of *Total Recall*: Quaid and his female revolutionary companion rush to kiss right before the final credits begin to unfold on the screen, out of fear that Quaid might after all turn out to be, not unlike the spectators of the film sitting in their Hollywood "dream transplant" seats, strapped in Total Recall's chair, only dreaming of the victorious revolution. The end of the film transforms the earlier certainty, provided by the gaze of the psychiatrist's drop of sweat, into yet another possible truth within a plurality of truths. The two alternative truths insert Truth into a *mise-en-abyme* that not only makes the film open-ended but also opens the path toward its sequel. Seriality—capitalism's mode of production (as well as one of the conditions for structure)—has as its epistemological double uncertainty.[2]

The standard leftist critique of *Total Recall's* denouement is well known: the film is conformist because, even though its plot presupposes and stages a point of development in capitalism that leads to such an aggravation of the workers' conditions of life that the revolution occurs, and even though the revolution is eventually presented as victorious, the film's denouement subverts this message by reintroducing uncertainty as to whether all this is a sheer reverie caused by the Total-Recall-Hollywood "dream transplant." According to the present argument, however, even if Quaid's life on Mars were not guided by a revolutionary mission, even if his mission on Mars were only to hunt exotic Martian animals, the film would still be conformist, as long as it would conclude inconclusively, reinserting its eventual declaration of truth into a *mise-en-abyme* of radical uncertainty.

The biopolitical function of uncertainty forces us to revise the traditional notion of the "happy ending." A properly secular capitalist happy ending does not consist in the certainty of a happy future but in a radical uncertainty thanks to which the same story could be retold indefinite times, without an ultimate anchoring point that could bring this eternal recurrence of the same to a halt. The allusion here is not Nietzsche but Marx: truth is yet another exchange-value "appropriate for commencing the valorization [*Verwertung*] process" in a constantly "renewed movement," in which "the movement of [both] capital [and truth] is therefore limitless" (Marx 1990, 252–253).

Postmodern Bioracism

Exporting Mortality

Whether we call the object of biopolitics "gaze" or "labor-power" or "surplus-enjoyment," we always refer to a single biopolitical mechanism: the administration of the subject's relation to mortality and immortality. Several Lacanian theorists have begun to stress the centrality of enjoyment as a factor in the sustenance of capitalism, but the biopolitical essence of enjoyment as a factor in producing and sustaining the illusion of immortality is not addressed. Yet, the latter lurks in the background as the inevitable logical consequence of some of their arguments. The first step in grasping the logic of the secular capitalist subjectivity consists, of course, as Yannis Stavrakakis has argued, in shifting the emphasis from so-called "false needs" to the administration of desires and enjoyment (see Stavrakakis 2003). And, as Todd McGowan remarks, in consumer society, "the moment of acquiring the object represents the end, not the beginning, of our enjoyment" (2004, 3). For, as Ceren Özselçuk and Yahya Madra infer from McGowan's position, "consumption as a means of enjoyment is bound to fail," but "this dissatisfaction is not a reason to abandon shopping"; on the contrary: "as long as the subjects of capitalism continue to believe that an ultimate enjoyment is possible, capitalism will continue to feed off of the very disappointment that the act of consumption produces[,] and shopping will go on ceaselessly" (82). Bringing together Özselçuk/Madra's and McGowan's insights, we can infer that if shopping goes on forever it is because each act of shopping, each acquisition of the object, puts an end to enjoyment, and that enjoyment can therefore emerge only in the anticipation or the potentiality of shopping, which must then start anew after each of its actualizations. Enjoyment is possible only if actualization is subordinated to the subsequent moment of potentialization, and hence only if life goes on forever.

But in the last chapter of the present work I would like to approach another mechanism of the biopolitical administration of surplus-enjoyment, which is at least as crucial as consumerism, and which directly relates to the question whether, and how, the postmodern or advanced capitalist mode of production effects the mechanisms of biopolitics. Michael Hardt and Antonio Negri have argued that in today's informatized capitalism, which is dominated by "the computerization of production" and its "immaterial labor":

> the heterogeneity of concrete labor [say, tailoring versus weaving, to refer to two of Marx's favorite examples] has tended to be reduced. . . . [All kinds of labor] involve exactly the same concrete practices—that is, manipulation of symbols and information. . . . Through the computerization of production, then, labor tends toward the position of abstract labor. (2000, 292)

Now, one could justifiably object to Hardt and Negri's argument that, as we have seen Marx argue, labor-power, whether it uses weaving machines, needles, book printers or computers, is sheer "potentiality," that is, "abstract," and has been so not since the shift from industrial to informatized capitalism but since the inception of capitalism. Yet, there is a grain of truth in Hardt and Negri's observation, namely, there has indeed been a shift through the computerization of production; not, however, a shift from material to immaterial or from actual to potential labor, but one in which the first shift introduced by capitalism, which transplanted the abstract concept of potentiality into the empirical socioeconomic field, now *metastasizes beyond labor itself to infest the raw material of the means of production, as well as the products of production*: symbols, information, in short, language. While in the past, the material means of production were, as such, subject to the linear time of physical decay—production-time—now this realm is colonized by abstract symbols, "language and communication" (Hardt and Negri 2000, 404), and, hence, is imbued by their temporality: synchrony or circulation-time. This would mean, to return to the "general formula for capital," that if in the past, production-time and its material objects (C) were eliminated from the formula M—C—M′ so that it appeared as M—M′, only because they were repressed or fetishistically disavowed, now they *appear* to have been actually eliminated.

This conclusion is true only insofar as it describes one of the several biopolitical illusions—hence "*appear*" in italics—that occur in the translation or the transition from the metaphysical to the ontic level, not unlike the one that, as we have seen, allows (metaphysical) eternity to appear ontically as immortality. For, as we saw in the chapter "Matter," ontologically, in their function as raw materials and products (use-values), information, language, and all symbols or semantic values, however (classically) immaterial they may be, are not the for-itself but the in-itself. It is because the ontic level is still conceived and described in ways that differentiate the in-itself from the for-itself on the basis of chemical criteria, that one tends to assume that language and its cognates are immaterial (the for-itself), regardless of whether they occupy a position in the process of production or in circulation. Thus, the illusion is produced that late or informatized capitalism constitutes in its entirety a universe of immortal immaterial values in circulation-time, with no room for the in-itself, production-time, and mortality (except, as we have seen, as exiled in a presumed transcendence of oppressive imperial biopower *qua* thanatopolitics).

But if one accepts that the generation and sustenance of this secular illusion of immortality is indeed a central biopolitical mechanism that finds its culmination in informatized capitalism, then one will have to undermine its generality or universality. To see why, let us examine further Hardt and Negri's argument. They "distinguish three types of" informatized labor: (1) "industrial production," which too "has been informationalized"; (2) the "labor of analytical and symbolic tasks"; and (3) the "production and manipulation of affect" (2000, 293). The latter two dominate the mode of production in advanced capitalist countries, while the first, "industrial production[,] has declined in the dominant countries [and] has been effectively exported to subordinate countries, from the Unites States and Japan, for example, to Mexico and Malaysia." This difference, Hardt and Negri continue, "should not lead us back to an understanding of the contemporary global economic situation in terms of linear stages of development," which would assume, for instance, that "an auto factory built by Ford in Brazil in the 1990s might be comparable to a Ford factory in Detroit in the 1930s." For, unlike the latter, the factory in Brazil today is "based on the most advanced and most productive computer and informational technologies available" (287). However true this may be, the difference between the two worlds remains *incommensurable as far as the biopolitical illusion is concerned,* whose success depends on *sustaining the classical distinction between the in-itself and the for-itself,* according to which cars are taken for material and information for immaterial objects, even when they both function as use-values. For the biopolitical machine of secular immortality to function, industrial products—however informationalized their mode of production may be—must be perceived as material, while the products of analytical and symbolic or affect production must be perceived as immaterial, including in their aspect as use-values. And this means that in certain parts of today's world—the subordinate countries, and, possibly considerable subordinate pockets of population within the dominant countries—the (perceived) materiality of the products determines the collective and individual imaginary in ways that provide their inhabitants with access to production-time and mortality. By contrast, in the advanced capitalist countries, in which the dominant mode of production tends to involve only (so the illusion goes) "abstract" raw materials and products, circulation-time becomes the dominant, increasingly exclusive, mode of temporality, reassuring ever increasing parts of this population of their immortality. In short, what *the dominant countries are exporting,* along with industrial production, *is mortality.*

We have seen that throughout capitalism, the two *representable* sides of capitalist circulation exhaust themselves within *Darstellung*: on the one hand, there is the commodity, *not* as an object of utility, but as abstract exchange-value, and, on the other hand, there is direct exchange-value (capital), whereby objects of utility (C) drop out of circulation, and the movement of capital appears in its abridged form, as M—M'. The representation of the commodity as an object of utility, like that of the specific commodity of labor-power *qua* use-value—*Vertretung*—remains repressed. The informatization of production in late capitalism consummates this repression, as its raw materials and products are (mis)taken for abstract values. Thus, the universe of informatized capital comes to appear as the exclusive kingdom of circulation-time, out of which materiality and mortality are finally exorcised.

In such a global world configuration, when, in spite of everything, specific gazes do erupt with their claims to certainty—and their concomitant threat of mortality—they are expectedly perceived as manifestations of (repressed) *Vertretung*, that is, as signs of a presecular mode of representation which is the past "other" of our own world. What is more, such gazes are even denied as our past, as this *Vertretung* is invariably projected, depending on the current political situation, onto any "subordinate" part of the present world. Žižek's comments, in his comparison of the representation of the collapse of the World Trade Center towers and the representation of death and violence in the Third World, are not irrelevant to this biopolitical dualistic use of *Darstellung* and *Vertretung*:

> A "derealization" of the horror went on after the WTC collapse: while the number of victims—3,000—is repeated all the time, it is surprising how little of the actual carnage we see—no dismembered bodies, no blood, no desperate faces of dying people . . . in clear contrast to reporting on Third World catastrophes, where the whole point is to produce a scoop of some gruesome detail: Somalis dying of hunger, raped Bosnian women, men with their throats cut. These shots are always accompanied by an advance warning that "some of the images you will see are extremely graphic and may upset children"—a warning which we never heard in the reports on the WTC collapse. Is this not yet further proof of how, even in this tragic moment, the distance which separates Us from Them, from their reality, is maintained: the real horror happens *there*, not *here*? (2002, 13)

When it comes to "Us," death is represented vicariously in the representations of immortality that make us "begin to experience 'real reality' itself as a virtual entity": "For the great majority of the public, the WTC explosions were" not only fairly bloodless events, but also "events on the TV screen . . . reminiscent of spectacular shots in catastrophic movies," so that there would be "an element of truth" in inferring that "the 'terrorists' themselves did not do it primarily to provoke real material damage, but *for the spectacular effect of it*" (Žižek 2002, 11). When it comes to "Them," though, things change drastically, so that "their reality" in its entirety is represented exclusively as "real horror." I would only add to Žižek's commentary that, for biopolitics, the "real horror" by now includes even the most natural death.

In one of their characteristically optimistic moments, Hardt and Negri conclude that because of its "cooperative interactivity through linguistic, communicational, and affective networks . . . immaterial labor . . . seems to provide the potential for a kind of spontaneous and elementary communism" (2000, 294). I wish they were right . . . but this will not be my conclusion. Mine will pass through Foucault's afore-cited observation that: "racism . . . is in fact inscribed in the workings of all . . . modern States" (i.e., all biopolitical states). Foucault also added that the racism in question is "not a truly ethnic racism, but racism of the evolutionist kind, biological racism." He had in mind the administration of life and death, "the idea that the essential function of society or the State, or whatever it is that must replace the State, is to take control of life, to explore and reduce biological accidents and possibilities" (2003, 260–262). I think we are way beyond that point. The level on which biopolitics operates is not biology; rather, it is surplus-enjoyment. Just as its true agenda, whatever other tasks it may perform in the process, is to administer not (actual) death and life but (illusions of) mortal-ity and immortality. And the racism in question is certainly not "truly ethnic" but also not "biological"; it is properly biopolitical—a biora-cism, in which the super-biorace of the immortals launch war against the sub-biorace of the mortals. For, if in the late informatized capitalist mode of production, "humans" means immortals, then mortals are not humans—and, then, the immortals feel entitled to kill with impunity the mortals. Today this battle is called the "war against terrorism"; tomorrow it may have another name. But, whatever its name, it is a bioracial war.

Notes

Preface

1. In another work I focus on the differences between Sartre and Heidegger, which, I argue, lie primarily in the fact that the gaze, as well as the unconscious, are operative in Sartre's theory but not in Heidegger's (with important consequences for their respective conceptions of historical time) (see Kordela forthcoming).

2. Incidentally, this revised conception of representation entirely bypasses the problematic set up by Quentin Meillassoux, as the impasse of "correlationism," that is, the idea held by all post-critical or post-Kantian philosophy, "according to which we only ever have access to the correlation between thinking and being, and never to either term considered apart from the other" (Meillassoux, 5). This post-critical premise, as Meillassoux argues, causes correlationism's inability to conceive of an "absolute reality [that] is an *entity without thought*," and, hence, to take at face value scientific statements about "any reality anterior to the emergence of the human species," such as "the age of the universe, the formation of stars, or the accretion of the earth" (36, 26, and 10). It is because Meillassoux, not unlike the orthodox post-critical tradition that he criticizes, equates thought with human consciousness that he deems necessary the intervention of what has been termed "speculative materialism," that is, the claim to the existence of "absolute reality" beyond and prior to thought. But if one understands that thought is value, that is, a system of differential relations that is itself beyond and prior to consciousness, already pertaining to "absolute reality," then one does not need the presence of consciousness—"an 'ancestral witness,' an attentive God," as Meillassoux puts it, "who turns every event into a phenomenon"—in order to take "ancestral statements" at face value (10–11). For, as we shall see in the main body of this work, to say that representation or thought is value and, hence, to comprehend that it involves not only linguistic signs but also exchange-values, amounts to acknowledging that "absolute reality" or nature itself thinks—which, to avoid misunderstandings, is far from

claiming that nature has consciousness. I shall not elaborate any further here on the inadequacy of Meillassoux's position, as I am doing so in my current book project, under the tentative title "Biosemantics," particularly in the introductory section "In Response to Contemporary Debates."

Part I   Monist Meta-Phenomenological Ontology

Being and Time

1. I intentionally use the term "flesh" here to allude to the fact that it was on the basis of Sartre's exposition of the gaze that Maurice Merleau-Ponty developed his own theory of the gaze as the "flesh of the world," according to which the body is inseparable from the rest of the world, and which (theory) was, along with Sartre, a major inspiration for Lacan's concept of the gaze in his eleventh seminar (see Merleau-Ponty).

Monist Being and Atheism

1. Unless otherwise noted, brackets in quotations are mine.
2. Methodologically, the present work relies heavily on the construction of expanding chains of equivalent terms. In this operation, the conceptual distinction between the terms within a chain of equations must be maintained alongside with their quasi-synonymity. That is, each term must retain its distinctiveness, and yet it must at all times bear within it, as a potential that can at any time be reactivated, the further properties attributed to it by all other members of the chain of equation of which it is part. The inevitability with which this approach marks the present work owes at least partly to its conceptual reliance on Lacan's work, in which, as Jameson discerningly observes, there is a "slippage of meanings within the space of A," as, for instance, the space of the "Symbolic" order in Lacan, or of the entire series of appearances here, which "might better be thought of as a shifting of gears from one power or logic to another." This transition between powers or logics "is predicated on this very 'chain or ladder of signifieds'" that are linked together and allow for a "movement [from an old space] into a new space," such that it "carries properties of the old along with it" (Jameson 2006, 288–289). However, one of the intentions of the present work is to designate as explicitly as possible the specific plateau in which a term is used each time, by inserting it in its, at times momentary and at times more permanent, epistemological or ontological frame. Such designations may include the distinction between immanence and transcendence or, as we shall see later, attributive and modal levels, and entail that all equivalent terms associated with the term in question should

also be conceived at that given instance in the same frame, with all entailed modifications. I hope this sounds in the abstract more complicated than it is in its concrete applications.

Value—Being—Surplus

1. Though it should be added that, as I point out elsewhere, the inception of unconscious thought in philosophical discourse is to be found already in Friedrich Wilhelm Joseph Schelling's 1800 work, *System of Transcendental Idealism* (see also Kordela 2013).

2. More extensively, Marx distinguishes circulation-time from production-time as follows: "*Circulation time* is the part of capital which may be regarded as the time it takes to perform its specific motion as capital, as distinct from production time, in which it reproduces itself; and in which it lives not as finished capital which must merely pass through formal metamorphoses, but as capital-in-process, creative capital, sucking its living soul out of labour" (1993, 660). In circulation-time, the "metamorphoses" of capital—"transformation of commodity into money, transformation of money into commodity, etc."—are purely "formal," for there capital is already "finished capital," that is, even the material objects we call commodities can enter the space and temporality of circulation taken only as exchange-values, abstract symbols with no inherent material qualities (660). By contrast, unfinished "capital-in-process" lives in the space and time of production, in which it is "creative," producing products out of concrete materials and the specific "labour" of human laborers, its "living soul," both of which are subject to physical decay. Production-time is marked by "*continuity*," while circulation time "is the *interruption* of continuity" brought about by "capital as circulating," and whose tendency is "*circulation without circulation time*," that is, simultaneity or synchronicity, a mode of time in which the instant and infinity coincide (663 and 659). In short, in production-time everything has a finite life within continuous linear time, while in circulation-time everything is an immaterial, unaging, immortal abstraction.

3. As we shall see later, there is room for the being-in-itself-for-itself also in Sartre's phenomenology, but only as a human ideal (moral value), rather than as the fundamental structure of being, which, as such alone can explain the emergence of this human ideal.

Historical Time

1. See Macherey 1979 or 2011; for an earlier English translation of the second chapter of this book, see Macherey 1997.

2. See Kordela 2006. In this article I also present a critique of stage theories of capitalist development, a critical elaboration of Gilles Deleuze's con-

ceptualization of time as presented in his two cinema books, and a critique of the teleological conception of historical time developed by Michael Hardt and Antonio Negri in *Empire*, a more extensive version of which is included in my book *$urplus: Spinoza, Lacan* (see Deleuze 1991 and 1995; Hardt and Negri 2000; and Kordela 2007).

3. Although never referred to as such, Freud's "belatedness [*Nachträglichkeit*]" is an application of immanent causality on history (see "Aus der Geschichte einer infantilen Neurose," particularly chapter 4: "Der Traum und die Urszene," in Freud, Vol. XII, 54–75). One can arguably read Benjamin's conception of history also as a rearticulation of immanent causality, even as other readings are also offered, as we shall briefly see in the chapter "Historiographical Project." Whether properly or not, this Spinozian conception of history has had, notably since Louis Althusser, a significant impact on a line of Leftist thinkers (regarding Althusser, see 1996, particularly the section "The Historical Problem," 71–86).

4. In making this distinction between empirical fantasy and real fantasy I am alluding to the distinction between fantasy as ideological illusion and primary fantasy as the mechanism through which the subject and the object (reality) are constituted as distinct. This mechanism of the primary fantasy, as Jean Laplanche and J. B. Pontalis have argued, is the object of psychoanalysis, and its temporality, as Deleuze has shown, is that of the death drive. I am not presenting these connections in more detail here, but I should note that the temporality of the primary fantasy is described by Deleuze as the "third synthesis of time" or the temporality of the death drive, and, as we shall see in part 2 in the context of ethics, in the terms of the present work it is also the attributive temporality of surplus or substance, to which Spinoza refers as the species of eternity, and of which diachrony and synchrony are the two modes of its empirical manifestation. (See Laplanche and Pontalis; and Deleuze 1994, particularly the second chapter, "Repetition for Itself," 70–128.)

5. As we shall see in the chapter "Whence the Need for a Meta-Phenomenological Ontology?" in Sartre's scheme, the in-itself, insofar as it is constitutive of the for-itself, is in truth not facticity but lack, and the latter emerges also in Sartre from nothing other than value (even as Sartre conceives of value exclusive in human terms, i.e., as moral value). This link between, in fact an indissoluble intertwining of, facticity and lack offers us a premonition of the nature of facts in secular history, which will examine in the chapter "Meta-Phenomenological Fact."

6. As far as the function of historical contingency on the determination of semantic value is concerned, Saussure's account is not undermined but rather reinforced by Lacan's notorious subversion of the Saussurean sign. That is, the sliding of the signified under the chain of signifiers only intensifies the contingency of the constitution of the linguistic fact, while foregrounding, of

course, also the multifaceted character of history itself, which, like everything else, reveals a different appearance to different subjects.

Meta-Phenomenological Fact

1. Notable among seventeenth-century philosophers representative of this thesis are Blaise Pascal and Spinoza, particularly their works published in 1670 (see Pascal; and Spinoza 1951, especially the fourteenth chapter of *A Theologico-Political Treatise*, 182–189).

2. As a European variant of what is currently happening in the USA, one may want to consider the Netherlands' post-9/11 resuscitation of the Enlightenment as the genealogical anchoring point for its current self-representation as a "liberal" society that, by the same token, cannot tolerate "non-liberal" attitudes. As Ian Buruma puts it: "It was the attacks on the World Trade Center on September 11, 2001 . . . that brought the Enlightenment back to the center of political debate, especially in Holland, one of the countries where it all began more than three hundred years ago. Not just academics but politicians and popular columnists saw the Enlightenment as the fortress to be defended against Islamist extremism" (28).

Historiographical Project

1. Several Lacanian theorists concur that the discourses of the Master and the University represent the precapitalist and capitalist eras, respectively. (See, for instance, Justin Clemens and Russell Grigg, particularly the articles by Alenka Zupančič and Juliet Flower MacCannell, 155–178 and 195–215.)

2. This is the logic of fetishism as defined by Freud, that is, as the logic through which the subject disavows something it knows to be true ('I may know very well that X is true, but nevertheless I act as if I did not know'). This conception of Freud's fetishism represents the basis of ideology, including the cynical ideology of more recent stages of capitalism, according to which 'I keep doing X even as I am aware of the truth about it.' Marx's commodity fetishism, even though it refers to something that people "do . . . without being aware of" it (Marx 1990, 166–167), actually goes, as Étienne Balibar has shown, beyond ideology, for, unlike ideology that employs "an 'idol,' an abstract representation which seems to exist all on its own in the ethereal realm of ideas (Freedom, Justice, Humanity, Law)," fetishism operates on the basis of the " 'fetish,' " that is, "a material thing which seems to belong to the earth, to nature, while exerting an irresistible power over individuals (the commodity and, above all, money)" (Balibar, 76). As I argue in my current book project (tentatively titled "Biosemantics"), fetishism constitutes indeed a realm beyond

ideology, and this is the properly biopolitical domain of capitalism. For Freud's concept of fetishism, see his article "Fetischismus [Fetishism]," in Freud, Vol. XIV, 311–317. Moreover, Freud's fetishism relates to the 'as-if-principle,' as derived from Jeremy Bentham's "Philosophy of the 'As If,' " and as revised by the neo-Kantian philosopher Hans Vaihinger (see Bentham; and Vaihinger). Octave Mannoni further developed the 'as-if-principle' as the logic of the "je sais bien, mais quand même . . . [I know well, but, nevertheless . . .]" (see Mannoni, particularly the chapter "Je sais bien, mais quand même . . ."). The 'as if' logic has had a significant impact on the works of, among others, Lacan, Althusser, and Žižek (see Lacan 1981, 163 and 1992, 12, 187, and 228; Althusser 1971, particularly "Ideology and Ideological State Apparatuses," 127–186; and Žižek 1989, particularly 36–47).

3. As Žižek points out, conscious belief is in fact a defense against the real of one's desire. See the chapter "*Psycho*'s Moebius Band," in Žižek 1992, 226–231.

4. Lacan elaborates on the function of this fantasy particularly in his third seminar (see Lacan 1993, chapter 10, 130–142).

5. In part 2 we shall see in more detail the mechanism of this fantasy, as well as its relation to surplus-enjoyment and to the ultra-ideological biopolitical forms of power.

Whence the Need for a Meta-Phenomenological Ontology?

1. In other words, what after all eludes Sartre in his discovery of the (body *qua*) gaze is that it emerges as the surplus of a structural network of values, economic or semantic. We should also note here that the gaze is the core concept through which Sartre attempts to undermine Heidegger's phenomenological scheme. As Sartre writes, by proposing *Dasein* "immediately as *care*" and as always already "*Mitsein*," a "*being-with-others*," Heidegger glosses over the conditions required for the "*experience* of the 'we' " (134 and 536–537). Sartre emphatically opposes both Heidegger's assumption that the experience of the "we" is "the foundation of our consciousness of the Other," and the "we" conceived as "an inter-subjective consciousness" or "a new being which surpasses and encircles its parts as a synthetic whole in the manner of the collective consciousness of the sociologists" (536). In his search for "the foundation of the consciousness of the Other," Sartre eventually replaces *Dasein qua Mitsein* with the *gaze*—the herald of both Merleau-Ponty's and Lacan's eponymous concept. Nevertheless, the limitations of his discovery consist in the fact that in his attempt to account for the experience of the "we" Sartre remains trapped within the Hegelian dialectic, since from the outset he postulates that "in order for a consciousness to get the consciousness of being engaged in a 'we,' it is

necessary that the other consciousnesses which enter into community with it should be first given in some other way; that is, either in the capacity of a transcendence-transcending or as a transcendence-transcended" (536). "Transcendence-transcending" and "transcendence-transcended" are Sartre's terms for the master and the slave, respectively. Being predicated on the dialectic of the master and the slave, Sartre's "Concrete Relations with Others," as the title of the third chapter of the third part of *Being and Nothingness* puts it, turn out to converge in masochism, sadism, and "conflict," as the exhaustive list of relations in which empirical human beings can enter (555). In other words, Sartre falls short of grasping that the gaze as the foundation of the experience of the "we" determines above all not our relations with other concrete human beings but our relation with the Other. It was Lacan who first established that it is from this primary relation of the subject to the Other (which can be not only sadistic or masochistic but also neurotic, hysteric, or psychotic) that relations among human beings derive.

Recapitulation in Other Words

1. Though it is not within the scope of the present work, it must be noted at least in passing that the paradigms of pan-spiritualism (and partly paganism) must be distinguished from those of monotheism as veritably distinct historical blocks. In the former case, all immanence is subsumed under transcendence, in the mode of what Georges Bataille aptly likens to the state of "water in water" that characterizes the animal but also humans as long as they conceive of spirit such that, even though, "by definition, the supreme being has the highest rank," things, humans, and spirits, "all are of the same kind, in which immanence and [transcendent] personality are mingled; all can be *divine* and endowed with an operative power; all can speak the language of man," so that, "in spite of everything, they basically line up on a plane of equality" (34). It is in monotheism that the dualist split between immanence and transcendence is established and that the function of surplus is relegated to the latter. In other words, strictly speaking, pan-spiritualism is a historical block in which the surplus *is* operative within the plane of immanence, but, unlike in our block, there the plane of immanence *is* that of transcendence (which is why the effects of surplus there are not surplus-value and the imaginary in its secular mode, but the endowment of the world with magical and supernatural powers). To my knowledge, the work that describes at its clearest the centrality of the function of surplus in archaic societies is Marcel Mauss's *The Gift* (see Mauss).

2. This thesis alone suffices to explain the importance of religion in Marx's thought. On this topic, see Karatani's commentary on Marx's notorious, and widely misread, analogy between religion and the "opium of the

people" (Karatani 1995, particularly the afterword, 185–188), as well as Alberto Toscano's more extensive commentary on Marx's approach to religion in terms that, in my opinion, correspond to a proper understanding of Marx's broader conception of commodity fetishism (see Toscano 2010).

Part II   Bios: Biopolitics and Ethics

Bios in Extant Biopolitical Theories

1. As discussed in the preface here, it remains irrelevant to my line of argument whether one could show that this biological or natural body is ultimately reducible to discursive constructions. Moreover, this conception of bios as fundamentally biological or natural life is also shared by Roberto Esposito, although, as I maintain in the review essay of his trilogy that I am currently working on for Cultural Critique, what underlies Esposito's conception of bios as its underside is not discursive construction but specific logical models that are indeed constitutive of biopolitics (see Esposito 2008, 2010, and more importantly, 2011).

2. For the teleological character of Negri's thought in general, see Macherey 1982–1983. I also address more extensively the teleological character of Hardt and Negri's thought in Kordela 2007.

3. To avoid misunderstandings, let me add here that I could not share more Hardt and Negri's desire and determination to criticize and condemn the current mechanisms of policing and violent control in the name of " 'nation building,' " as "in countries like Afghanistan and Iraq," including all imperial interventions into the lives of individuals and communities, up to the level of arbitrarily "dividing up the globe and drawing the maps," as all "colonial powers" do with "their subject territories" (2004, 23). My objection concerns the method through which such a criticism can really be effective. My position is that whatever method we may choose to employ, it cannot rely on any dualism, including the transcendence of biopower and the immanence of biopolitics, which is why in the present work these two terms are employed as basically interchangeable terms. This is not to say that in certain contexts this distinction may not be useful and desirable, but only as long as it is not predicated on dualism.

4. I address elsewhere the necessarily transhistorical aspect of biopolitics as a form of power that is in fact entailed already in the primary law of the incest prohibition, which grounds the formation of any society since the most archaic times (see Kordela 2011). In other words, it is precisely as biological life (in-itself) that bios has always been the object of biopolitics, but, as we shall see, in secular capitalist modernity it is bios as a specific modulation of the being-in-itself-for-itself that becomes its proper object.

Bios: Surplus qua *Labor-Power*

1. Elsewhere I expand on several other concepts that appear or become dominant first in postmodern empirical reality, while being structurally constitutive of capital since its inception (see Kordela 2007a).

Double Representation of Bios: Darstellung *and* Vertretung

1. Note that to say that *Vertretung* is the repressed of capitalism is not the same as saying that it is its unconscious. As we saw in the chapter "Value—Being—Surplus" in part 1, the unconscious of capital is surplus-value. We shall clarify the difference between the unconscious and the repressed in subsequent chapters.

Modal Aspects of the Unconscious: Conscious Darstellung *and Repressed* Vertretung

1. Foucault concurs with Marx as to the historical moment at which this identity between thing and representation is *fully* broken, that is, the eighteenth century, in which parliamentarism, as Marx stresses, was introduced. Nevertheless, as we have seen, Foucault also acknowledges that the loosening of the link between things and words had already begun since the seventeenth-century advent of the secular, binary, and arbitrary sign in both language and economy. To explain, however, the epistemological shift from classical secular philosophy and philology to the more modern problematic of representation, which is essentially established since Kant's excommunication of the thing-in-itself from representation in the late eighteenth century, Foucault maintains that, its arbitrariness notwithstanding, representation somehow continued throughout "the *Classical episteme*" of "seventeenth- and eighteenth-century thought" to reveal the things adequately and without arbitrary distortions, due to the presupposed metaphysical principle of a "continuum of representation and being, an ontology defined negatively as an absence of nothingness, a general representability of being, and being as expressed in the presence of representation" (1970, 206). I agree with Foucault's position, but I see its value only on the level of changes that are internal to the historical block of secular capitalism. That is, the formal or structural possibility of *Darstellung* is already in place once the arbitrary binary sign has been introduced, so that the full potential of the Classical episteme is always already *Darstellung*—not, of course, because of any diachronic teleology, but due to the monistic principle that the sole *telos* of all stages within a given historical block is to maximize the realization of the formal structures of the block to which they belong (as was explained in the chapter "Historiographical Project," in part 1, here).

2. See again Kordela 2007, the chapter "Is It Possible Not to Hate Representation? (Another Look at *Empire*)," 123–131.

3. Here we can specify further the distinction introduced in that chapter between the discourses of the Master and the University by adding that in the former the unconscious is not operative precisely because its attribute of *Vertretung* is not repressed. Rather, *Vertretung* takes there the form of absolute transcendence—"spirit" in the archaic or theocratic sense—so that its Marks are considered, by consciousness and official discourse alike, to be established by it.

Discourse, or the Symptom of the Repressed, and Language

1. At this stage, when in 1955–1956 Lacan offers his third seminar, he has not yet developed a clear distinction between the real and the imaginary, as is evident in formulations such as: "His [the neurotic's] real, or his imaginary, enters into the discourse" (1993, 155). Nor has he yet defined the real as "the impossible" (1981, 167). Thus, there is an apparent confusion as to the status of meaning, which Lacan presents sometimes as imaginary and sometimes as real, as follows from his assertion that "within the phenomenon of speech we can integrate the three planes of the symbolic, represented by the signifier, the imaginary, represented by meaning, and the real, which is discourse that has actually taken place in a diachronic dimension" (63). If the discourse is real, and if it is the discourse that supplies the relationship between meaning and signifier, then the latter should also be real. One could arguably maintain that Lacan implies a distinction between meaning itself, which is imaginary, and the relation between meaning and signifier, which he presents as real. However, his explanation why meaning is by nature imaginary reads: "Meaning is, like the imaginary, always in the end evanescent, for it is tightly bound to what interests you, that is, to that in which you are ensnared" (54). I do not see how the pure "groups of opposition" of the synchronic system of language could possibly "ensnare" the subject, that is, produce a lack and hence a desire in the subject, without involving a fantasy, because of which alone the subject could begin to prefer this rather than the other group involved in what otherwise would remain purely neutral oppositions. Given that it is a system (set), the synchronic dif-ferentiality of language involves lack, but because it consists of entirely neutral oppositions it cannot provide the fantasy required to fill in this lack. As we have seen, although the structure that constitutes fantasy is synchronic, the content of fantasy is always presented as a diachronic narrative, and if there were no fantasy the subject would not even know which of the signifiers to pick first in its speech, let alone what to desire. In fact, Lacan admits as much already in the third seminar: "When he speaks, the subject has the entire material of language at his disposal, and this is where concrete discourse begins to be formed. Firstly, there is a synchronic whole, which is language . . . then there is what occurs diachronically . . . , which is discourse. . . . If I read this page starting from

the bottom reading up, backwards, the effect won't be the same as if I read it in the right direction, and in certain cases this may give rise to an extremely serious confusion" (1993, 54). As far as the pure synchronicity of the "groups of opposition" is concerned, one could read "this page" by starting at any random point, or, rather, one should read all of them at once, synchronically. If I read it by starting at the top it is because we have established the convention that this is how pages are to be read within diachrony. And this convention is supported not on the real but on fantasy, as is evident in the fact that there are plenty of languages in which the convention as to how to read a page is different. Yet, such a fantasy, though impossible from the perspective of the real (i.e., there is no ground in the real as to which of all possible reading conventions one should adopt) is necessary for people to be able to read. In short, like ideology, meaning is real precisely insofar as it is imaginary (impossible) and necessary. It is this fact that is expressed in the third seminar as an ostensible contradiction. Be this as it may, nothing would change if one wanted to accept the aforementioned distinction between meaning, as imaginary, and the relation between meaning and signifier, as real. For what matters is never meaning without the support of the signifier, but meaning insofar as it is attributed to the signifier, or more accurately, as Lacan has stressed (by inverting Saussure's formula of the sign, so that the signifier stands above the signified or meaning), it is the signifier that has the priority, introducing the possibility of meaning in the first place (see Saussure, 114–115; and Lacan 1977, 151). Meaning, then, emerges from the outset in relation to the signifier, and it is imaginary with real effects.

Attributive Aspect of the Unconscious: The Temporality of Potentiality and Ethics

1. It is crucial to note that the ethical pertains to the level of the death drive and its temporality only insofar as the death drive or "Thanatos is completely indistinguishable from the desexualization of Eros"—which "desexualization," in the terms of the present work, is the elimination of intentionality or *telos* from the Marks of *Vertretung* (Deleuze 1994, 113). Only "the complementarity between the narcissistic libido [Eros] and the death instinct defines the third synthesis" of time, which, as I mentioned in an endnote in the chapter "Historical Time" in part 1, is Deleuze's term for the attributive temporality of surplus or substance and, hence the temporality of the metaphysical (ethical) dimension of the human being, and not its ontic dimension in which desire and libido are directed according to the being's interests and are, thus, reinscribed in the teleological temporality of diachrony. We shall approach in more detail Deleuze's account of the third synthesis of time shortly. For now, let us also note that this relation of quasi-indistinguishability between Thanatos and Eros reflects the relation between drive and desire, which is why the argument—

advanced by certain Lacanians, notably by Alenka Zupančič, in an otherwise insightful work—that there is a shift in Lacan's work from his early ethics of desire to his late ethics of the drive and the real, is untenable (see Zupančič 2000). Lacan's ethics remains throughout his work an ethics of desire which—once it is understood that, like Thanatos and Eros, desire and drive are not distinct tendencies—at the same time is an ethics of the drive. If in an earlier work I sided with the ethics of desire it was, I realize now, because of the false problematic of distinguishing between desire and drive (see again Kordela 2007, particularly the introduction, n. 8).

2. "NS" refers to *De Nagelate Schriften van Benedict de Spinoza*, that is, as the editor and translator of the collection, Edwin Curley, notes, "the contemporary Dutch translations which appeared in the other posthumous edition [of the *Ethics*] in 1677" (Spinoza 1985, x).

Battlefield of Biopolitics: Gazes of Immortality and Lethal Certainty

1. It is not an accident but contingency—in the sense specified here—that, while labor-power was a central concept for Marx, the gaze became pivotal in psychoanalytic theory through the work of Lacan. It is also contingent that psychoanalysis is the field of knowledge to which Foucault's various genealogies of biopower invariably converge, as the discourse through which madness, delinquency, and sexuality become the loci of truth. If psychoanalysis is a privileged mode of knowledge, so intrinsically saturated with power, it must by the same token also be a highly invested locus of resistance. It is for this reason that in order to tackle, disclose, and unravel the mechanisms of biopower, Foucault always proceeded on the basis of the most intrinsically psychoanalytic premises. For instance, the first volume of *The History of Sexuality*, which led Foucault to a more systematic consideration of biopower, is predicated on three central such premises. First, Foucault's entire approach to sexuality by means of undermining or subverting what he calls the "repressive hypothesis" is an application on the level of sexuality of the basic psychoanalytic premise that "repression and the return of the repressed are one and the same thing, the front and back of a single process" (Lacan 1993, 60). If there is no repressed prior to its return through the defiles of its own repression, then, there must have been no sexuality prior to its return via the defiles of the mechanisms of power that were repressing it. Second, "that was [capitalism's] starting point: getting rid of sex" (Lacan 1990, 30). Given that sex in Lacanian psychoanalysis indicates precisely that which escapes discourse (in Foucault's sense, from representation and knowledge to the mechanisms of power), to subsume sex under the mechanisms of power, as Foucault did, is *one* way of interpreting capitalism's tendency to get rid of sex. And, third, the entire deployment of sex within the tension between what

Foucault calls the "will to knowledge" (the incentive to speak) and the "will to non-knowledge" (the incentive to conceal) replicates the basic structure of the hysteric (i.e., "normal") subject, whose desire is the desire for truth, "the dimension of" which, however, emerges "as establishing itself in, and even by, a certain lie" (Lacan 1981, 138).

2. For the self-referential character of the gaze (and of being) see the chapter "Being and Time" in part 1, here.

3. See the second of the "Meditations" (Descartes, 102–112).

4. The Master-*Vertretungs*-Mark is what Freud calls *Vorstellungsrepräsentanz*, which Lacan translates as "représentant de la représentation," and Alan Sheridan as the "representative of the representation" (Lacan 1973, 243; 1981, 218). This is the "signifier [that] constitutes the central point of the *Urverdrängung* [primary repression]—of what, from having passed into the unconscious will be . . . the point of *Anziehung*, the point of attraction, through which all the other repressions will be possible, all the other similar passages in the locus of the *Unterdrückt* [repressed], of what has passed underneath as signifier" (Lacan 1981, 218). When Lacan says that the "*Vorstellungsrepräsentanz* is the binary signifier," he of course does not mean it in the Foucauldian sense or, in our terms, as the binary arbitrary signifier of *Darstellung*. Rather, he calls this exceptional signifier that structures the process of repression binary because it is the indissoluble link of two elements, the concept and the thing. This is why in the *Vorstellungsrepräsentanz* "[t]here is . . . a matter of life and death," as it introduces "the division of the subject," because of which "when the subject appears somewhere as meaning, he is manifested elsewhere as 'fading,' as disappearance" of being *qua* in-itself or material existence (1981, 218). In our terms, when the subject appears in *Darstellung* as signifier (value), it disappears in *Vertretung*, which has as its "effect the *aphanisis* of the subject," the disappearance or effacement of it as material body, so that it emerges as immortal (218). Note that the word *aphanisis* in Greek can designate that somebody is literally missing, exterminated, presumed dead, killed.

5. Which is also to say that, unlike ideology that can intervene on the levels of consciousness and all secondary repressions, biopolitics intervenes on the level of *Urverdrängung* (primary repression). Just as everything that does not relate to the administration of the gaze pertains to ideology, everything that does not relate to the administration of mortality and immortality pertains, and can be explained by reference, to ideology.

6. Although I do not use the term "biopolitics" in that context, I show elsewhere that the difference between the ethical and the biopolitical gazes can be explained formally through the difference between set theory and Kant's mathematic antinomy, respectively (see Kordela 2007, particularly the chapters "The Rule of Representation and Sex" and "Set Theory and Being," 93–108).

Enjoyment (Jouissance) and Utilitarianism

1. This is indicated, for instance, in the scene in which Guido is getting dressed to go and meet the cardinal, and other fellows are asking him to bargain forgiveness with the cardinal also for them: "put in a good word for me too," says one, followed by another who wants the cardinal's "dispensation" so as to get his "Mexican divorce." One is reminded of the corruption of indulgences that Luther protested against—I guess, this could be called Protestant irony.

2. As Bruce Fink writes in his translation of Lacan's twentieth seminar, the verb *jouir* from which the noun *jouissance* derives, "means 'to come' in the sexual sense: 'to reach orgasm,'" and in the syntactical pattern *jouir de*, it also "means to enjoy, take advantage of, benefit from, get off on, and so on" (Lacan 1998, 3n8).

3. In fact, I would suggest that humanity has never enjoyed, at least since antiquity. During theocracy, enjoyment was relegated to the heavenly afterlife, and in antiquity, as Aristotle's οικονομια indicates, life was subjected to the law (νομοσ) of the household, which is the law of using goods for satisfying one's needs, and is, as such, a utilitarian law, albeit of a different kind due to its limited character, as we saw in the chapter "Aristotle's Discourses: Οικονομια versus Χρηματιστικη" in part 1. Rather than expressing a historically actualized mode of existence, pure enjoyment is a hypothesis that emerges through its subjection to the law, because of which it is always adulterated.

4. Given *jouir*'s aforementioned double entendre, we must add that today, in late capitalism with its imperative to enjoy sex, biopolitical control has reached the point at which one must not only not come too much but also not come too little. Utilitarianism defines the proper amount of bodily excretions, and anything more *or less* than that is a waste.

Enjoyment and Uncertainty

1. For the two senses of "consistency" see the chapter "Modal Aspects of the Unconscious: Conscious *Darstellung* and Repressed *Vertretung*," here.

2. This structure of a closed set formed through an exception is often associated with Kant's dynamic antinomy. Joan Copjec argues so in the context of sexual difference (see Copjec, particularly the chapter "Sex and the Euthanasia of Reason," 201–236). I also elaborate in more detail on the difference between the ontological not-all and the ontic all (closed set), as well as the ontic diachronically open set—as in the indefinite sliding of gazes—through the difference between set theory and Kant's antinomies (see Kordela 2007, particularly the chapters "The Rule of Representation and Sex" and "Set Theory and Being," 93–108).

Part III   Biocinema and Bioracism

Biocinema: A Drop in Total Recall

1. Read, for instance, *Time Magazine*'s article "2045: The Year Man Becomes Immortal" on the Singularity movement, from which I quote here a short excerpt: "Once hyper-intelligent artificial intelligences arise, armed with advanced nanotechnology, they'll really be able to wrestle with the vastly complex, systemic problems associated with aging in humans. Alternatively, by then we'll be able to transfer our minds to sturdier vessels such as computers and robots. He and many other Singularitarians take seriously the proposition that many people who are alive today will wind up being functionally immortal. It's an idea that's radical and ancient at the same time. In 'Sailing to Byzantium,' W. B. Yeats describes mankind's fleshly predicament as a soul fastened to a dying animal. Why not unfasten it and fasten it to an immortal robot instead?" (Grossman 2011). Note also that, as is typically the case with literature that envisions immortality on the basis of scientific claims, skepticism about such claims is dismissed as being predicated on retrograde remnants of our philosophical and religious traditions.

2. For seriality as one of the conditions of structure, see Deleuze 2004. The relevance of this point to the present argument lies in the specifically secular character of structuralist thought, whose condition of possibility—even as its development into a systematic mode of thought and theory did not occur prior to the twentieth century—is evidenced in philosophical thought for the first time in Spinoza. As Alexandre Kojève astutely put it, Spinoza's philosophical edifice constitutes a "*total* . . . 'systematic' . . . 'circular' Knowledge," which, as is the case of structuralist thought, "is *impossible in Time*," understood as diachrony (Hegel's historical time) (122). (I elaborate extensively on the structuralist nature of secular thought in my current book project, "Biosemantics," and the idea is also introduced in my essay on aesthetic theory; see Kordela 2013).

Works Cited

Agamben, Giorgio, 1993. *Infancy and History: Essays on the Destruction of Experience.* Trans. Liz Heron. London: Verso.

———, 1998. *Homo Sacer: Sovereign Power and Bare Life.* Trans. Daniel Heller-Roazen. Stanford: Stanford University Press.

Althusser, Louis, 1971. *Lenin and Philosophy and Other Essays.* Trans. Ben Brewster. New York: Monthly Review Press.

———, 1996. *For Marx.* Trans. Ben Brewster. New York: Vintage.

Aristotle, 1992. *The Politics.* Trans. T. A. Sinclair. Rev. Trevor J. Saunders. London: Penguin Books.

Badiou, Alain, 2001. *Ethics: An Essay on the Understanding of Evil.* Trans. Peter Hallward. London: Verso.

Balibar, Étienne. *The Philosophy of Marx.* Trans. Chris Turner. London: Verso, 2007.

Bataille, Georges, 1989. *Theory of Religion. Trans. Robert Hurley.* New York: Zone Books.

Benjamin, Walter, 1969. "Theses on the Philosophy of History." In *Illuminations,* ed. Hannah Arendt, trans. Harry Zohn. New York: Schocken. 253–264.

Bentham, Jeremy, 1932. *Theory of Fictions.* Ed. C. K. Ogden. London: Kegan Paul, Trench, Trubner & Co.

Blumenberg, Hans, 1985. *The Legitimacy of the Modern Age.* Trans. Robert M. Wallace. Cambridge: MIT Press.

Burke, Kenneth, 1970. *The Rhetoric of Religion: Studies in Logology.* Berkeley: University of California Press.

Buruma, Ian, 2006. *Murder in Amsterdam: Liberal Europe, Islam and the Limits of Tolerance.* New York: Penguin Books.

Casarino, Cesare, 2003. "Time Matters: Marx, Negri, Agamben, and the Corporeal." *Strategies* 16:2, 185–206.

Clemens, Justin, and Russell Grigg (eds.), 2006. *Jacques Lacan and the Other Side of Psychoanalysis: Reflections on Seminar XVII.* Durham: Duke University Press.

Copjec, Joan, 1994. *Read My Desire: Lacan against the Historicists.* Cambridge: MIT Press.

Deleuze, Gilles, 1988. *Spinoza: Practical Philosophy.* Trans. Robert Hurley. San Francisco: City Lights Books.

———, 1991. *Cinema 1: The Movement—Image.* Trans. Hugh Tomlinson and Barbara Habberjam. Minneapolis: University of Minnesota Press.

———, 1994. *Difference and Repetition.* Trans. Paul Patton. New York: Columbia University Press.

———, 1995. *Cinema 2: The Time—Image.* Trans. Hugh Tomlinson and Robert Galeta. Minneapolis: University of Minnesota Press.

———, 2004. "How Do We Recognize Structuralism?" Trans. Melissa McMahon and Charles J. Stivale. In *Desert Islands and Other Texts 1953–1974,* ed. David Lapoujade. Los Angeles: Semiotext(e).

Deleuze, Gilles, and Félix Guattari, 1987. *A Thousand Plateaus: Capitalism and Schizophrenia,* vol. 2. Trans. Brian Massumi. Minneapolis: University of Minnesota Press.

Derrida, Jacques, 1976. *Of Grammatology.* Trans. Gayatri Chakravorty Spivak. Baltimore: The Johns Hopkins University Press.

Descartes, René, 1968. *Discourse on Method and the Meditations.* Trans. F. E. Sutcliffe. London: Penguin Books.

Esposito, Roberto, 2008. *Bios: Biopolitics and Philosophy.* Trans. Timothy Campbell. Minneapolis: University of Minnesota Press.

———, 2010. *Communitas: The Origin and Destiny of Community.* Trans. Timothy Campbell. Stanford: Stanford University Press.

———, 2011. *Immunitas: The Protection and Negation of Life.* Trans. Zakiya Hanafi. Cambridge: Polity Press.

Evans, Dylan, 1996. *An Introductory Dictionary of Lacanian Psychoanalysis.* London: Routledge.

Fink, Bruce, 1995. *The Lacanian Subject: Between Language and Jouissance.* Princeton: Princeton University Press.

Foucault, Michel, 1970. *The Order of Things: An Archaeology of the Human Sciences.* New York: Vintage.

———, 1990. *The History of Sexuality. Volume 1: An Introduction.* Trans. Robert Hurley. New York: Vintage Books.

———, 2003. *"Society Must Be Defended": Lectures at the Collège de France, 1975–1976.* Trans. David Macey. New York: Picador.

Freud, Sigmund, 1999. *Gesammelte Werke.* Ed. Anna Freud. [London: Imago 1952] Frankfurt/M: Fischer.

Grossman, Lev, 2011. "2045: The Year Man Becomes Immortal." *Time* (February 10) http://www.time.com/time/magazine/article/0,9171,2048299-4,00.html

Hardt, Michael, 1991. "Translator's Foreword: The Anatomy of Power." In Antonio Negri, *The Savage Anomaly: The Power of Spinoza's Metaphysics and Politics*, trans. Michael Hardt. Minneapolis: University of Minnesota Press. xi–xvi.

Hardt, Michael, and Antonio Negri. 2000. *Empire*. Cambridge: Harvard University Press.

———, 2004. *Multitude: War and Democracy in the Age of Empire*. New York: Penguin.

Hegel, G.W.F., 1977. *Phenomenology of Spirit*. Trans. A. V. Miller. Oxford: Oxford University Press.

———, 1988. *Phänomenologie des Geistes*. Ed. Hans-Friedrich Wessels and Heinrich Clairmont. Hamburg: Felix Meiner.

Heidegger, Martin, 1960. *Der Ursprung des Kunstwerkes*. Stuttgart: Reclam.

———, 2006. *Sein und Zeit*. Nineteenth Edition. Tübingen: Max Niemeyer.

———, 2008. *Being and Time*. Trans. John Macquarrie and Edward Robinson. New York: Harper.

———, 2008a. *The Origin of the Work of Art* [Excerpts]. In *Aesthetics: A Comprehensive Anthology*, ed. Steven M. Cahn and Aaron Meskin. Oxford: Blackwell. 344–357.

Holland, Eugene, 1998. "Spinoza and Marx." *Cultural Logic* 2:1 (Fall) http://clogic.eserver.org/

Hughes, Joe, 2008. *Deleuze and the Genesis of Representation*. London: Continuum.

Jameson, Fredric, 1991. *Postmodernism, or, The Cultural Logic of Late Capitalism*. Durham: Duke University Press.

———, 1992. *The Geopolitical Aesthetic: Cinema and Space in the World System*. Bloomington: Indiana University Press.

———, 2006. "Lacan and the Dialectic: A Fragment." In *Lacan: The Silent Partners*, ed. Slavoj Žižek. London: Verso. 365–397.

Kant, Immanuel, 1977. *Prolegomena to Any Future Metaphysics That Will Be Able to Come Forward as Science*. Trans. James Ellington. Indianapolis: Hackett.

Karatani, Kojin, 1995. *Architecture as Metaphor: Language, Number, Money*. Ed. Michael Speaks, trans. Sabu Kohso. Cambridge: MIT Press.

———, 2003. *Transcritique: On Kant and Marx*. Trans. Sabu Kohso. Cambridge: MIT Press.

Kelsen, Hans, 1929. *Vom Wesen und Wert der Demokratie*. Tübingen: J.C.B. Mohr.

Kojève, Alexandre, 1980. *Introduction to the Reading of Hegel: Lectures on the Phenomenology of Spirit*. Assembled by Raymond Queneau, ed. Allan Bloom, trans. James H. Nichols Jr. Ithaca: Cornell University Press.

Kordela, A. Kiarina, 2006. "Capital: At Least It Kills Time (Spinoza, Marx, Lacan, and Temporality)." *Rethinking Marxism* 18:4 (October), 539–563.

———, 2007. *$urplus: Spinoza, Lacan*. Albany: State University of New York Press.

———, 2007a. "Marx's Update of Cultural Theory." *Cultural Critique* 65 (Winter), 43–66.

———, 2011. "(Psychoanalytic) Biopolitics & Bioracism." *Umbr(a)* (2011), 10–25.

———, 2013. "Value." In *Keywords in German Aesthetics*, ed. J. D. Mininger and Jason M. Peck. Cambridge: Harvard University Press.

———, forthcoming. "Unconscious and Gaze in Heidegger and Sartre." In *Heidegger and Lacan: A New Conversation*, ed. Nathan Gorelick and Lydia R. Kerr.

Lacan, Jacques, 1973. *Livre XI: Les quatre concepts fondamentaux de la psych-analyse*. Ed. Jacques-Alain Miller. Paris: Seuil.

———, 1977. *Écrits: A Selection*. Trans. Alan Sheridan. New York: W. W. Norton & Co.

———, 1981. *The Four Fundamental Concepts of Psychoanalysis*. Ed. Jacques-Alain Miller, trans. Alan Sheridan. New York: W. W. Norton.

———, 1988. "Seminar on 'The Purloined Letter,'" trans. Jeffrey Mehlman. In *The Purloined Poe: Lacan, Derrida, and Psychoanalytic Reading*, ed. John P. Muller and William Richardson. Baltimore: The Johns Hopkins University Press. 28–54.

———, 1990. *Television: A Challenge to the Psychoanalytic Establishment*. Ed. Joan Copjec, trans. Denis Hollier, Rosalind Krauss et al. New York: W. W. Norton.

———, 1991. *Le Séminaire. Livre XVII: L'envers de la psychanalyse, 1969–1970*. Ed. Jacques-Alain Miller. Paris: Seuil.

———, 1991a. *Book II: The Ego in Freud's Theory and in the Technique of Psycho-analysis 1954–1955*. Ed. Jacques-Alain Miller. Trans. Sylvana Tomaselli. New York: W. W. Norton.

———, 1992. *Book VII: The Ethics of Psychoanalysis, 1959–1960*. Ed. Jacques-Alain Miller. Trans. Dennis Porter. New York: W. W. Norton.

———, 1993. *Book III: The Psychoses, 1955–1956*. Ed. Jacques-Alain Miller. Trans. Russell Grigg. New York: W. W. Norton.

———, 1998. *Book XX: Encore, 1972–1973: On Feminine Sexuality; The Limits of Love and Knowledge*. Ed. Jacques-Alain Miller, trans. Bruce Fink. New York: W. W. Norton.

———, 2002. *Écrits: A Selection*. Trans. Bruce Fink, with Héloïse Fink and Russell Grigg. New York: W. W. Norton.

———, 2007. *Book XVII. The Other Side of Psychoanalysis*. Ed. Jacques-Alain Miller, trans. Russell Grigg. New York: W. W. Norton.

Laclau, Ernesto, and Chantal Mouffe, 2001. *Hegemony and Socialist Strategy: Towards a Radical Democratic Politics*. 2nd Edition. London: Verso.

Laplanche, Jean, and J. B. Pontalis, 2003. "Fantasy and the Origins of Sexuality." In *Unconscious Phantasy*, ed. Riccardo Steiner. London: Karnac. 107–143.

Macherey, Pierre, 1979. *Hegel ou Spinoza*. Paris: François Maspero.

———, 1982–1983. "De la mediation à la constitution: description d'un parcours speculatif." *Cahiers Spinoza* 4 (Winter), 9–37.

———, 1997. "The Problem of the Attributes." Trans. Ted Stolze. In *The New Spinoza*, ed. Warren Montag and Ted Stolze. Minneapolis: University of Minnesota Press. 65–94.

———, 2011. *Hegel or Spinoza*. Trans. Susan M. Ruddick. Minneapolis: University of Minnesota Press.

Mannoni, Octave, 1969. *Clefs pour l'imaginaire ou l'autre scène*. Paris: Seuil.

Marx, Karl, 1990. *Capital: A Critique of Political Economy, Volume 1*. Trans. Ben Fowkes. London: Penguin Books.

———. 1993. *Grundrisse: Foundations of the Critique of Political Economy (Rough Draft)*. Trans. Martin Nicolaus. London: Penguin Books and New Left Review.

———, 1998. *The Eighteenth Brumaire of Louis Bonaparte*. New York: International Publishers.

———, 2009. *Das Kapital: Kritik der politischen Ökonomie*. Intro. Karl Korsch. [Unabridged version of the 1872 second edition] Köln: Anaconda.

Mauss, Marcel, 2000. *The Gift: The Form and Reason for Exchange in Archaic Societies*. Trans. W. D. Halls. New York: W. W. Norton.

McGowan, Todd. 2004. *The End of Dissatisfaction? Jacques Lacan and the Emerging Society of Enjoyment*. Albany: State University of New York Press.

Meillassoux, Quentin, 2008. *After Finitude: An Essay on the Necessity of Contingency*. Trans. Ray Brassier. London: Continuum.

Merleau-Ponty, Maurice. 1968. *The Visible and the Invisible*. Ed. Claude Lefort, trans. Alphonso Lingis. Evanston: Northwestern University Press.

Negri, Antonio, 2003. "The Constitution of Time." In *Time for Revolution*, trans. Matteo Mandarini. New York: Continuum.

Özselçuk, Ceren, and Yahya M. Madra, 2007. "Economy, Surplus, Politics: Some Questions on Slavoj Žižek's Political Economy Critique of Capitalism." In *Did Somebody Say Ideology? On Slavoj Žižek and Consequences*, ed. Fabio Vighi and Heiko Feldner. Newcastle: Cambridge Scholarly Publishing. 78–107.

Pascal, Blaise, 1995. *Pensées*. Trans. A. J. Krailsheimer. London: Penguin Books.

Pfaller, Robert, 1998. "Negation and Its Reliabilities: An Empty Subject for Ideology?" In *Cogito and the Unconscious*, ed. Slavoj Žižek. Durham: Duke University Press. 225–246.

Ricoeur, Paul, 1977. *Freud and Philosophy: An Essay on Interpretation*. Trans. Denis Savage. New Haven: Yale University Press.

Rush, Fred, 2005. "Jena Romanticism and Benjamin's Critical Epistemology." In *Walter Benjamin: Critical Evaluations in Cultural Theory, Volume II*, ed. Peter Osborne. London: Routledge. 63–81.

Sartre, Jean-Paul, 1992. *Being and Nothingness: An Essay on Phenomenological Ontology.* Trans. Hazel E. Barnes. New York: Washington Square Press.

Saussure, Ferdinand de, 1966. *Course in General Linguistics.* Ed. Charles Bally et al., trans. Roy Harris. London: Duckworth.

Shepherdson, Charles, 1994. "The Role of Gender and the Imperative of Sex." In *Supposing the Subject,* ed. Joan Copjec. London: Verso.

Simmel, Georg, 1990. *The Philosophy of Money.* 2nd edition. Ed. David Frisby, trans. Tom Bottomore and David Frisby from a first draft by Kaethe Mengelberg. London: Routledge.

Sohn-Rethel, Alfred, 1978. *Intellectual and Manual Labor.* Trans. Martin Sohn-Rethel. London: Macmillan.

Sophocles, 1993. *Antigone.* Trans. Sir George Young. New York: Dover.

Spinoza, Baruch/Benedict de, 1951. *A Theologico-Political Treatise and A Political Treatise.* Trans. R. H. M. Elwes. New York: Dover.

———, 1985. *The Collected Works of Spinoza.* Ed. and trans. Edwin Curley. Princeton: Princeton University Press.

———, 1990. *Die Ethik: Lateinisch/Deutsch.* Trans. Jakob Stern. Stuttgart: Reclam.

Stavrakakis, Yannis, 2003. "Re-activating the Democratic Revolution: The Politics of Transformation beyond Reoccupation and Conformism." *Parallax* 9:2, 56–71.

Toscano, Alberto, 2010. "Beyond Abstraction: Marx and the Critique of the Critique of Religion." *Historical Materialism* 18: 3–29.

Vaihinger, Hans, 1924. *The Philosophy of "As-If."* Trans. C. K. Ogden. 2nd ed. New York: Harper & Row.

Virno, Paolo, 2004. *A Grammar of the Multitude: For an Analysis of Contemporary Forms of Life.* Trans. Isabella Bertoletti, James Cascaito, and Andrea Casson. New York: Semiotext(e).

Žižek, Slavoj, 1989. *The Sublime Object of Ideology.* London: Verso.

———, 1991. *For They Know Not What They Do: Enjoyment as a Political Factor.* London: Verso.

———, 1992. *Everything You Always Wanted to Know About Lacan (But Were Afraid to Ask Hitchcock).* London: Verso.

———. 1993. *Tarrying with the Negative: Kant, Hegel, and the Critique of Ideology.* Durham: Duke University Press.

———, 1996. "Lacan with Quantum Physics." In *FutureNatural: Nature, Science, Culture,* ed. George Robertson, Melinda Mash, et al. New York: Routledge. 270–289.

———, 2002. *Welcome to the Desert of the Real: Five Essays on September 11 and Other Related Dates.* London: Verso.

Zupančič, Alenka, 2000. *Ethics of the Real: Kant, Lacan.* London: Verso.

Index

Made in the USA
Lexington, KY
12 May 2015